GPU-based Parallel Implementation of Swarm Intelligence Algorithms

GPU-based Parallel Implementation of Swarm Intelligence Algorithms

Ying Tan

AMSTERDAM • BOSTON • HEIDELBERG • LONDON
NEW YORK • OXFORD • PARIS • SAN DIEGO
SAN FRANCISCO • SINGAPORE • SYDNEY • TOKYO
Morgan Kaufmann is an imprint of Elsevier

Morgan Kaufmann is an imprint of Elsevier
50 Hampshire Street, 5th Floor, Cambridge, MA 02139, USA

British Library Cataloguing in Publication Data
A catalogue record for this book is available from the British Library

Library of Congress Cataloging-in-Publication Data
A catalog record for this book is available from the Library of Congress

ISBN: 978-0-12-809362-7

For information on all MK publications
visit our website at http://store.elsevier.com/

Working together
to grow libraries in
developing countries

www.elsevier.com • www.bookaid.org

Publisher: Todd Green
Acquisition Editor: Simon Tian
Editorial Project Manager: Naomi Robertson
Production Project Manager: Nicky Carter
Designer: Maria Inês Cruz

To my family, Chao Deng and Fei Tan

Contents

Preface

Swarm intelligence algorithms (SIAs) are a family of intelligent optimizers inspired by the collective behavior of a swarm in nature under the umbrella of the well-known swarm intelligence (SI), which is to deal with the collective behavior of a swarm with the properties of decentralization, self-organization, and cooperation. Generally speaking, a typical SI system consists of a population of simple individuals which can communicate with each other by acting on their local environment. Though the individual in a swarm follow very simple rules, the interactions between such individuals can lead to the emergence of very complicated global behavior, far beyond the capability of single individual agent.

In SIAs, a swarm is generally made up of multiple simple individuals. The individuals can exchange heuristic information through direct or indirect local interaction. It is such interaction that, in addition to certain stochastic elements, generates the behavior of adaptive and efficient search, and finally leads to global optimization for a very complicated problem.

The two most popular SIAs are particle swarm optimization (PSO), which is inspired by the social behavior of bird flocking or fish schooling, and ant colony optimization (ACO), which simulates the foraging behavior of ant colony. Besides, many novel SIAs with differently specific search mechanisms have also been proposed continuously and achieved great successes on a number of specific problems. They are fireworks algorithm (FWA), brain storm optimization (BSO), bacterial foraging optimization (BFO), bee algorithm (BA), fish schooling search (FSS), cuckoo search, artificial bee colony (ABC) algorithm, and firefly algorithm (FA), to name a few.

Nowadays, SIAs have become efficient approaches for solving very complicated optimization problems and an effective complement of the traditional optimization methods which are prone to get trapped into local minima and can only be used for a limited range of problems. Nevertheless, SIAs suffer from the serious drawbacks of slow convergence and high computational amount, which make it infeasible for SIAs to tackle large-scale and complex problems. Therefore, it is a critical task to accelerate SIAs greatly enough to make them applicable in more scenarios.

On the other hand, current multicore revolution encourages the community to start looking at heterogeneous solutions. Heterogeneous computing, which refers to systems that use more than one kind of processor, has entered the computing's mainstream systems while diverse heterogeneous combinations have been applied in the scientific domain. The general-purpose computing on the graphics processing unit (GPGPU) is one of the most important heterogeneous solutions.

Initially designed for addressing highly computational graphics tasks, the graphics processing unit (GPU), from its inception, has many computing cores and can provide massive parallelism with thousands of cores at a reasonable price.

In the past decade, GPU has evolved into a general-purpose computing device with many cores, and has become an indispensable weapon in the arsenal of high-performance computing (HPC). Although the attempt on leveraging GPUs' massively parallel computing power can date back to the first day of GPGPU, significant progress had not been achieved until the emergence of high-level programming platforms such as compute unified device architecture (CUDA) and open computing language (OpenCL).

Based on the local interactions within population, SIAs are naturally amenable to parallelism. SIAs' such intrinsic property makes them very suitable to run on the GPU in parallel, thus achieving a remarkable performance improvement.

In the past few years, different implementations of diverse SIAs were proposed. With the excellence in performance, GPU-powered SIAs have been applied to many complex real-world problems, such as computer vision, image processing, machine learning, data mining, parameter optimization, economy as well as many other problems. Because of the significant speedup, SIAs now can be used to solve many tasks which were previously unmanageable by the original algorithm in a reasonable time.

Nowadays, all computing systems, from mobile to supercomputers, are becoming heterogeneous, massive parallel computers for higher power efficiency and computation throughput, and GPU and its likes are everywhere you are. Therefore, GPU-based SIAs (GPU-SIA) can easily find their efficient computing platform and play a very important role in many complex and large-scale problems.

Thanks to the inherent parallelism of SIAs, it is promising to leverage the highly parallel GPU to enormously speedup SIAs. The author of the book has kept track of the state-of-the-art of both domains for more than 8 years and combines them organically. Especially, in applying GPU to accelerate SIAs, we deeply studied the application of GPU to accelerate PSO, for the first time in 2009. This work has been cited more than 130 times by Google Scholar, that is a high-cited work in this domain. Very recently, we also developed a GPU-based fireworks algorithm (GPU-FWA) which achieved a beneficial of 200+ times speedup. In the year of 2015, by making full use of the cutting-edge dynamic parallelism mechanism provided by CUDA in the latest GPU platform, an attract-repulse fireworks algorithm (AR-FWA) is proposed by introducing an efficient adaptive search mechanism (AFW Search) and a nonuniform mutation strategy for spark generation, which can be implemented on the GPU easily and efficiently. Currently, it has become a popular topic to study GPU-based SIAs, which has great impact on the solving of large-scale, complicated problems.

So I think it is the time for me to organize those works, published in a variety of journals and conferences, together, which also triggered me to write this book for researchers, engineers, and graduates with interests in parallel implementation of the novel SIAs.

This monograph specifically focuses on the implementation of SIAs on the GPU, which is a very popular and promising interdisciplinary topic of academic and industrial significance. Almost all of the content of this monograph are excerpted from the research works and academic papers published by myself and my supervised graduate students. In particular, this book begins by introducing SIAs, GPU, and combination of SIAs and GPU, with some perspectives of mine. Then a detailed description of GPGPU is presented along with a brief review. Four parallel models for GPU-based implementations of SIAs are proposed in the following chapter with examples for each model in literature, with which SIAs can be implemented easily and conveniently. Chapter 4 presents the parallel performance metrics, i.e., rectified efficiency and speedup, for a desirable objective and fruitful comparison. Then Chapter 5 points out some necessary and important considerations in implementing SIAs when using GPUs. The following successive four chapters describe in detail the typical GPU's parallel implementations of SIAs, including GPU-PSO, GPU-FWA, AR-FWA, as well as GPU-GA, GPU-DE, and GPU-ACO briefly. The Chapter 10 is devoted to the generation of random numbers, one of the most important parts of SIAs. The widely used algorithms for generating random numbers are presented followed by the empirical study on the impact of different methods on the performance of PSO. With the excellent performance, GPU-powered SIAs have been applied to many real-world and complicated problems which are previously unmanageable by the original algorithm in reasonable time. Chapter 11 presents some real-world applications which benefit greatly from the GPU parallelism. At last, it is well known that benchmarking is a key for developing and comparing varieties of optimization algorithms, so the last chapter gives a CUDA-based real-parameter optimization benchmark, i.e., cuROB, with which the test functions with diverse properties are also included and implemented efficiently with CUDA.

This monograph, at present, is an unique book dealing with the combination of SIAs and GPU, and gives such an organic organization of plenty of related GPU-SIAs' material scattered in different journals and conferences, which can definitely attract a lot of readers who are eager to accelerate SIAs based on the cheaper and powerful GPU platform.

The book provides a particular horizon which is hardly realized from the perspective of GPGPU or SIAs solely. I believe that this book will be a bridge to connect the researchers from the separate domain and can be beneficial for both.

To give the readers a thorough knowledge of this emerging interdisciplinary research area, the book not only introduces the GPGPU in sufficient detail, but gives out the concrete considerations on the implementation of SIAs on the GPU. To make it self-contained, we introduce some popular SIAs when they are first met in the book.

This book features:

1. Concise but sufficient introduction to GPGPU is able to help layman to get familiar with this emerging computing technique.
2. Implementation details of SIAs on GPU are very useful and helpful for readers to easily utilize the techniques to accelerate their programs for a promising speedup.
3. Readers from the domain of HPC can find the relatively young research domain, i.e., SIAs, very interesting, and the HPC plays a increasing key role in the emerging area.
4. Many applications presented in the book are of great help for reader to decide whether or not SIAs or GPGPU can be used in their tasks at hand.

This book is suitable for researchers and practitioners of SIAs, who want to accelerate the execution of algorithms. However, for those who are interested in GPGPU alone can also find many techniques and tips for GPU programming.

Although much effort has been made, research of GPU-SIAs is still in its infancy and rising phase, especially good and convincible performance criteria as well as canonical paralleled schema are yet to be developed. In order to better understand what achievements have been made and how it is a useful insight on the future development, I try to collect the most important and latest works published by my leading group of CIL@PKU after a detailed literature review on this field. Hopefully, light can be shed on the trends of SIAs on GPU.

Due to my limited specialty knowledge and capability, a few errors, typos, and inadequacy may appear in the book, therefore valuable comments and suggestions are warmly welcome to ytan@pku.edu.cn.

Beijing, August 2015   *Ying Tan*

Acknowledgments

I would like to deliver my thanks to my past graduates, Mr. You Zhou and Dr. Ke Ding who conducted extensive and deep research on the project of GPU-based swarm intelligence algorithms under my guidance in the past 8 years.

I want to thank Dr. Simon Tian, Acquisition Editor of Elsevier S&T Books, for his kind coordination and help in reviewing the proposal and the manuscript of this book.

While working on the topics of this book, I was supported by the Natural Science Foundation of China (NSFC) under grant no. 61375119 and the Beijing Natural Science Foundation under grant no. 4162029, and partially supported by National Key Basic Research Development Plan (973 Plan) Project of China under grant no. 2015CB352302.

Acronyms

ACO	ant colony optimization
AFW	adaptive firework
APOD	assess, parallelize, optimize, deploy
APU	accelerated processing unit
AR	attract-repulse
AR-FWA	attract-repulse fireworks algorithm
BA	bee algorithm
BFO	bacterial foraging optimization
BSO	brain storm optimization
CA	cellular automata
CCPSO	cooperative coevolutionary particle swarm optimization
CMR	combined multiple recursive generator
CPSO	clonal particle swarm optimization
CS	cuckoo search
CUDA	compute unified device architecture
DE	differential evolution
DP	double precision
ERS	elitism random selection
FSS	fish schooling search
FWA	fireworks algorithm
GA	genetic algorithm
GFSR	generalized feedback shift register
GPGPU	general-purpose computing on the GPU
GPU	graphics processing unit
GPU-FWA	GPU-based fireworks algorithm
GPU-MOPSO	multiobjective particle swarm optimization on graphics processing unit
GPU-PSO	GPU-based particle swarm optimization
LCG	linear congruential generator
MCG	multiplicative congruential generators
MOO	multiobjective optimization
MOPSO	multiobjective particle swarm optimization
MRG	multiple recursive generator
MT	mersenne twister
OpenCL	open computing language
PDF	probability distribution function
PSO	particle swarm optimization
RE	rectified efficiency
RNG	random number generator

RWS	roulette-wheel selection
SIA	swarm intelligence algorithm
SIMT	single instruction multiple thread
SMP	streaming multiple processor
SP	streaming processor
SP	single precision
SPSO	standard particle swarm optimization
TSP	traveling salesman problem
VEGA	vector evaluated genetic algorithm
VEPSO	vector evaluated particle swarm optimization

Chapter 1
Introduction

Contents

1.1 Swarm Intelligence Algorithms (SIAs)

Swarm intelligence is the collective behavior of decentralized, self-organized systems. A typical swarm intelligence system consists of a population of simple agents which can communicate (either directly or indirectly) locally with each other by acting on their local environment. Though the agents in a swarm follow very simple rules, the interactions between such agents can lead to the emergence of very complicated global behavior, far beyond the capability of individual agents [54, 55]. Examples in natural systems of swarm intelligence include bird flocking, ant foraging, and fish schooling.

Inspired by swarm's such behavior, a class of algorithms is proposed for tackling optimization problems, usually under the title of swarm intelligence algorithms (SIAs) [203]. In SIAs, a swarm is made up of multiple artificial agents. The agents can exchange heuristic information in the form of local interaction. Such interaction, in addition with certain stochastic elements, generates the behavior of adaptive search, and finally leads to global optimization.

The most respected and popular SIAs are particle swarm optimization (PSO) which is inspired by the social behavior of bird flocking or fish schooling [87, 19], and ant colony optimization (ACO) which simulates the foraging behavior of ant colony [52, 51]. PSO is widely used for real-parameter optimization while ACO has been successfully applied to solve combinatorial optimization problems, for instance, the most well-known combinatorial optimization problems are the traveling salesman problem (TSP) and quadratic assignment problem (QAP).

Novel SIAs with particular search mechanisms have been proposed and achieved success on specific problems. Some instances of novel SIAs are bacterial foraging optimization (BFO) [145], bee algorithm [148], fish schooling search (FSS) [57], cuckoo search [204], fireworks algorithm (FWA) [180–182, 185], brain storm optimization (BSO) [174], and the list is increasingly long.

In essence, SIAs are iterative-based stochastic search algorithms where heuristic information is shared in order to guide the search in the following iterations.

A simplified general framework of SIAs is depicted in Fig. 1.1. For a particular SIAs, the sequence of each phase may be different and some phases can be included several times in a single iteration.

Though different SIAs utilize different interaction mechanisms and various heuristic information in quite different ways, we think this framework is capable of embodying the essential philosophy underlying SIAs, thus can be used as the reference frame for discussing various parallel implementations on the graphics processing unit (GPU).

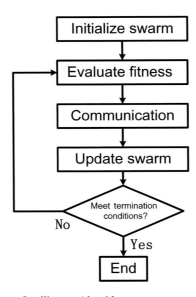

Fig. 1.1 Framework of Swarm Intelligence Algorithms

Take standard PSO for example. After randomly initializing the population, the fitness value of each particle is evaluated. In the following communication phase, fitness values are communicated among particles according to certain topology (global topology, ring topology, etc.). Then each particle updates its private and neighborhood best information (if necessary), and its velocity and position vector in swarm updating phase. The loop continues until termination conditions (e.g., meeting the presetting accuracy or reaching the maximum number of fitness evaluations) are satisfied.

In the case of typical ACO, ants communicate with one another indirectly via pheromone updating. Each ant needs to construct a feasible path before it can evaluate the fitness (cost of the path). This path construction step may be quite different from PSO and other SIAs for real-parameter optimization at the first glance. However, thinking this step under the proposed reference frame, the path construction is nothing but a stochastic updating mechanism. As the ant has no private "memory," it must build the new solution from scratch with the pheromone as heuristic guide. Once the path is constructed, the calculation of the fitness value is trivial.

More often, for combinatorial optimization problems, the fitness value is calculated as the same time as the path is under construction. In this case, fitness evaluation phase and swarm updating can be viewed as emerged into one single phase.

For a particular SIA, each phase enjoys parallelism of various degree, thus should be mapped onto the most suitable processors (CPU, GPU, or other devices) for optimal performance [182].

1.2 Graphics Processing Units (GPUs)

Facing technical challenges with higher clock speeds in fixed power envelope, modern computer systems increasingly depend on adding multiple cores to improve performance [35, 160]. Initially designed for addressing highly computational graphics tasks, the GPU, from its inception, has many computational cores and can provide massive parallelism (with thousands of cores) at a reasonable price. As the hardware and software for GPU programming grow mature, GPUs have become popular for general-purpose computing beyond the field of graphics processing, and great success has been achieved in diverse domains, from embedded systems to high-performance supercomputers [141, 5, 138]. Today's GPUs greatly outperform CPUs in both arithmetic throughput and memory bandwidth. GPUs can offer great performance at a very low price, and meanwhile GPUs can also be integrated into high-performance computing (HPC) systems without much difficulty [38, 10]. Moreover, GPUs also have great performance/watt, which is key for achieving super computing performance. In the latest (as of April 2015) Green500 list,[1] 9 of the top 10 systems on the Green500 are accelerated with GPUs. Much effort has been made to harness the enormous power of GPUs for general-purpose computing, and a great success has been achieved.

Many platforms and programming models have been proposed for GPU computing, of which the most important platforms are compute unified device architecture (CUDA) [136] and OpenCL [88]. Both platforms are based on C language and share very similar platform model, execution model, memory model, and programming model.

1.3 SIAs and GPUs

When SIAs are applied to complex problems, many function evaluations are needed to get an acceptable solution. To tackle this issue, in recent years, GPUs are used to speedup the optimization procedure. Thanks to their inherent parallelism, SIAs are very suitable for the GPU platform.

---

[1] http://green500.org/lists/green201411

Based on interactions within population, SIAs are naturally amenable to parallelism. SIAs' such intrinsic property makes them very suitable to run on the GPU in parallel, thus gain remarkable speedup.

Many GPU-based parallel implementations of SIAs have been proposed in the literature. The first attempts to implement SIAs on GPU hardware were reported by Li et al. [106] and Catala et al. [31].

Li et al. implemented standard PSO on the GPU. Particles' operations were mapped into the texture-rendering process. The proposed implementation was tested on three preliminary benchmark functions, and a $4.3\times$ speedup was reported when number of particles is large (6400 particles).

Catala et al. presented two ACO implementations, which utilized, respectively, the vertex shader and fragment shader of GPU for building ants' paths (solutions) in parallel. Both implementations were tested by solving orienteering problem and $1.3\times$ and $1.45\times$ speedup were observed, respectively.

When these early research works were conducted, high-level frameworks for GPU programming like CUDA and OpenCL were not available yet. These implementations relied upon direct graphics APIs (OpenGL, DirectX, etc.) by using high-level shading language (HLSL) [140]. Attempts on using GPU accelerating SIAs through graphics APIs can also be found in [107, 84, 85, 217, 9, 198].

Limited by hardware architecture and software tools, in these early attempts, some key components (eg, random number generation, sorting) were still completed by CPU. For the components running on GPU, the proposed implementations were much more complex than their CPU counterparts and could not scale very well. Moreover, in these implementations, the overall speedup achieved was relatively small. So, graphics API-based proposals were hardly applicable for real-world optimization. In spite of all these drawbacks, these proof-of-concept works demonstrate the great potential to accelerate SIAs using the GPU as computational device.

In the end of 2006, NVIDIA released CUDA [136]. CUDA provides a packaged solution for mapping applications on GPU without using graphics API, thus changes the pattern of general-purpose computing on the GPU (GPGPU). Until then, GPUs really drew widely interest in SI community and research and applications of GPU-based SIAs began to flourish.

Earliest research on using CUDA accelerating SIAs are reported by Zhou and Tan [213], Veronese et al. [142], and Zhu and Curry [216].

Zhou and Tan [213] proposed a parallel PSO within CUDA platform for the first time. In this work, all real computation was offloading onto GPU except for random number generation. The authors adopted the strategy of structure of arrays (SoA) for efficient global memory access, which is widely used in following GPU-based implementations of SIAs. Speedup against population size and problem scale (dimension) were empirically studied. The authors also presented some interesting analysis on the solution quality comparison between CPU and GPU and with respect to population size. Since then, Veronese et al. presented a similar parallel SPSO implementation with well-annotated CUDA C code and a breakdown timing of parallel and sequential parts was given for analyzing the speedup.

Zhu et al. proposed a GPU-specific implementation of ACO for nonlinear continuous function optimization. A variation with pattern search (PS) as local search component was adopted for parallelizing. Path construction, cost evaluation, and PS steps were offloaded onto GPU to accelerate ACO for optimizing benchmark functions. The implementation used the task parallel model, i.e., each ant was mapped to one CUDA thread. The proposal achieved remarkable speedups (up to $260\times$). Solution quality was compared with time limited to 1 s and the GPU version outperformed its sequential counterpart.

Though convenient to use, CUDA is only aimed at NVIDIA's GPUs. OpenCL [88] was proposed later for the sake of cross-vendor and cross-platform.

Comparative study on performance on CUDA and OpenCL was conducted by Arun et al. [8]. In their work, a multi-objective PSO (MOPSO) was implemented on CUDA and OpenCL. The performance of both implementations was compared with sequential implementation of MOPSO through simulations, the two implementations were compared with respect to speedup and throughput. The results show that CUDA and OpenCL implementations behave differently in terms of data size.

Franz et al. [59, 60] studied multiswarm PSO for ask matching problem and implemented the algorithm using OpenCL on accelerated processing unit (APU), which fuses the CPU and GPU together on a single chip. The authors investigated optimizations to increase kernel occupancy, leverage vectorization, optimize memory access, reduce register usage, and so on. Special attention was drawn on APU's special architecture to improve memory efficiency by eliminating the traditional PCIe bottleneck. The results show that CUDA throughput is increasing and OpenCL throughput tends to decrease with respect to data. Here we point out that the disparity may be caused by the immaturity of OpenCL runtime then, as according to recent research, OpenCL and CUDA can achieve almost the same performance if programming with care [53].

Many proposals of GPU-accelerated PSO and ACO have been reported. Besides, GPU-based parallel implementations of diverse novel SIAs are also proposed, such as FSS [111], FA [75], ABC [129], BA [113], CS [83], and FWA [49]. In light of the specific architecture of GPUs, new search mechanisms are introduced, which enjoy the benefit of significant speedup as well as improving the solution quality in comparison with the sequential implementations (such as [49, 201]).

1.4 Some Perspectives

As we have come into an era of multi- and many-core era, single thread is not a reasonable assumption any more. Parallel implementation will dominate the design and implementation of SIAs both on CPU and GPU. Little interest and attention will be focused on sequential version for academic research and industrial applications.

Though performance measures are key for evaluating and improving GPU-based parallel algorithms, good performance criteria are yet to be developed. We propose rectified efficiency for measuring parallel performance. As for the algorithm performance, it is more reasonable and practical to compare solution quality under limited time or compare the consumed time given accuracy.

It is more rational and practical to compare algorithm under limited time. Thus parallelism will be a key factor for evaluating different algorithms, as algorithms with better parallelism can operate the same number of function evaluations in shorter time with parallel computing devices. Which is of little significance in serial ear when algorithms are always compared under limited function evaluations.

Multi-objective optimization is a hot topic in swarm intelligence community, however, only few implementations (several proposals can be found in [215, 8, 28]) leveraged GPU's computational powers. As multi-objective problems are usually more computationally intensive than single-objective ones, thus accelerating problems will be useful for algorithm design and applications.

As GPUs are used for solving large-scale problems successfully, multi-GPU and GPU cluster will be popular for implementing SIAs. Several preliminary works have be reported in [187, 89]. Fortunately, the hardware infrastructure is mature and software is ready to use [168, 197].

Though CUDA is the dominating platform for implementing SIAs on GPUs by now. It suffers the drawback of closed environment, only NVIDIA's GPUs are supported. Since diverse hardware platforms are at hand for accelerating SIAs, from embedded systems [121, 122] to super computers, a more universal solution will be applaudable. OpenCL is a good candidate for addressing this need and a competitive alternative for CUDA. OpenCL can be as efficient and productive as CUDA is [53]. Besides, supported by multiple vendors, OpenCL enjoys the advantage of portability. With no or very little modification, program written in OpenCL can run all these hardware. In near future, more and more researches and applications will be based on OpenCL.

The work by Cagnoni et al. [24] had shown the portable power of OpenCL. The authors implemented PSO with OpenCL, and run it on both GPU and multicore CPU without any modification. Great performance improvements were achieved on both platforms.

APUs: New advances in the combination of GPU and CPU are gaining momentum in the industry; these new processors will open research to deal with asynchronous algorithms profiting from the two kinds of components. It will then be possible to run collaborative parallel meta-heuristics both on GPU and CPU, and even connect them in a single computer. This powerful system-on-a-chip will also allow us to create new unseen search models for complex problems, and can be one way to arrive at the computation of solutions in just a few seconds for problems that take days at present.

1.5 Organization

This book focuses on the implementation of SIAs on the GPU platform. The remainder of the book is organized as follows.

In order to give the reader a working knowledge of GPU computing, we, first of all, introduce GPGPU in Chapter 2. The basic parallel models for GPU implementation are presented in Chapter 3 and Chapter 4 gives out the performance metrics suitable in the scenario of GPU. Chapter 5 discusses some general considerations when implementing SIAs on the GPU. In the successive two chapters, we will focus on the SIAs under active research, PSO and FWA. Both the algorithms and their GPU implementations will be discussed in detail. Other popular SIAs will be briefly introduced in Chapter 9. Chapter 10 will discuss random numbers generators and their impact on SIAs. Some real-world applications powered by GPU-based SIAs will be shown up in Chapter 11. In the last chapter, an efficient GPU-based benchmark for optimization is given for practitioners.

Chapter 2
GPGPU: General-Purpose Computing on the GPU

Contents

2.1 Introduction

Graphics processing units (GPUs) were at first designed especially for the purpose of image and graphic processing on computers, where compute-intensive and highly parallel computing is required. Driven by the insatiable demand for realtime high-definition graphics, GPUs have evolved into highly parallel and many-core processors and are able to execute tens of hundreds threads concurrently. The performance and capabilities of GPUs have been increasingly improved in recent years. Today's GPU is not only a powerful graphics engine but also a highly parallel and programmable device that can be used for general-purpose computing application. With its tremendous computational horsepower and very high memory bandwidth, the GPU has become a significant part of modern mainstream, general-purpose computing systems [140, 178], and great success has been achieved.

2.1.1 Multi- and Many-Core Era

In the single-core CPU period, programmers have relied on enormous extension on the advances in hardware to accelerate their applications; as a new generation of processors is introduced, the same software just runs faster. However, due to energy-consumption and heat-dissipation issues, the increase of the clock frequency and the level of productive activities that can be performed in each clock period within a single CPU is significantly limited [160] (observe Fig. 2.1). Virtually CPU vendors switched to models where multiple processor cores are used in each chip to increase the processing power. We have entered a multicore period and have to parallelize the legacy serial program to fully exploit the horsepower of the new generation of CPUs.

Modern processor architectures have embraced parallelism as an important pathway to increased performance. In the last two decades, GPUs have also evolved from fixed function rendering devices into programmable parallel processors. GPUs enjoy several advantages over single- and multicore CPUs.

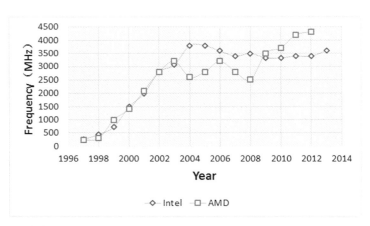

Fig. 2.1 Trend of CPU's Clock Frequency

2.1.2 GPUs as General-Purpose Computing Units

Initially designed for graphics tasks, GPUs contribute more transistors on compute unit instead of controlling and cache (observe Fig. 2.2). Thus GPUs are more powerful than CPU and CPU-based devices with respect to computational capability [80]. In the meantime, in order to satisfy the high-data throughput demanded by graphics, the GPU's bandwidth is much higher than the CPU since its inception.

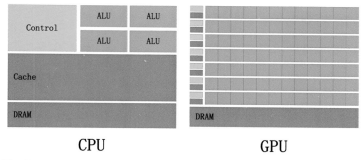

Fig. 2.2 The GPU Devotes More Transistors to Data Processing

As the GPU is designed with many cores from its inception, it is quite effective in utilizing parallelism and pipelining. It takes many advantages over both single- and multicore CPUs [136].

2.1.2.1 Powerful

GPU computes faster than CPU. GPU devotes more transistors to data processing rather than data caching and flow control, which enables it to do much more float-point operations per second than CPU.

Fig. 2.3 demonstrates a comparison between GPUs and CPUs year by year. In the same period, the theoretical peak floating-point computing power of the GPU is an order of magnitude higher than CPUs. GPUs enormous computing power to make high-performance computing (HPC) has been widely used. Among world's fastest supercomputers, the China's Tianhe-1A supercomputer and Oak Ridge Laboratory's TITAN supercomputer rely heavily on GPUs to improve the performance. The GPU provides a new huge development potential HPC.

The GPU is more suitable for data-parallel computations. It is especially well suited to solve problems that can be expressed as data-parallel computations with high arithmetic intensity — the ratio of arithmetic operations to memory operations.

2.1.2.2 Low Price

GPUs can offer great performance at a very low price. Traditionally, enormous computing power is provided by distributed computing infrastructure. For instance, the cluster at Institute of Theoretical and Applied Geophysics, Peking University[1] has 46 computing nodes (Dell PowerEdge M610), 368 CPU cores in total with theoretical peak 3326.72 GFLOPS. Obviously, even resource of this relatively moderate level is beyond the reach of many researchers and small businesses. GPUs offer

---

[1] http://blade.geophy.pku.edu.cn/

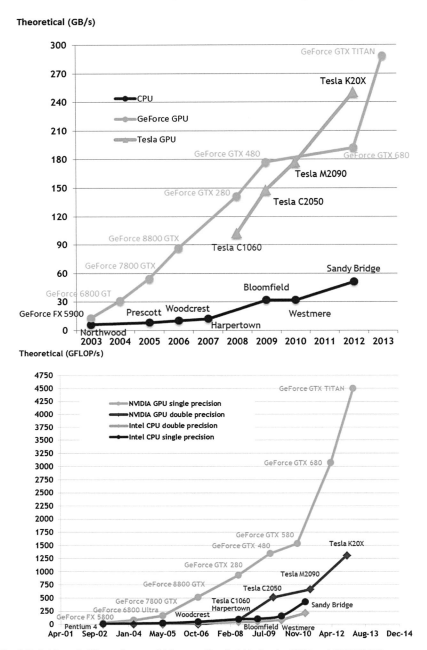

Fig. 2.3 Arithmetic Throughput and Memory Bandwidth for the CPU and GPU [136]

an alternative approach to HPC. As a comparison, AMD's HD 7970 owns 2048 processing elements (computing cores), and its theoretical peak is as high as 4096 GFLOPS for single precision float operation and 1024 GFLOPS for double precision. Many GPUs can be integrated into HPC systems without much difficulty [10, 38].

2.1.2.3 High Efficiency

GPUs also enjoy great performance/watt, which is key to achieve super computing performance. In the latest (as of November, 2013) Green500 list,[2] all of the top 10 systems on the Green500 are heterogeneous systems (GPUs to be exactly). For the first time, a supercomputer has broken through the 4 GFLOPS/WATT barrier.

2.1.2.4 Ubiquitous

As portable devices dominate in the domain of PC [27] and wearable devices become increasingly popular, GPUs are intruding into embedded systems [67, 114]. Effort is made to leverage the computational power of these embedded devices [172]. Besides, GPU-enabled servers will arm the data center in the future. In one word, GPUs are becoming as ubiquitous as CPUs.

2.2 GPGPU Development Platforms

Initially, the GPU is a device with fixed functions, and can only execute specific tasks in the graphics pipeline, thus lack programmability. At this point, in order to take advantage of the GPU for general-purpose computing, computational tasks must be packaged as graphics processing tasks, and then delivered to the GPU. This can be implemented by low-level assembler commands (low-level shading language). More efficiently, we can use high-level shading languages such as OpenGL, Cg, and other graphical programming interface.

But even with the high-level shading language, there is also a lot of inconvenience. First, developers need to be familiar with graphics processing and master a series of graphics interface which is completely unrelated to the problems considered. Second, the graphics interface is a specific programming interface thus lack the flexibility required by general-purpose computing.

To simplify GPU programming, programming models with higher-level abstraction have been proposed. The GPU's specific unified shader is abstracted processor unit that can execute threads in parallel in a particular way. GPU's memory, texture caching and other storage units, are abstracted to a memory hierarchy.

---

[2] http://www.green500.org/lists/green201311

The abstraction enables us to use high-level language for GPU programming and perform common computing tasks.

We first introduce the stream processing mode. After that, we turn to introduce the popular programming languages and tools for GPGPU. Compute unified device architecture (CUDA) and open computing language (OpenCL) will be described in the following sections.

2.2.1 Stream Programming Model

Stream programming model is a programming model similar to SIMD (single instruction multiple data).

As Fig. 2.4 shows, the major difference between stream model and SIMD is that, for SIMD, basic operator unit is instruction while kernel (a sequence of instructions) for stream mode. Data stream (input stream) together with the kernel are loaded into the processors, the kernel is executed simultaneously by the processors and generate the output data (output stream).

Stream and kernel are the two most important concepts in stream programming mode. A stream is a collection of data elements which are processed in the same or similar manner. A kernel is a sequence of operations (instructions) which determines how each data should be processed. For the GPU platform, texture unit acts the role of stream. The data to be processed are read and manipulated by the stream processor in the form of a two-dimensional texture. Many problems can be naturally mapped to two-dimensional textures, such as matrix algebra, physics simulation, and so on. Programmable shaders act as kernels.

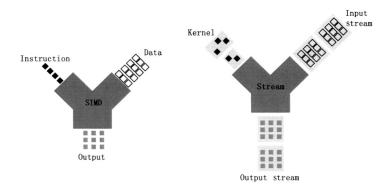

Fig. 2.4 Stream Programming Mode vs. SIMD

By organizing the data into a stream and formulating operations on the data into a kernel, stream model can exploit the inherent parallelism of the task. By stream model, developers can easily use GPU, FGPA, and other hardware with parallel computing capability without explicitly dealing with memory allocation, synchronization, and communication. For application with good data parallelism, stream model can achieve good performance [86].

The programming model for GPU is illustrated in Fig. 2.5. A shader program operates on a single input element stored in the input registers, and after all the operations are finished, it writes the execution results into the output registers. This process is done in parallel by applying the same operations to all the data, during which the data stored on other memory patterns such as texture and temp registers can also be retrieved.

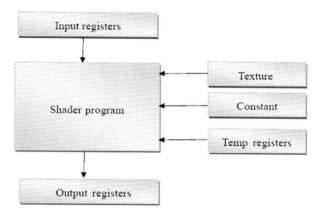

Fig. 2.5 Programming Model for GPU

2.2.2 GPGPU Development Platforms

As today's computer systems often include highly parallel CPUs, GPUs, and other types of processors, it is important to enable software developers to take full advantage of these heterogeneous processing platforms. Creating applications for heterogeneous parallel processing platforms is challenging as traditional programming approaches for multicore CPUs and GPUs are very different. General-purpose GPU programming models address complex memory hierarchies and vector operations but are traditionally platform, vendor, or hardware specific. These limitations make it difficult for a developer to access the compute power of heterogeneous CPUs, GPUs, and other types of processors from a single, multiplatform source code base.

2.2.2.1 Shading Language

At the very beginning of GPU computing in 2001, general-purpose programming on GPU mainly relied on shading languages. A shading language is a C-like high language, which wrappers the low-level graphical rendering operators and is used to program code to manage the graphic processing.

A general computing problem is mapped to several shaders (a sequence of graphical rendering operations) that process in parallel, while the input and output data are stored as textures. The programming model of GPU for general purpose can be illustrated in Fig. 2.5.

A shader program operates on a single input element stored in the input registers, then it writes the extension result into the output registers. And this process is done in parallel by applying the same operations to all the data.

Among numerous shading languages, OpenGL shading language (GLSL), DirectX high-level shading language (HLSL), and Cg programming language are the most widely used ones.

GLSL is a companion to OpenGL 2.0 and higher and part of the core OpenGL 4.3 specification [167]. It was created to give developers more direct control of the graphics pipeline without having to use assembly language or hardware-specific languages. Programs written by GLSL are compiled into OpenGL shader programs and must run through OpengGL APIs.

Analogous to the GLSL used with the OpenGL standard, HLSL is developed by Microsoft for cooperating with the Microsoft Direct3D API.

Cg (short for C for graphics) is another shading language developed by NVIDIA in close collaboration with Microsoft. It is very similar to GLSL and HLSL, but unlike the former two shading languages dependent of specific APIs, it can works with both DirectX and OpenGL APIs.

While this GPU computing model can leverage the computing power of GPUs greatly, it faces several drawbacks. First, one needs not only to have a good knowledge of the problem to be solved, but also to possess intimate knowledge of graphics API and GPU architecture. Second, problems have to be expressed in terms of vertex coordinates, textures and shader programs, greatly increasing program complexity. Third, basic programming features such as random reads and writes to memory are not supported, which greatly restrict the flexibility of the programming model.

To address these problems, various programming platforms and technologies have been introduced. Instead of programming GPUs with graphical APIs, the programmer can now write programs in C or other high-level programming languages and target a general purpose and massively parallel processor.

2.2.2.2 Brook

Brook was a compiler and runtime implementation of a stream programming language targeting modern graphics hardware, to be used for program highly parallel

GPUs. BrookGPU is an implementation of Brook stream programming language, which is a variant of ANSI C.

The Brook was an early attempt to enable general-purpose computing on graphics processing units and effect CUDA and OpenCL much [21].

2.2.2.3 OpenACC

OpenACC [2] is a programming standard for parallel computing developed by Cray, CAPS, NVIDIA, and PGI. The standard is designed to simplify parallel programming of heterogeneous CPU/GPU systems. Like OpenMP, OpenACC is a directive-based HPC parallel programming model, but designed for performance on many types of platforms. By now, OpenACC is mainly supported by commercial compilers. Despite, an open source compiler is also developed by the University of La Laguna [154]. GNU GCC is also working on adding OpenACC support. In the future, OpenACC may merge into OpenMP specification to create a common specification which extends OpenMP to support accelerators [139].

2.2.2.4 C++ AMP

C++ accelerated massive parallelism (C++ AMP) is a library implemented on DirectX 11 and an open specification from Microsoft for implementing data parallelism directly in C++. It is intended to make programming GPUs easy for the developer by supporting a range of expertise from none (in which case the system does its best) to being more finely controllable, but still portable. Code that cannot be run on GPUs will fall back onto one or more CPUs instead and use Streaming SIMD (Single Instruction Multiple Data) Extensions (SSE) instructions. The Microsoft implementation is included in Visual Studio 2012, including debugger and profiler support. Support for other platforms and hardware may become available from Microsoft or other compiler or hardware vendors. As far as this paper is written, C++ AMP is mainly supported by Microsoft on the Windows platform.

OpenACC, C++ AMP are easy to use, however, they suffer the drawback of inefficiency. To make the most use of GPUs' computational power, OpenCL and CUDA are proposed.

2.3 Compute Unified Device Architecture (CUDA)

CUDA was created by NVIDIA and implemented in NVIDIA's GPUs. CUDA is very easy to use as far as programming procedure is concerned. It just like conventional C/C++ except adding few GPU platform specific keywords and syntax. The ecosystem of CUDA is relatively mature. There exit interfaces to other high-level languages, like pyCUDA for Python and through Jacket toolbox, programmer can accelerate Matlab Codes utilizing CUDA under the hood.

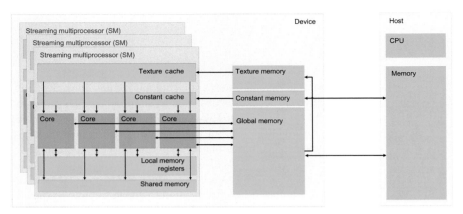

Fig. 2.6 NVIDIA GPU

Fig. 2.6 illustrates the main components of NVIDIA GPU. Referring to Fig. 2.6, we give a detail description of major concepts of CUDA.

2.3.1 Kernels

Kernel is a core concept of the CUDA programming model. A kernel is a function that explicitly specifies data parallel computations to be executed on a device (GPU) that operates as a co-processor to the host (CPU) running the program. When a kernel is launched on the GPU, it is executed by a batch of threads.

2.3.2 Thread Hierarchy

When programming through CUDA, the GPU is viewed as a compute device capable of executing a very high number of threads in parallel. A function in CUDA is called as a *Kernel*, which is executed by a batch of threads. The batch of threads is organized as a grid of thread blocks. A thread block is a batch of threads that can cooperate together by efficiently sharing data through some fast shared memory and synchronizing their execution to coordinate memory accesses.

Threads are organized into independent blocks, and blocks in turn constitute a grid, as illustrated in Fig. 2.7. Threads can be identified by a set of intrinsic thread-identification variables (eg, threadIdx, blockIdx, blockDim, gridDim). To help with complex addressing based on the thread, an application can also specify a block as

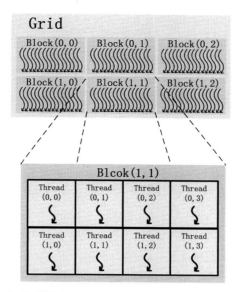

Fig. 2.7 Thread Hierarchy in CUDA

a two- or three-dimensional array of arbitrary size and identify each thread using a two- or three-component index instead. For a two-dimensional block of size $D_x \times D_y$, the thread ID of index (x, y) is $y * D_x + x$.

2.3.3 Memory Hierarchy

The memory model of CUDA is tightly related to its thread bathing mechanism. There are several kinds of memory spaces on the device:

- Read-write per-thread registers
- Read-write per-thread local memory
- Read-write per-block shared memory
- Read-write per-grid global memory
- Read-only per-grid constant memory
- Read-only per-grid texture memory

CUDA threads may access data from multiple memory spaces during their execution as illustrated in Fig. 2.8. Each thread has private registers and local memory. Each thread block has shared memory visible to all threads of the block. All threads have access to the same global memory. Shared memory has the same lifetime as the block, while the global, constant, and texture memory spaces are persistent across kernels.

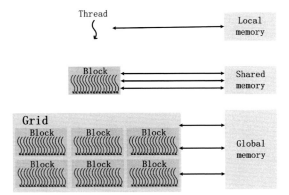

Fig. 2.8 Memory Hierarchy

There are also two additional read-only memory spaces accessible by all threads: the constant and texture memory spaces. They are little relevant to scientific computing, so we leave them out to interesting readers (refer to [136]).

2.3.4 Single-Instruction, Multiple-Thread (SIMT)

A CUDA-enabled GPU can have a scalable array of multithreaded streaming multiprocessors (SMs), which is roughly equivalent to CPU cores. Each SM can have certain number of scalar processors (i.e., streaming processors, SPs) with respect to the specific architecture.

When a CUDA program on the host CPU invokes a kernel grid, all blocks are distributed equally to the SMs with available execution capacity. The threads of a thread block execute concurrently on one multiprocessor in the entire execution period as a unit, and multiple thread blocks can execute concurrently on one multiprocessor. As running blocks finish the execution, inactive blocks are launched on the vacated SMs, as illustrated in Fig. 2.9.

To manage such a large amount of threads, it employs a unique architecture called single-instruction, multiple-thread (SIMT).

The multiprocessor creates, manages, schedules, and executes threads in groups of 32 parallel threads called warps. Individual threads composing a warp start together at the same program address, but they have their own instruction address counter and register state and are therefore free to branch and execute independently.

When a multiprocessor is given one or more thread blocks to execute, it partitions them into warps and each warp gets scheduled by a warp scheduler for execution. The way a block is partitioned into warps is always the same; each warp contains threads of consecutive, increasing thread IDs with the first warp containing thread 0.

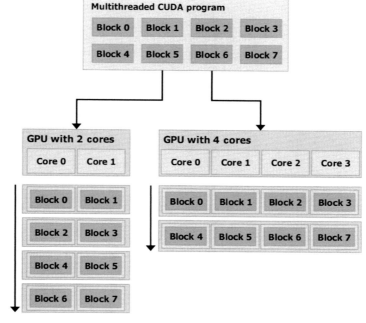

Fig. 2.9 Automatic Scalability

A warp executes one common instruction at a time, so full efficiency is realized when all 32 threads of a warp agree on their execution path. If threads of a warp diverge via a data-dependent conditional branch, the warp serially executes each branch path taken, disabling threads that are not on that path, and when all paths complete, the threads converge back to the same execution path. Branch divergence occurs only within a warp; different warps execute independently regardless of whether they are executing common or disjoint code paths.

2.3.5 Libraries

Besides a C-based programming language, CUDA SDK provides many useful libraries.

2.3.5.1 Thrust

Thrust is a C++ template library for CUDA based on the standard template library (STL). Thrust allows you to implement high-performance parallel applications with minimal programming effort through a high-level interface that is fully interoperable with CUDA C.

Thrust provides a rich collection of data parallel primitives such as scan, sort, and reduce, which can be composed together to implement complex algorithms with concise, readable source code. By describing your computation in terms of these high-level abstractions you provide Thrust with the freedom to select the most efficient implementation automatically. As a result, Thrust can be utilized in rapid prototyping of CUDA applications, where programmer productivity matters most, as well as in production, where robustness and absolute performance are crucial.

2.3.5.2 cuBLAS

The CUDA basic linear algebra subroutines (cuBLAS) library is a GPU-accelerated version of the complete standard BLAS library that delivers $6\times$ to $17\times$ faster performance than the latest MKL BLAS. cuBLAS provides complete support for all 152 standard BLAS routines with single, double, complex, and double complex data types. Building on the GPU-accelerated BLAS routines in the cuBLAS library, heterogeneous LAPACK implementations such as CULA tools and MAGMA are also available.

2.3.5.3 cuFFT

The fast Fourier transform is an efficient algorithm for computing discrete Fourier transforms of complex or real-valued data sets. The NVIDIA CUDA fast Fourier transform library (cuFFT) provides a simple interface for computing FFTs up to $10\times$ faster. cuFFT provides familiar API similar to FFTW advanced interface and support 1D, 2D, 3D transforms of complex and real data types.

2.3.5.4 cuRAND

Random numbers are widely used in computer science and engineering. The cuRAND library provides facilities that focus on the simple and efficient generation of high-quality pseudorandom and quasirandom numbers. It can be used to generate random numbers of uniform distribution and many other nonuniform distribution, such as Gaussian, Cauchy, Poison, etc.

2.3.5.5 cuDNN

cuDNN is a GPU-accelerated library of primitives for deep neural networks. NVIDIA cuDNN is designed to be integrated into higher-level machine learning frameworks, such as UC Berkeley's popular Caffe software [81]. It is optimized for

NVIDIA GPU architectures and supports all major neural network related operators. The simple, drop-in design allows developers to focus on designing and implementing neural net models rather than tuning for performance, while still achieving the high-performance modern parallel computing hardware affords.

In addition to the libraries described above, there are a large number of third-party libraries to choose from. These libraries cover the fields of basic algebra, numerical computation, statistics, image processing, machine vision, video codec, GIS, and so on. The number and range of these libraries is constantly increasing, the latest developments can be found in [138].

2.3.6 Debugging and Profiling

Debugging and optimization is a difficult task for GPU programming. To simplify debugging and optimization processes, CUDA provides a range of software tools to improve development efficiency.

Parallel Nsight provides tools for both debugging and profiling. Nsight can be integrated in Visual Studio (for Windows) and Eclipse (for Linux) for interactive debugging. In the Linux environment, developers can also utilize cuda-gdb debugger in the command mode, or the cuda-gdb used in conjunction with the IDE. In addition, CUDA SDK also provides cuda-memcheck for checking the memory access error.

Beside Nsight, Visual Profiler can also be used for performance analysis. It is capable of visualizing the running time of various parts of the program, to help find performance bottlenecks.

2.4 Open Computing Language (OpenCL)

OpenCL is an open, royal-free specification aimed on heterogenous programming platforms. OpenCL is portable and supported by diverse hardware, GPUs (both NVIDIA and AMD), CPUs, accelerators (eg, Intel Phi), FPGA, and so forth [199]. As smart phones, tablets, and wearable devices are increasingly popular, there are good chances that OpenCL on these novel, embedded compute devices [67, 114].

Both based on the proof-of-conception platform of Brook [21], OpenCL and CUDA share very similar platform model, execution model, memory model and programming model. Most concepts in both platforms can be connected [90].

2.4.1 Device Hierarchy

OpenCL defines a hierarchical heterogenous parallel model.

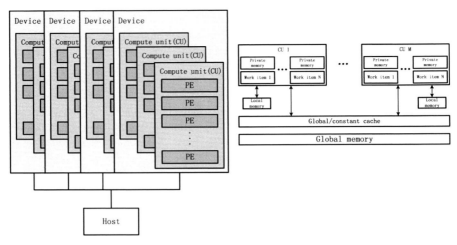

Fig. 2.10 OpenCL Device Model

As illustrated in Fig. 2.10, the system defined by OpencCL includes a host and multiple devices. Each device includes several compute unit (CU). CU can be the compute unit in AMD's GPUs or SM for NVIDIA's GPUs. Also, CU can be a CPU's core or other computing device like DSP and FPGA. CU can be made up of several processing element (PE).

OpenCL define the hierarchy for memory. Global and constant memory can be assessed globally, local memory and private memory can only be accessed locally.

Table 2.1 lists the mapping of OpenCL's memory types to CUDA's memory types.

Table 2.1 Mapping Between OpenCL and CUDA Memory Types

OpenCL Memory Type	Memory Type
Global	Global
Local	Shared
Private	Local
Constant	Constant

2.4.2 Data Parallel Mode

OpenCL defines the execution mode for the program. Fig. 2.11 demonstrates the data model in OpenCL. In OpenCL, the execution units are organized hierarchically: work items make up of a working group, and work groups constitute a an index

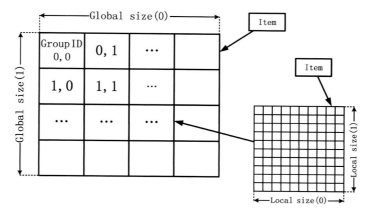

Fig. 2.11 OpenCL Abstract Parallel Model

space — NDRange. The mapping of concepts between OpenCL and CUDA is listed in Table 2.2.

Table 2.2 The Mapping Between OpenCL and CUDA's Parallel Model

OpenCL	CUDA
Kernel	Kernl
Host	Host
Work item	Thread
Work group	Block

Like CUDA, work item and work group are also identified by indexes.

2.4.2.1 Device Management and Kernel Launch

The kernel in OpenCL is identical to CUDA by large.

When kernel launched, each work item kernel executes the instructions simultaneously. As OpenCL is hardware independent, the launch of kernel is a bit complex than CUDA is. (In CUDA work is carried by CUDA driver and runtime.)

OpenCL requires a context to manage the devices with each device a context (see Fig. 2.12). The context provides a uniform interface to the host. When the host launch a kernel, the kernel is put into a command queue for executing. If a kernel finish the execution, another kernel in the queue will be fetched and executed. More detailed description can be found in [63, 123].

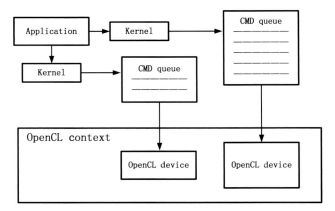

Fig. 2.12 OpenCL Manage Kernel Execution Through Command Queue and Context

2.4.3 Libraries

Many libraries are available for OpenCL.

2.4.3.1 Bolt

Bolt is an STL compatible library of high-level constructs for creating accelerated data parallel applications. Code written using STL or other STL compatible libraries (eg, TBB) can be converted to Bolt in minutes. With Bolt, kernel code to be accelerated is written in-line in the C++ source file. No OpenCL API calls are required since all initialization and communication with the OpenCL or C++ AMP device is handled by the library. Bolt includes common compute-optimized routines such as sort, scan, transform, and reduce operations.

2.4.3.2 Math Lib

clMath is the open-source project for OpenCL-based BLAS and FFT libraries clMath provides the complete set of BLAS level 1, 2, and 3 routines and FFT with 1D, 2D, and 3D support for both real and complex values.

Based on clMath, MAGMA provides high-level matrix operation, like LUQR and Cholesky decomposition, eigenvalue calculation.

2.4.4 Profiling and Analysis Tools

There are many excellent tools for debugging and optimizing OpenCL programs. CodeXL, distributed with AMD APP SDK, contains a set of software tools to help developers make full use of GPU. CodeXL includes a powerful debugger, which is capable of monitoring both CPU and GPU code and analyzing kernels dynamically. CodeXL can be integrated into Visual Studio, or it can be used alone.

2.5 Programming Techniques

In this section, we introduce some important operators and data structure in GPU computing.

2.5.1 Parallel Primitives

2.5.1.1 Map/Reduce

Map and Reduce are basic operations for parallel computing. Map/Reduce, as a programming model, has become the mainstream tools for developing parallel and distributed algorithms on clusters [43].

Map applies an operation to every element in a collection. For example, scale the pixel values from $[0, 1]$ to $[0, 255]$ for display. A parallel implementation can reduce the time required by applying the operation to many elements in parallel.

Reduce repeatedly applies a binary associative operation to reducing a collection of elements to a single element or value. For example, get the sum of a sequence. Reduce can be conducted with time complexity $O(n)$, in parallel mode with p compute unit, reduce can be completed in $O(n/p * log(n))$. Thus, reduce can be implemented efficiently on the GPU.

2.5.1.2 Scatter/Gather

Gather and scatter are two fundamental data-parallel operations, where a large number of data items are read (gathered) from or are written (scattered) to given locations. Given input array *Rin* and output array *Rout* and index array *L*, gather can be formulated as $Rout(L(i)) = Rin(i)$ and scatter as $Rin(L(i)) = Rout(i)$ (observe Fig. 2.13).

In essence, the scatter operation consists of a series of random read and sequential write, and gather operation contains a series of sequential reads and random writes [69]. Due to limitations of the hardware design, random read/write can be

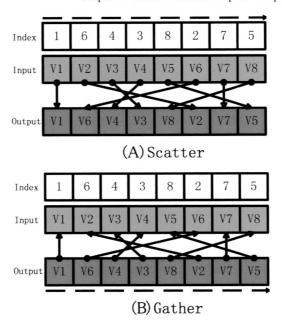

Fig. 2.13 Gather and Scatter

very inefficient for the GPU. Therefore, scatter and gather operations should be optimized according to the actual problems accordingly [69].

2.5.1.3 Scan (Prefix Sum)

Scan, alternative named Prefix-Sum, is a basic building blocks for many parallel algorithms.

Scan involves two operators: a binary operator $\odot$ and an array a with n elements. Given $\odot$ and $a_i, i = 1, 2, \ldots, n$ the target of scan is to get the following output sequence [17]:

$$[a_1, (a_1 \odot a_2), \ldots, (a_1 \odot a_2 \ldots \odot a_{n-1})]$$

For instance, given $\odot$ the common plus operation, then the output of sequence $[1, 3, 5, 7, 9]$ is $[1, 4, 9, 16, 25]$.

Scan can be completed naively in linear time. After dedicated consideration, scan can be completed parallel with time complexity of $log(n)$. GPU implementation of scan can be found in [68].

2.5.1.4 Sort and Search

Sorting is the process of arranging items according to a certain sequence. Many efficient sorting algorithms have been proposed for CPU [92]. Limited by the specific memory access mode, these classical algorithms are not suitable for GPU without dedicated consideration. However, some old algorithms are recovered to be efficient for the GPU (notable bitonic merge sort are [140, 14]).

Search is the process of locating a given element in a certain sequence. Efficient search heavily rely the data organization. We use conduct a search linearly on average if the sequence is not sorted, while the search can be completed in the $log(n)$ if sorted. Searching a specific domains (such as K-D tree [72, 64]) usually needs specific data structures to make the process efficiently.

2.5.2 Data Structures

2.5.2.1 Array of Structures and Structure of Arrays

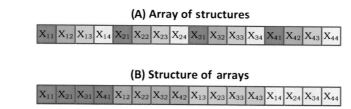

Fig. 2.14 Array of Structures vs. Structure of Arrays

In the traditional CPU programming, associated data are often organized as structures, and several of these structures are stored together to form an array. However, memory organization of this kind could be very insufficient for GPU.

For instance, in Fig. 2.14, assume that a 4-tuple is organized into a structure, on the conventional CPU, the structure will form as an array of structures (Fig. 2.14A). If we are going to add 1 to each element, then in the stream programming model, while each kernel function is treated with an element in the same dimension. In the case of GPU, this operation involves discrete memory read and write operations thus will result in a waste of memory bandwidth and increase the data transmission delay, thereby reducing the overall performance. If the data are organized in the form of structure of data (Fig. 2.14B), the data of the same dimension are stored together to form arrays, and all arrays are organized into a larger structure. In the way, the operation of each dimension only continuous read and write operations, higher utilization of the bandwidth.

The most proper data structure depend on the specific task at hand. However, memory organization is critical factor which should be considered carefully.

2.5.2.2 Matrix

Matrix is the basic data structure in the computing domain As aforementioned, GPU's memory is accessed in a specific way, so when the memory is stored in the matrix, specific factors should be considered wisely. For dense matrix, the matrix's elements generally are stored in memory linearly. For the sake of data alignment, some extra space is padded in the end of each row or column.

For sparse matrices, the situation is more complex. According to the characteristics of sparse matrix, a variety of storage formats have been proposed [15].

2.6 Some Discussions

2.6.1 Limits of GPU

First, not all tasks are suitable for GPU. GPU is applicable in the scenarios where there is enormous data parallelism and no complex logic dependency between the data (such as the typical matrix calculation). For tasks with complex logic or random read/write, GPU may not be the best choice.

Second, GPU's support for arithmetic is yet to be improved. Although mainstream GPUs support IEEE-compliant floating-point arithmetic, but the support of the double-precision floating-point is to be improved. For example, in the application of artificial neural networks, experiences have shown that, for the same network structure and training methods, the use of single-precision arithmetic error probability is significantly higher than that of double-precision arithmetic. Meanwhile, the commodity GPUs do not support ECC. So care should be taken when apply them to tasks that require high reliability.

Like with conventional parallel programming, GPU's highly parallelism makes debugging a difficult task. Despite a number of tools can be used to aid debugging, the debugging of logic errors remains a formidable challenge.

In addition, the portability of GPU program is yet to be improved. Due to its simplicity and relatively sound ecology, CUDA dominates in GPGPU, but it only supports NVIDIA's GPU. As an open standard, OpenCL program is portal in theory. However, the performance of OpenCL depends on the hardware platform. Currently, hardware and software vendors's support to OpenCL is getting better. In the coming years, GPU programming portability is expected to gradually improve.

2.6.2 Perspectives

Due to the popularity of smart phones, tablets, and wearable devices and the increasing demand for voice, video, and other multimedia resources, GPU has been widely used in these relatively new fields. In the future, it can be expected that GPU will bring a revolution to these fields. As these nontraditional computing devices tend to be emended and low power, GPUs will face new challenges [67, 114]. Also, GPU would be used to data center as a solution for the more and more data scale.

2.7 Summary

In this chapter, the basic knowledge of GPU and GPU computing was introduced. Especially, CUDA and OpenCL, two major platforms for GPGPU, were presented in detail. With this knowledge, we will discuss GPU-based swarm intelligence algorithms (SIAs) in a concrete way in the following chapters.

Chapter 3
Parallel Models

Contents

3.1 Previous Work

Before we present our parallel models for the parallel implementation of swarm intelligence algorithms, we first take a brief review of previous work on how to model or classify the implementations in literature.

Laguna-Sánchez et al. [98] proposed four typical parallel particle swarm optimization (PSO) implementations on the graphics processing unit (GPU), which are widely used in the domain of swarm intelligence algorithms' (SIAs) parallelization. Solution quality, convergence, speedup rate, and efficiency were empirically compared under different conditions.

Pedemonte et al. [146] proposed a taxonomy for classifying parallel ant colony optimization (ACO) algorithms. Based on this taxonomy, the authors made a systematic literature review of parallel ACO implementation. Only CPU-based implementations (on multiprocessors and clusters) were covered in the article. Complementing the work of Pedemonte et al., Delisle [45] reviewed existing parallel

ACO models relating more closely to high-performance computing architectures. GPU-based ACO implementation was discussed but in a very coarse level.

Bastos et al. [11] reviewed the GPU-based PSO before 2009. The authors implemented PSO with various topologies and compared empirically their performance in terms of both solution quality and running time. Some considerations when modeling PSO on GPU were discussed.

Krömer et al. [95] provided a brief overview of the research on the design, implementation, and applications of GPU-based PSO. The authors concluded that there were ongoing efforts to implement fine-grained data parallel PSO on GPUs and compute unified device architecture (CUDA) was the major platform for these implementations. Only works published in 2012 and 2013 were reviewed in the paper, and each group of algorithms were described independently.

Angelo et al. [78] presented and discussed different parallelization strategies for implementing ACO on GPU. A list of references on previous works on this area was also provided. Special attention was given to OpenCL by the authors.

Alba et al. [4] grouped metaheuristics into two categories: trajectory- and population-based metaheuristics. Three important parallel models for population-based metaheuristics, to which SIAs belong, were concluded: (a) master-slave, (b) distributed, and (c) cellular models. Novel computing platforms including GPU were described and the best practices expected from researchers were also defined. Different parallelization strategies and communication patterns of metaheuristics on the GPUs were presented too.

Extending the work of Alba et al., Krömer et al. [96] provided a brief survey of recent studies dealing with GPU-powered GA, DE, PSO, and simulated annealing (SA) and the applications of these algorithms to both research and real-world problems. In their review, each group of algorithms were reviewed independently instead of under a uniform framework.

Valdez et al. [194] implemented on the GPU a set of bio-inspired optimization methods (PSO, GA, SA, and pattern search). Experiments on five benchmark functions demonstrated that GPU-based algorithms could achieve good results and are much faster than the CPU-based ones. However, implementation details were not described.

Reviewed several evolutionary computing methods, respectively, Majd and Sahebi [115] summarized four general frameworks for the parallelization of EC methods. No real implementation or specific hardware were involved.

These previous reviews are either focused on more generalized population-based/meta-heuristic algorithms [4, 96] or limited to certain particular SIAs [98, 146, 78]. The proposed taxonomies are mainly aimed at CPU-based parallel platforms [4], which is not suitable for GPU-based SIAs.

Inspired by those previous works, we come up with a new taxonomy based on the perspective of parallel optimization, which is very suitable for GPU platform. With the taxonomy, SIAs of different kinds are classified and surveyed extensively.

3.2 Basic Guide for Parallel Programming

The basic idea for parallel programming is to find the bottleneck and do optimization accordingly. In this section, we follow the parallel design process introduced in [135], name APOD.

As illustrated in Fig. 3.1, APOD, short for Assess, Parallelize, Optimize, Deploy, which is a cyclical process: initial speedups can be achieved, tested, and deployed with only minimal initial investment of time, at which point the cycle can begin again by identifying further optimization opportunities, seeing additional speedups, and then deploying the even faster versions of the application into production.

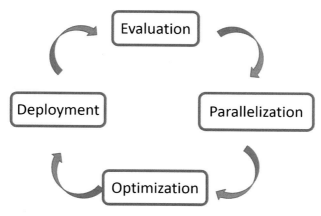

Fig. 3.1 Cycle Process of APOD

3.2.1 Assessment

In this first step, we assess the application to identify the hotspot, i.e., the parts of the code that consumes most of the execution time. This can be done by breakdown timing or some specific profilers. This knowledge enable us to evaluate the bottlenecks for parallelization and start to investigate GPU acceleration. Also, based on Amdahl's and Gustafson's laws, we can estimate the upper bound of performance improvement before the real parallelization begins.

3.2.2 Parallelization

Depending on the original code, this can be as simple as calling an existing GPU-optimized library (eg, use cuRand for efficient random number generation) or it could be as simple as adding a few preprocessor directives as hints to a parallelizing compiler (eg, parallelize function evaluation simply by parallel primitive of OpenMP in the case of coarse-grained parallelization).

On the other hand, some applications' designs will require some amount of refactoring to expose their inherent parallelism. For instance, in the case of GPU-based fireworks algorithm (refer to Chapter 7), new mechanisms are introduced for better parallelism.

3.2.3 Optimization

After each round of application parallelization is complete, we can move to optimizing the implementation to improve performance.

Optimizations can be applied at various levels, from overlapping data transfers with computation all the way down to fine-tuning floating-point operation sequences. The available profiling tools are invaluable for guiding this process, as they can help suggest a next-best course of action for the developer's optimization efforts and provide references into the relevant portions of the optimization section of this guide. Chapter 5 gives some important tips for optimization.

3.2.4 Deployment

Finally the optimized code can be delivered to application. Note that, for APOD, program optimization is an iterative process. It is not necessary for a programmer to spend large amounts of time memorizing the bulk of all possible optimization strategies prior to seeing good speedups. Instead, strategies can be applied incrementally as they are learned.

The idea of APOD will be clear when introducing our four models for GPU-based implementation of swarm intelligence algorithms.

3.3 GPU-Oriented Parallel Models

Different from previous taxonomies for parallel implementations of SIAs, we propose four cascading parallel models from the perspective of parallel optimization [135]. We think the models are more helpful for those who want to leverage GPUs' enormous parallel computing power for accelerating SIAs of specific kind as well as more practical for real-world applications. In accordance with how each phase is mapped onto processors (the CPU or the GPU), the GPU-oriented parallel models fall into four major categories [182]:

1. Naïve parallel model
2. Multi-kernel parallel model
3. All-GPU parallel model
4. Island parallel model

Each model can expose more parallelism of SIAs compared to its previous models. In the following sections, each model will be discussed in detail.

3.4 Naïve Parallel Model

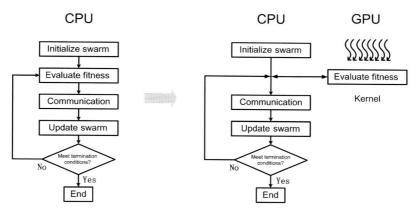

Fig. 3.2 Naïve Parallel Model

Many SIAs are designed for black-box optimization problems. In such case, algorithms know nothing about the objective function, but only require that the corresponding fitness value (cost) can be returned by giving a trail solution. Most SIAs except ACO fall into this category. For nontrivial problems, evaluating a fitness function for every agent is usually very time consuming. Typically, each fitness is evaluated in a parallel, independent way. Thus, according to the Amdahl's Law [7], significant speedup can be obtained by parallelized fitness evaluation. By an breakdown timing of each part of the algorithm, the potential speedup can be derived easily before real parallelization begins.

So considering the basic principle in parallel programming — locate the bottleneck and optimize it, the straightforward optimization strategy to accelerate SIAs is to offload the fitness evaluations onto the GPU for parallel running. Compared to other more complicated strategies (as will be discussed later) which can utilize more parallelism in specific algorithms, such an implementation is relatively naïve and can be used by almost any SIA, so we name it naïve parallel model as illustrated in Fig. 3.2.

An example will make this discussion clear. Assume that we will optimization the Weierstrass function using PSO. Weierstrass function is defined as follows:

$$f(\mathbf{x}) = \sum_{i=1}^{D} \left(\sum_{k=0}^{k_{max}} a^k \cos\left(2\pi b^k(\mathbf{x}_i + 0.5)\right) \right) - D \cdot \sum_{k=0}^{k_{max}} a^k \cos\left(2\pi b^k \cdot 0.5\right), \qquad (3.1)$$

where $a = 0.5$, $b = 3$, $k_{max} = 20$, and $D = 30$. Weierstrass function is a widely used function for optimization. It is multimodal and continuous everywhere but differentiable on no point.

In this case, we use PSO with different population sizes to optimize the Weierstrass function. Fig. 3.3 illustrates the ratio of function evaluation and other operations. As can be seen, in all setup, the function evaluation takes up near 90% of the running time.

Obviously, the hotspot of this task is the function evaluation operations. By following the naïve model, we port the evaluation onto the GPU side. Fig. 3.4 shows the speedup ratio achieved. Up to $16\times$ speedup is obtained.

Implementation using naïve parallel model can be coarse-grained (task parallel) or fine-grained (data parallel).

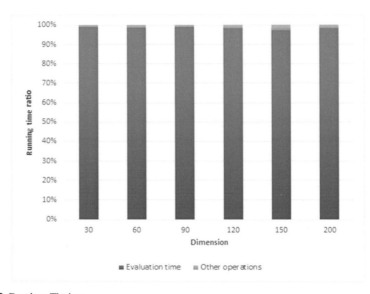

Fig. 3.3 Breakup Timing

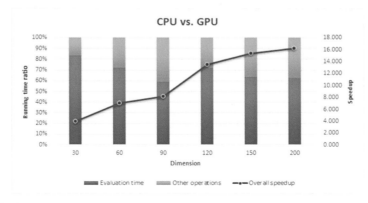

Fig. 3.4 The Overall Speedup Achieved by GPU-Based Implementation Using Naïve Model

When the fitness function lacks parallelism or there are many independent evaluations to be performed simultaneously, the coarse-grained parallel can be adopted. Under this condition, each evaluation task is mapped to one thread (see Fig. 3.5(A)).

Naïve parallel model is particularly interesting when the fitness function can be parallelized. In that case, the function can be viewed as an aggregation of a certain number of partial functions that can be run in parallel, i.e., a fine-grained implementation (see Fig. 3.5(B)). Many implementations for optimizing benchmark functions fall into this category (cf. [84, 30, 48]), so do many real-world applications [74].

Naïve as this parallel model is named, it can be very useful in both academic research and industrial applications. As only fitness evaluation is selected for parallel implementation, legacy serial codes need change very little, thus simplify the programming and debugging process while greatly reducing the running time of the program. Besides, the parallelized fitness evaluation component is "pluggable." Researchers can implement different swarm algorithms without worrying too much about the performance, and plug the GPU-parallelized fitness evaluation with for fast execution. This can greatly accelerate the process of comparing different algorithms and developing novel algorithms.

A recent instance is from Blecic et al. [16]. The authors applied a specifically designed cooperative coevolutionary particle swarm optimization (CCPSO) to the automatic calibration of cellular automata (CA) models for simulating land-use

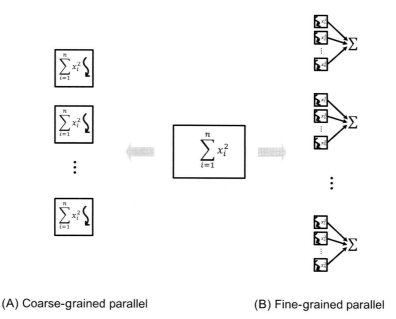

(A) Coarse-grained parallel   (B) Fine-grained parallel

Fig. 3.5 An Example for Coarse- and Fine-Grained Parallel

dynamics in urban planning. The proposed GPU-based parallel version of the CA model achieved speedup of over 100, compared to the corresponding sequential implementation on a standard workstation. The great speedup makes it possible to use PSO for the fast and accurate optimization of calibration.

3.5 Multi-Kernel Parallel Model

Naïve parallel model offers a useful starting point when considering GPU-based parallelization of SIAs, and is popular due to its easy implementation. However, acceptable acceleration may not be obtained with this model.

As the case of ACO, the algorithm implementation is intensively coupled with the task to be solved. So there is usually no such thing as a single fitness evaluation phase, and parallelism exits in the process of path construction, pheromone updating.

In the case of other fitness evaluation oriented algorithm such as PSO, once the explicit parallel part is parallelized and highly optimized, the percentage of the serial part of the program (scaled serial ratio) will increase correspondingly [173]. In this case, further mining the parallelism of the remainder part can be beneficial. In these cases, with reasonable design, more efficient implementation is possible, thus able to fully leverage GPU's computing power.

In the so-called multi-kernel parallel model, attempts are made to offload computation from different phases with explicit or implicit parallelism onto GPU (observe Fig. 3.6).

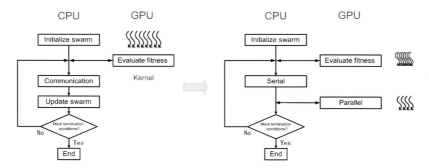

Fig. 3.6 Multiphase Parallel Model

Observing Fig. 3.4, after parallelizing the function evaluation, the ratio of function evaluation takes up only about 50% of the overall running time. The time consumed by other operations cannot be ignored any more. Following the multi-kernel model, we can parallel other operations, such as velocity and position update. The speedup achieved by this implementation is illustrated in Fig. 3.7. The speedup increase from the naïve model's 16 to about $30\times$.

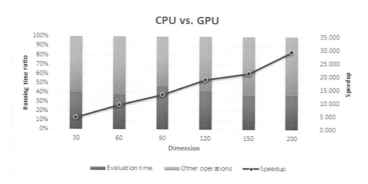

Fig. 3.7 The Overall Speedup Achieved by GPU-Based Implementation Using Multi-Kernel Model

Unlike the case of naïve parallel model which is universal for all SIAs, multi-kernel parallel model is algorithm dependent at large. Multiple kernels can be implemented for parallelizing different phases, and different kernels can take different parallel strategies and granularity to best fit to the specific tasks.

3.5.1 Vector Update

For PSO and many SIAs, moving is a major operation for searching the solution efficiently. Positions as well as other relevant data such as velocity can be updated in parallel. Usually, this can be implemented in a very fine-grained data parallel way, i.e., each entry of the vector is updated by a single thread. Such a technique is very straightforward and trivial, so adopted by all SIA implementations reviewed.

3.5.2 Path Construction

For ACO, the path construction is inherently parallel. When using ACO for traveling salesman problem (TSP), the key to efficiently parallelize the construction process is how to select the next unvisited city which is classically implemented via roulette-wheel selection. Many proposals have been reported for addressing this issue.

In [31], the state transition rule was directly implemented on the GPU as vertex or fragment rendering process via graphics API. Another similar work was reported in [198] using Cg for GPU programming.

Cecilia et al. [33] observed the existence of redundant computation and thread divergences in such task-parallel approach used in [31]. A fine-grained data-parallel approach was used to enhance construction performance for solving the TSP. A new method called I-Roulette (independent roulette) was proposed to replicate the classic roulette wheel while improving GPU parallelism. In this design, intercity probabilities need to be calculated only once and stored into an additional memory to avoid repeated computation. A tiling technique was proposed to scale this method to problems with large numbers of cities. Experiments showed that the quality of the solution obtained by I-Roulette ACO was comparable to roulette-wheel-based ACO for solving TSP. More details on data structures and memory usage were discussed in [32, 34]. Before the work of Cecilia et al., Fu et al. [61] implemented the same method which the authors called All-In-Roulette (AIR) by using Matlab Jacket.

Following the work in [33], Dawson and Stewart [41] proposed a novel parallel implementation of roulette-wheel selection algorithm (double-spin roulette, DS-Roulette) to tackle some drawbacks of I-Roulette. DS-Roulette, in effect, is a two-phase prefix-sum-based implementation of roulette-wheel selection by leveraging the fast shared memory. Experiments showed that it greatly reduced the execution time for constructing paths.

Uchida et al. [191] described a group of implementation strategies for path construction. Different from [33], only one random number is needed and a straightforward roulette-wheel based on prefix-sum is adopted for city selection. A compressed mechanism was proposed to remove the visited cities before prefix-sum. To avoid performing prefix-sum for every selection (as the case of the former two methods and [41]), stochastic trial was proposed. In this proposal, before path construction starts, the prefix sums for each city are calculated. When selecting city, regular roulette-wheel selection is performed until a unvisited city is picked out. Finally, a hybrid method of the three methods was proposed for better performance.

As roulette-wheel selection is widely used for other population-based heuristic algorithms, so the proposed techniques may be used in this areas such as GA and ABC [129].

3.5.3 Pheromone Update

Pheromone update comprises two major tasks: pheromone evaporation and pheromone deposit.

Pheromone evaporation is easy to be implemented in a fine-grained parallel manner, i.e., a single thread can independently lower each entry of the pheromone matrix by a constant factor. However, pheromone deposition is sort of problematic, as different ants may try to depot pheromone onto the same edge at the same time.

The straightforward solution to tackle this issue is to use atomic instructions to prevent race conditions when accessing the pheromone matrix. In this manner, Cecilia et al. [33] implemented pheromone update directly on GPU.

Another implementation based on atomic operation was proposed by Uchida et al. [191]. A special data structure was introduced to present the constructed path. With this structure, pheromone update for each city can perform indecently. In this design, the atomic operations happen in shared memory instead of in the global memory as the case of [33].

Atomic operations on float numbers may not be supported by some GPUs, especially older devices. Cecilia et al. [33] proposed a scatter to gather transformations technique to perform pheromone deposition without atomic operations, at the cost of drastically increasing the number of accesses to device memory ($O(n^4)$ in comparison with $O(n^2)$ in the atomic-instruction implementation). Experimental results in [33, 34] showed that this implementation is significantly inefficient ($\sim$10-fold slower) than the atomic operation-based implementation.

3.5.4 Other Parallelism

Optional components may be added into a SIA to enhance the optimization process. These diverse steps with various parallelism are potential candidates for parallelization.

Local search is an optional component for ACO. This mechanism can improve the solution quality greatly at the cost for enormous computation time. As each solution is being improved independently of others, this step is very suitable for task parallel. Tsutsui et al. proposed an ACO variant (cAS) with tabu search [188, 190] and 2-opt search [189] as local search component, respectively. A technique called move-cost adjusted thread assignment (MATA) was introduced to further accelerate calculating the cost in the process of local search at the cost of extra memory space.

Arun et al. [8] described an implementation of multiobjective PSO (MOPSO) on GPU. A density-based guide selection technique, which is more suitable for parallelization on GPU, was proposed to replace the sequential crowding distance method.

Other common operations, such as finding the top n maximum/minimum values, sorting, etc., can also be parallelized on GPUs with diverse efficiency.

3.6 All-GPU Parallel Model

Compared to the fast computational speed of GPU, the communication between GPU and CPU is very slow. The overhead of frequent kernel launching is also a potential factor that may harm GPU's overall efficiency. So it may be beneficial to combine multiple kernels into single one thus a whole program can run on the GPU only (see Fig. 3.8). In this case, serial code is deported onto the GPU. Though it is not the priority of GPU, compared to the communication and kernel launch overhead, the offload will pay off if the serial code is not too computational intensive, thus the overall performance can get improved.

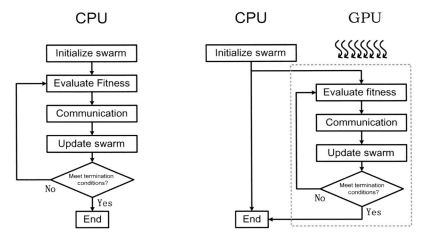

Fig. 3.8 All Device Parallel Model

3.6.1 Coarse-Grained Strategy

One difficulty that prevents kernel merging is the data synchronization. Data dependency may exist between different phases. Before a phase starts, the previous phase must complete and the data must be written back correctly. For instance, in PSO with global topology, only until particles have completed updating their private best (position and velocity) and all data are written back to the proper memory, the operation of finding the best particle can be started.

However, GPU cannot synchronize between different thread blocks, so we must stop the kernel to explicit make sure the synchronization just as in the common cases of multiphase parallel model.

To tackle this issue, a direct way is to organize all thread into one single block, i.e., the swarm is mapped into one thread block, and each particle is mapped into one thread [126, 26]. A bonus of thus a coarse-grained design is that fast shared memory can be used for communication thus better performance can be obtained.

However, as a block must be assigned to one single SMs and one SM can only support limited threads and blocks. This strategy only reasonable for small swarm size. Therefore, coarse-grained all-device parallel strategy is often adopted as a component of island parallel model which will be discussed below.

3.6.2 Fine-Grained Strategy

As aforementioned, if fitness function can be implemented in parallel, fine-grained parallel can be taken, in which case each particle is mapped to one thread block.

Each thread executes some part of the function evaluation and the partial results are reduced to get the final value.

As the hardware synchronization is not supported by GPU, two solutions can be used to tackle the issue: (a) remove data-dependency and (b) utilize software synchronization.

Mussi et al. [128] proposed an asynchronous PSO (APSO). In APSO, interparticle communication is removed, every particle updates its velocity just according to its private best. The implementation was applied to solve body tracking problem [127].

3.6.3 Persistent-Thread Strategy

Gupta et al. [66] introduced the concept of persistent thread (PT). In PT, all thread have the same time cycle, and thread synchronization is implemented by software method (atomic operators). PT was reported to reduce kernel launch overhead, and CPU communication [66]. Though implementation using PT is yet to be reported, we point out that the PPSO proposed in [26] can be easily modified to use PT model.

3.7 Island Parallel Model

SIAs can be plagued by a rapid deterioration of their optimization capabilities as the problem scale and dimensionality of the search space increases. The effective approach consists of decomposing the problem to smaller subproblems and then running on them multiple search instances, which corporate with each other by sharing information. Meanwhile, a computing device with hundreds, even thousands of processing cores, GPUs can support enormous number of threads at the same time, thus are able to run thousands of agents simultaneously.

So for high-dimensional and large-scale problems, island parallel model comes as a natural way not only to reduce the search time but also to improve the quality of the solutions provided. Instead of running one single swarm, in the island parallel model, the swarm is divided into a few subswarms, and each of them evolves separately utilizing different thread or group of threads (see Fig. 3.9). Thus the island model can be called multiswarm parallel model alternatively. Compared to a single swarm with a large population, algorithms using multiple smaller swarms may perform better in terms of both solution quality and running time [98].

Island model can be divided into two groups: (a) solo island model, where multiple independent copies of the same algorithm execute in parallel and swarms are free to converge toward different suboptima, and (b) collaborative island model, where communication of certain form is allowed among swarms.

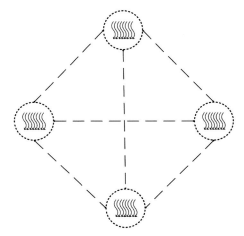

Fig. 3.9 Island Parallel Model

3.7.1 Solo Island Model

Multiswarm implementations can be memory bounded, thus introduce challenges for GPU platform. One strategy to address this issue is to run multiple independent subswarm independently, and choose the best solution of all.

Musssi et al. [125] proposed a GPU-based implementation of PSO for road sign detection. In their proposal, three swarms (one per each sign class under consideration) composed by 64 particles were employed simultaneously. An asynchronous mechanism was introduced into PSO [124] for further reducing the communication overhead. The results of the proposed method were comparable to conventional computer vision algorithms, and often better in terms of correct detections. The algorithm is more robust with respect to environmental changes. Accelerated by GPU, it can effectively detect traffic signs in real time.

Bai et al. [9] provided a multicolony implementation of MAXMIN Ant System (MMAS) where each colony has different parameters. In their proposal, the whole execution of each iteration is deported on the GPU. Each ant colony was mapped to one thread block and each thread within the block was mapped to an ant.

Calazan et al. [25, 26] described an implementation of multiswarm PSO (Swarm Grid PSO). Swarm Grid PSO, in essence, run several swarms independently for searching different subdomains in the solution space, and finally select the best result from all the swarms. A similar work was conducted by Rabinovich et al. [152]. In their work, Gaming PSO was implemented using GPU. In both Swarm Grid PSO and Gaming PSO, swarms adopted the global topology. Each swarm is mapped to one thread block, and every particle mapped to a thread. Different from Swarm Grid PSO which run a fixed number of iterations, in Game PSO, there was no division of the search space and the swarms exchanged information every several iterations to determine whether to stop or not.

Other work on independent swarms was reported by Rymut et al. [163]. They implemented a PSO enhanced by particle filter for human motion tracking. Multiple swarms execute the optimization independently in order to better maintain the multimodal distribution.

Roberge and Tarbouchi [157] provided a parallel PSO for real-time computation of optimal switching angles for multilevel inverters with several DC inputs while minimizing 50th first harmonics. The CUDA implementation of the multiple-swarm PSO utilized several kernels that were launched with one thread per particle and one thread block per independent swarm. Each swarm was due to one optimization task. A $115\times$ speedup was observed when compared to the sequential variant. Another application of the same algorithm was presented in [158].

Jovanovic and Tuba [83] presented a parallelized version of the cuckoo search algorithm. Multiple colonies were lunched simultaneously to exploit the power of massively parallel of GPU and partially as a consequence of limited shared memory capacity. Under the same number of evaluation, the proposed implementation outperformed the original one on tree benchmark functions.

3.7.2 Collaborative Island Model

Though suffering the drawbacks of data transfer and synchronization overhead, it may be beneficial for multiple swarms to cooperate other than totally independently.

Solomon et al. [175, 176] presented Collaborative multiswarm PSO (CMS-PSO) for task matching problem. In CMS-PSO, an immigrating mechanism was introduced into PSO. Every several generations, the worst particles were removed, and replaced by the best particle in the neighbor swarm.

Franz et al. [59, 60] utilized a multiswarm PSO variant, MPSO, for the same problem. The proposed method maintains several independent swarms, stopping periodically to migrate particles between them. Migrated particles maintain the memories of their personal best positions, and their current velocities. This creates an implicit form of communication between the swarms.

Nobile et al. [132] utilized a GPU-accelerated PSO for the estimation of parameters of reaction constants in stochastic models of biological systems. The authors used a multiple-swarm PSO to analyze the data. Each swarm was set up with different experimental conditions and they cooperated to find a set of kinetic values that would satisfy all experimental conditions as much as possible. The details of swarm cooperation used in the algorithm were described in more detail in [131]. The swarms exchanged at fixed iterations the gbest particles either following a ring communication topology or a dynamic communication topology randomly chosen at each migration step. The worst particle in one swarm was replaced by the received gbest.

Husselmann et al. [75] proposed a uniform-grid space partitioning strategy to localize interactions of agents. This mechanism allows separate swarms to search in parallel. Limited by dimension-curse, this spatial partitioning techniques is feasible only for low-dimension problems, thus is of less use for real-world optimization problems.

Souza et al. [177] implemented a multiswarm evolutionary PSO. In this proposals, the swarms were divided into a master swarm and several slave swarms. The master swarm shared its gbest particle with slave swarms to stimulate their evolution but no direct communication between slave swarms took place.

Ding et al. [49] proposed a GPU-based fireworks algorithm (GPU-FWA). In the proposal, each firework performs FWA search independently for local search. The FWA search is implemented by generating a shower of sparks via firework explosion. Every several iterations, all fireworks communicate their current best fitness values to update the amplitudes for FWA search.

Zhao et al. [209] used a multiswarm PSO for converter gas system parameter optimization in steel industry. The research used the CUDA platform and launched one thread block for every subswarm and one thread for each particle. Initially, N randomly generated particles are grouped into M subswarm in accordance with the fitness values. All subswarms run a fixed iteration asynchronously before a new grouping takes place. A novel best-so-far of subswarm item was introduced into the velocity update formula to affect the particles's search behavior.

Luo et al. [113] proposed a multicolony bees algorithm on GPU. To avoid high-latency communication, information was only exchanged between colonies located in the same thread block by using shared memory. As many colonies ran simultaneously, some conditions were relaxed for better performance.

As a special extreme condition, each subswarm may consist of only one agent. Wachowiak and Foster [196] described a global parallel APSO. Task parallel approach was taken for the implementation wherein each particle is represented by an individual thread running on the GPU. In the proposal, the GPU threads ran independently for a number of iterations and performed synchronization at specified intervals for the sake of minimizing communication among individual population members. The algorithm was employed to solve three complex but relatively low-dimensional realistic parameter estimation problems including toy protein folding, logistic function (regression benchmark problem) optimization, and the disequilibrium problem.

3.8 Summary

This chapter introduced four models for parallel implementation from a standpoint of optimization: naïve model, multiphase model, all-GPU model, and island model. In the perspective of optimization, the implementation was increasingly complex. Through the experiments and analyses, it is clear that the models should be selected in accordance with the specific application scenario. A naïve model may be a good start. If the speedup is very critical, other more complicated models can be carried out.

Chapter 4
Performance Metrics

Contents

4.1 Parallel Performance Metrics

Speedup and efficiency are the most common metrics used by the parallel community. Speedup can be defined as the ratio of the execution time of parallel implementation (T_p) and the execution time of the sequential one (T_s) (Eq. (4.1)), and efficiency is the normalized value of the speedup regarding the number of cores (m) executing a parallel algorithm (Eq. (4.2))

$$S = \frac{T_s}{T_p} \tag{4.1}$$

$$E = \frac{S}{m} \tag{4.2}$$

In conventional parallel computing, the speedup allows to evaluate how faster a parallel algorithm is compared to a corresponding sequential algorithm while the efficiency gives a platform-independent metric of different parallel implementations. But, in graphics processing unit (GPU) computing, the two metrics have different meanings.

As the execution times are tested on hardware platforms with totally different architectures — the CPU and the GPU, different researchers can use different GPUs and different CPUs, thus making the comparison of different implementations very hard if not impossible. Similarly, the efficiency is not as a useful metric as in CPU parallel analysis.

From the viewpoint of real-world applications, the speedup still makes good sense, as the metric reflects how fast an application can execute compared to its counterpart running on CPU-based hardware platforms. However, the speedup can also be misleading sometimes.

In some cases, the speedup is calculated on an unfair base. Considerable effort is expanded to optimize the code on the GPU while no effort whatsoever is made to optimize the sequential code on the CPU. It is really more of a comparison of a multithreaded, single instruction multiple data (SIMD) implementation with regular memory accesses to a single-threaded, single instruction single data (SISD) implementation, with unstructured memory accesses, or perhaps an implementation in a language like compute unified device architecture (CUDA) versus an implementation in a language like C without Streaming SIMD Extensions (SSE), without threads, and with an abundance of pointer chasing. In such case, inflating speedups by comparing to an poorly optimized sequential code, happens too often and has led to unrealistic expectations of the benefits of moving from a CPU to a GPU [104]. Fortunately, the issue of speedup inflation has been noticed and framework for fair comparison has been proposed in [24, 159].

4.2 Algorithm Performance Metrics

In conventional framework of CPU-based algorithms, there are two major ways to compare the performance of two algorithms. One way is to compare the accuracy of two algorithms to solve the same problem for a fixed number of function evaluations. Another way is to compare the number of function evaluations required by two different algorithms for a given accuracy. An implicit assumption underlying such a method is that, the number of function evaluations roughly reflect the running time of the algorithms.

However, such assumption does not hold when parallelization gets involved and abuse of the two methods leads to some confusions in the study.

In the literature, solution quality achieved by GPU-based implementation is always compared with the CPU counterpart with the same population size and evaluation times. If the problem to be solved is very complex, a normal population size can fully exploit the computational power, then this comparison makes sense. However, oftentimes the fitness function is not computationally intensive enough or problem scale is moderate. In such case, significant speedup is obtained only when population size is very large. Such a large population size is usually far from the reasonable one for conventional CPU configuration. For many swarm intelligence algorithms, the reasonable population size is relatively moderate. For instance, particle swarm optimization's (PSO) population size is usually between 20 and 100 [19].

The conventional iteration-oriented comparison is problematic in the context of GPU computing. From the standpoint of practice [this is what swarm intelligence algorithms (SIAs) are all about], the speedup calculated with this assumption cannot reflect its usage for real-world application. In the following, we will present our opinion for a practical criterion for comparison.

4.3 Rectified Efficiency

As the established comparison methods have drawbacks, we propose new criteria to improve the evaluation.

To evaluate the parallel performance, we propose a rectified efficiency to evaluate the parallel performance across different CPU and GPU platforms. To calculate the modified efficiency, we need the theoretical processing power ratio (denoted as R) of the target CPU and GPU. R is defined as

$$R = \frac{P_{gpu}}{P_{cpu}} \tag{4.3}$$

where P_{gpu} and P_{cpu} are the theoretical peak processing power (number of float operations per second) of GPU and CPU, respectively.

Rectified efficiency (RE) can be calculated as follows:

$$RE = \frac{S}{R} \tag{4.4}$$

where S is the speedup defined in Eq. (4.1). The larger RE is, the more efficient the parallel implementation is.

Note that in the scenario of symmetric multicore CPU, $R = (m * P_{cpu})/P_{cpu} = m$. So the rectified RE can be viewed as a generalization of efficiency E, thus play a similar role as E for parallel performance evaluation.

We suggest that the RE is used with efficiency to compare the parallel performance. The efficiency (multithreaded implementation against single-threaded implementation) functions as the quality of the CPU-based parallel implementation while the RE (GPU implementation against multithreaded implementation) functions as the quality of the GPU-based parallel implementation.

As for the algorithm performance, it is more reasonable to compare the accuracy under limited time or compare the consumed time before a given accuracy is achieved. The benefit GPU brings either accuracy improvement (within limited time) or acceleration (with given accuracy). Instead of giving a speedup with unreasonable setting and a comparison of solution quality under such a setting, a more insightful and practical comparison is CPU and GPU implementations, under each best setting, how good the solution is with limited time and how long it will take to reach a particular quality (when the optima is already known).

4.4 Case Study

In this section, we will revisit a pioneering work on GPU-based PSO [213] with the proposed criteria to verity their rationality for evaluating GPU-based SIAs. It will be clear very soon that with the help of the proposed RE concept, this early implementation was not efficient enough. Based on this observation, we come up with an improved version and thanks to the new criteria, we can prove that is more efficient than the original one despite the fact that we use very different hardware.

4.4.1 Case Study on Parallel Performance

Zhou and Tan [213] proposed one of the earliest GPU-based PSO implementation and discussed the speedup with respect to three benchmark functions ($f1 \sim f3$). The speedups (S) measured in this work are listed in Table 4.1 (Case 1). The speedups were tested on $f1$ (sphere function) with dimension 50 and various population sizes (rows). We calculate the RE according to the hardware specification (NVIDIA 8600 GT and Intel Core Duo 2).

If only speedup is considered, the GPU implementation seems quit good considering the GPU used is relatively less powerful than the updated GPUs. However, two factors make this conclusion suspectable and unreliable. First, though CPU of two cores was used in the experiments, only single thread implementation was used for comparison. As aforementioned, this was an unfair comparison, and speedup is overestimated. Second, as the RE implies (notice that the RE is also overestimated due to the inflating speedups), the power of GPU was not fully exploited in comparison with CPU. The inefficiency could be caused by at least two obvious factors. (1) One critical component of PSO, random number generator, is implemented by the CPU, which is much less efficient than GPU-based counterparts [47]. (2) Another factor is that, the CUDA driver then was not as efficient as nowadays.

To address these issues, we improve this implementation by generating random numbers on the GPU directly. Besides, in order to conduct a fair comparison, we implement CPU version with both single thread and multiple threads (using OpenMP) with different hardware (NVIDIA 560 Ti and Intel i5). The results are listed in Table 4.1 (Case 2A for speedups against single-threaded while Case 2B for multi-threaded).

Comparing the REs of Cases 1 and 2A, it is easy to get the conclusion that the new implementation improved the original implementation greatly, and such a conclusion cannot be achieved if only speedup is concerned. According to the RE of

Table 4.1 Speedup and Rectified Efficiency With Various Population Sizes ($f1$, Dimension = 50)

POP	Case 1		Case 2A		Case 2B	
	S	RE	S	RE	S	RE
400	3.74	0.10	4.37	0.32	1.59	0.12
1200	4.64	0.12	11.12	0.82	4.20	0.31
2000	4.54	0.12	18.43	1.35	6.62	0.49
2800	4.98	0.13	23.79	1.75	8.08	0.59

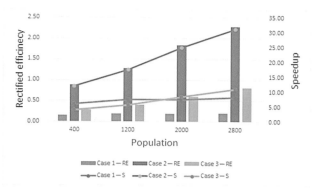

Fig. 4.1 Speedup and Rectified Efficiency With Various Population Sizes ($f2$, Dimension = 50)

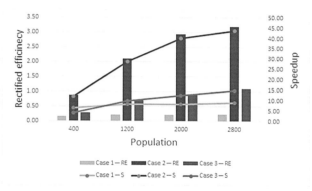

Fig. 4.2 Speedup and Rectified Efficiency With Various Population Sizes ($f3$, Dimension = 50)

Case 2B, the efficiency of the new implementation is still not very applaudable, thus more dedicated implementation can be expected.

These analyses hold for other experimental settings, as illustrated in Figs. 4.1 and 4.2. As $f2$ and $f3$ are more computationally intensive than $f1$, the GPU achieved better speedup and higher RE.

4.4.2 Case Study on Algorithm Performance

To show how GPU can significantly improve SIA's performance, in this case study, we try to utilize PSO to find the minimal of Weierstrass function. Weierstrass function is defined as follows:

$$f(\mathbf{x}) = \sum_{i=1}^{D} \left(\sum_{k=0}^{k_{max}} a^k \cos\left(2\pi b^k (\mathbf{z}_i + 0.5)\right) \right) \quad (4.5)$$

where $D = 50$, $a = 0.5$, $b = 3$, and $k_{max} = 20$.

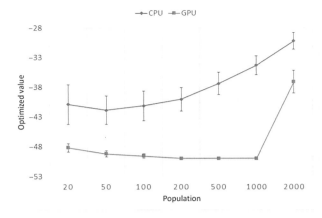

Fig. 4.3 Solution Achieved Under Different Conditions

Multithreaded and GPU-based PSO implementations in the last case study are reused here, and the testbed is also identical. For the CPU case, 10,000 function evaluations were conducted with different population sizes, and 35 independent trials were run for each population size. The GPU-based algorithm ran for roughly the identical time (around 11 s for each population size). The experimental results are illustrated in Fig. 4.3.

As can be seen, GPU-based PSO could obtain better solution than CPU-based one, even when the population size is relatively small.

Based on the results, some insightful conclusions below can be drawn. (1) For CPU-based PSO, it is better to choose population of moderate size (50 in our case), which agrees with the conventional empirical rule. (2) However, this rule of thumb is invalid for the GPU case. In our case, the best solution was achieved when the population size is 1000. (3) The speedup achieved by using GPU can lead to performance improvement, which is very important for GPU's application in real-world problems. (4) Care should be taken when pursuing high speedup since high speedup with very large population may deteriorate performance badly, just as our case when population size is 2000.

As has been seen from the case study above, the new criteria can result in more objective and insightful evaluation for GPU-based implementation, thus help us deploy the GPU-based algorithms to real-world applications.

4.5 Summary

Though performance measures are key for evaluating and improving GPU-based parallel algorithms, good performance criteria are yet to be developed. In this chapter, we reviewed the conventional metrics for parallel implementation, and pointed out that these metrics are problematic in the scenario of GPU computing. Then, a novel criteria, RE, was proposed for measuring parallel performance. As for the algorithm performance, it is more reasonable and practical to compare solution quality under limited time or compare the consumed time given accuracy. Thus parallelism will be a key factor for evaluating different algorithms, as algorithms with better parallelism can operate the same number of function evaluations in shorter time with parallel computing devices. Which is of little significance in serial era when algorithms are always compared under limited function evaluation. Based on these discussions, the proposed criteria can lead to more objective and fruitful comparisons.

Chapter 5
Implementation Considerations

Contents

5.1 Float-Point

Float-point (FP) arithmetic is ubiquitous in computer systems. However, it has been known that it is erroneous to compute with floating-point numbers and operations due to the finite precision.

5.1.1 Instabilities

FP suffers some well-known numerical instabilities [65]:

- Rounding generates an error.
- Non associativity. For instance, $(a + b) + c$ and $a + (b + c)$ are not necessarily identical.
- Cancellation. It happens when to subtract two very close FP numbers. It results in the loss of many accurate bits.
- Absorption. It happens when we add two very far FP numbers. It results in ignoring some or all the digits of the smallest one.

These instabilities make it not only tricky to program properly but also hard to verify the correctness [120].

5.1.2 Performance

Initially designed for graphics tasks which need just a low precision, graphics processing units (GPUs) own enormous computing capability for single precision (SP) float operations. The support of double precision (DP) float is a relatively new thing in recent years. DP float operations can be 1/3 to 1/16 slower on various particular hardware, and double memory space are needed for storage.

So if SP float can satisfy the precision requirement, running algorithms on SP float can fully leverage GPUs' full computing power. For the same reason, if low precision is acceptable, faster native math function can be used. Some mathematical operators (such as powf, sin) can drastically affect the overall performance of GPUs [46], fast low-precision native implementation (usually several fold faster than the conventional implementation) can improve the performance greatly but the precision loss depends on the specific device [34].

In one word, SP float and native functions should be the first consideration whenever the precision can satisfy the task at hand.

5.2 Memory Accesses

The GPU has a hierarchical memory structure as illustrated in Fig. 2.6 in Chapter 2, so threads may access data from multiple memory spaces during their execution. Each thread has private local memory. Each thread block has shared memory visible to all threads of the block and with the same lifetime as the block. All threads can access the same global memory. Texture and constant memories are read-only, and are cached for fast access.

Table 5.1 compares the data transfer rates of different memory spaces in NVIDIA GeForce 560 Ti GPU.

Table 5.1 Data Transfer Rates for GPU (NVIDIA GeForce 560 Ti, PCIe 2.0 x16)

	Memory	Global Memory	Shared Memory	Local Memory
Bandwidth	16 GB/s	128.26 GB/s	1024 GB/s	No latency

Different memories are quite different with respect to bandwidth (see Table 5.1 for the theoretical peak bandwidth). GPU can access host's memory via system bus (Table 5.1 lists the peak bandwidth for PCIe 2.0 bus with 16 lanes, which is widely used for today's PC). Global memory are off-chip DRAM which is usually connected to the GPU via GDDR5. Shared memory, in effect, is a block of programmable on-chip L1 cache with limited capacity. Local memory is the register, thus can be accessed without latency.

Each memory obeys its specific access pattern, so memory traffic must be carefully tuned to exploit the full bandwidth from all memory controllers. Below, we will briefly discuss the best practices on optimizing GPU memory accesses.

5.2.1 Device Memory

Communications between host and device always should be minimized, as there is a huge bottleneck on data transferring of this kind. If transfer is unavoidable, data should be transferred in bulk, as large transfer is much more efficient than multiple small transfers.

5.2.2 Global Memory

GPUs are equipped with a very large global memory bus, resulting in a very high bandwidth. However, this performance can only be achieved when the memory access pattern is fully coalesced, i.e., continuous locations in address space of the global memory are accessed in the same time (observe Fig. 5.1). As GPUs use a single instruction multiple thread (SIMT) model, special consideration should be taken when designing data structure.

For instance, we want to find the minimum of a function, say $\sum_{i=1}^{D} x_i$, by using swarm intelligence algorithm (SIA), say particle swarm optimization. Then multiple thread will calculate the function value with different inputs simultaneously. If a task parallel model is taken, i.e., one thread for one evaluation. If array of structures (AoS) model is taken of storage vectors which is the conventional style on CPU (see Fig. 5.2A). Then data must be accessed in a stride way, thus we can achieve only $1/D$ bandwidth at best. In this case, the structure of arrays (SoA) model is the better storage model (Fig. 5.2B). For the same reason, random global memory access will greatly deteriorate the performance, thus should be avoided.

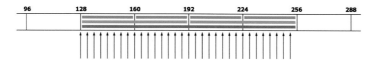

Fig. 5.1 Coalesced Access of Global Memory

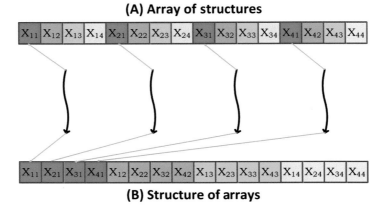

Fig. 5.2 Optimal Global Memory Access

5.2.3 Shared Memory

As shared memory is much faster than global memory, it can be used as a cache to hide the access latency of the global memory in practice. As the capacity is very limited, tiling is a widely used technique for tackling large-sized data. Data are divided into multiple smaller size blocks (tiling), then each block is loaded into shared memory for some calculations one after another. If the ratio of data reuse is high, bandwidth of shared memory other than global memory will be achieved.

When utilizing shared memory, a case should be avoided is the so-called bank conflict, which has a great effect on transfer rate. As the band conflict is not common as far as implementation is concerned and hardware dependent at large, further discussion on this topic is omitted here. Readers can refer to the specific manual for detailed information.

Shared memory is divided into equally sized memory modules (banks) that can be accessed simultaneously (as shown in Fig. 5.3). Therefore, any memory load or store of n addresses that spans n distinct memory banks can be serviced simultaneously, yielding an effective bandwidth that is n times as high as the bandwidth of a single bank (c.f. Fig. 5.3). However, if multiple addresses of a memory request are mapped to the same memory bank, the accesses are serialized. The hardware splits a memory request that has bank conflicts into as many separate conflict-free requests as necessary, decreasing the effective bank width by a factor equaling to the number of separate memory requests. The one exception here is when multiple threads in a warp address the same shared memory location, resulting in a broadcast.

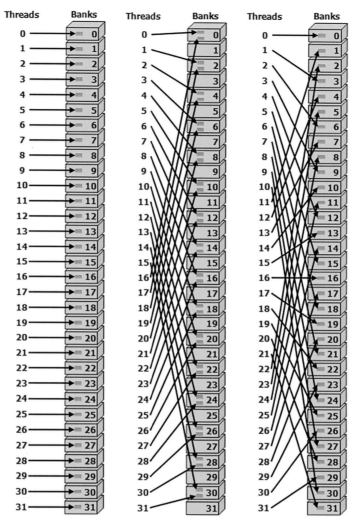

Fig. 5.3 Shared Memory Access

5.2.4 Read-Only Memory

Both constant memory and texture memory can only be read by the threads. Thanks to the existence of fast cache, both have smaller latency than global memory. The data used for read-only can be stored in read-only memory for faster access, such as random numbers and distance matrix in ant colony optimization (ACO) for the traveling salesman problem (TSP).

5.3 Random Number Generation

SIAs need random numbers of a minimum quality to perform well [12]. Conventional random number generators (RNGs) cannot be executed directly in parallel, since they need a current state and a seed to run. In early proposal [106, 213], this issue is tackled by pregenerating all random numbers needed to run the algorithm on the CPU and transfer to graphics memory. However, random numbers can be efficiently generated directly on the GPU in highly parallel manner [99], and handy library is also available [137]. In common CPU-based implementations, random numbers are typically generated as needed. In the case of GPUs, it is much more efficient to generate a bunch of random numbers once. For fast access, the random numbers can be stored in read-only memory.

A detailed discussion on RNG will be given in Chapter 10.

5.4 Branch Divergence

All GPU threads are organized into multiple groups (warps or wavefronts). Threads in a group execute the same instruction when selected. The GPU's performance drops off with the degree of divergence. So when to design algorithms, divergence should be avoided whenever possible. For instance, to avoid thread divergence, probability matrix was calculated by a separate kernel which executed prior to path construction [34].

5.5 Occupancy

Multithreading to saturate all cores. As a rule of thumb for GPU optimization, memory access latency is best to be hidden by computation. That is to say, in general, there should be more active threads than physical processing cores. Although there is no trivial relation between occupancy and the implementation efficiency and hardware utilization ratio, occupancy can be helpful in the design of algorithms on specific GPUs.

5.6 Summary

In this chapter, we discussed some general considerations which are critical for the GPU-based implementation of SIAs. High speedup achieved by GPU is no accident, it is the result of efforts and careful considerations on the characteristics of the GPU and application at hand. A bad implementation can be very inefficient even no speedup can be observed. Different algorithms may need to be optimized at different aspects. In practice, the proper optimization decision can only be drawn on the basis of careful profiling analysis.

Chapter 6
GPU-Based Particle Swarm Optimization

Contents

6.1 Introduction

Particle swarm optimization (PSO), developed by Eberhart and Kennedy in 1995, is a stochastic global optimization technique inspired by social behavior of bird flocking or fish schooling [87]. In the PSO, each particle in the swarm adjusts its position in the search space based on the best position it has found so far as well as the position of the known best-fit particle of the entire swarm, and finally converges to the global best point of the whole search space [207, 206].

Compared to other swarm-based algorithms such as genetic algorithm and ant colony algorithm, PSO has the advantage of easy implementation, while maintaining strong abilities of convergence and global search. In recent years, PSO has been used increasingly as an effective technique for solving complex and difficult optimization problems in practice. PSO has been successfully applied to problems such as function optimization, artificial neural network training, fuzzy system control, blind source separation, machine learning, and so on [179, 183].

In spite of those advantages, it takes PSO a lot of time to find solutions for large-scale problems, such as problems with large dimensions and problems which need a large swarm population for searching in the solution space. The main reason for this is that the optimizing process of PSO requires a large number of fitness evaluations, which are usually done in a sequential way on CPU, so the computation task can be very heavy, thus the running speed of PSO may be quite slow.

In this chapter, we present how to run PSO on graphics processing unit (GPU) in parallel using compute unified device architecture (CUDA). With a good optimization performance, the PSO implemented on GPU can solve problems with large-scale population and high dimension, speedup its running dramatically and provide users with a feasible solution for complex optimizing problems in reasonable time.

For single-objective optimization, experiments are conducted by running the PSO both on the GPU and the CPU, respectively, to optimize several benchmark test functions. The running time of the PSO-based GPU (GPU-PSO, for short) is greatly shortened compared to that of the PSO-based CPU (CPU-PSO, for short). A *40*$\times$ speedup can be obtained by our implemented GPU-PSO on a display card of NVIDIA GeForce 9800 GT, with the same optimization performance.

For multiple-objective optimization, a GPU-based parallel PSO for multiobjective problems is presented. Experiments on several two objective benchmark test problems are conducted. Compared with a sequential multiple-objective PSO (MOPSO) based CPU, our GPU-based parallel MOPSO is much more efficient in reducing the running time than the former, and speedups between 3.74 and 7.92 are reached. And the bigger the size of the swarm is, more nondominated solutions can be found, higher the quality of solutions may be, and bigger speedup can be obtained.

The remainder of this chapter is organized as follows: In Section 6.2, PSO is presented in details. Implementation and experimental results will be presented in Section 6.3 (single objective) and Section 6.4 (multiple objective), respectively. Finally, we summarize this chapter in Section 6.5.

6.2 Particle Swarm Optimization

6.2.1 Original Particle Swarm Optimization

In original PSO, each solution of the optimization problem is called a particle in the search space. The search of the problem space is done by a swarm with a specific number of particles.

Assume that the swarm size is N and the problem dimension is D. Each particle i ($i = 1, 2, \ldots N$) in the swarm has the following properties: a current position X_i, a current velocity V_i, and a personal best position $\tilde{P}_i$. And there is a global best position $\hat{P}$, which has been found in the search space since the start of the evolution. During each of the iteration, the position and velocity of every particle are updated according to $\tilde{P}_i$ and $\hat{P}$. This process in original PSO can be formulated as follows:

$$V_{id}(t+1) = wV_{id}(t) + c_1 r_1 (\tilde{P}_{id}(t) - X_{id}(t)) + c_2 r_2 (\hat{P}_d(t) - X_{id}(t)) \tag{6.1}$$

$$X_{id}(t+1) = X_{id}(t) + V_{id}(t) \tag{6.2}$$

where $i = 1, 2, \ldots N$, $d = 1, 2, \ldots D$. In Eqs. (6.6), (6.7), the learning factors c_1 and c_2 are nonnegative constants, r_1 and r_2 are random numbers uniformly distributed in the interval $[0, 1]$, $V_{id} \in [-V_{max}, V_{max}]$, where V_{max} is a designated maximum velocity which is a constant preset according to the objective function. If the velocity on one dimension exceeds the maximum, it will be set to V_{max}. This parameter controls the convergence rate of the PSO and can prevent it from growing too fast. The parameter w is the inertia weight, which is a constant in the interval $[0, 1]$ used to balance the global and local search abilities.

6.2.2 Standard Particle Swarm Optimization

In these two decades, many researchers have taken great effort to improve the performance of original PSO by exploring the concepts, issues, and applications of the algorithm. In spite of this attention, there has as yet been no standard definition representing exactly what is involved in modern implementations of the technique.

In 2007, Daniel Bratton and James Kennedy designed a standard particle swarm optimization (standard PSO, for short, SPSO) which is a straightforward extension of the original algorithm while taking into account more recent developments that can be expected to improve performance on standard measures [19, 183]. This standard PSO is intended for use both as a baseline for performance testing of improvements to the technique, as well as to represent PSO to the wider optimization community.

Standard PSO is different from original PSO mainly in two aspects.

6.2.2.1 Swarm Communication Topology

Original PSO uses a global topology as shown in Fig. 6.1A. In this topology, the global best particle, which is responsible for the velocity updating of all the particles, is chosen from the whole swarm population, while in standard PSO there is no global best, instead, each particle relies on a local best particle for velocity updating, which is chosen from its left and right neighbors as well as itself. We call this a local topology, which is shown in Fig. 6.1B.

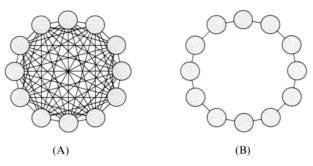

(A)   (B)

Fig. 6.1 Original PSO and Standard PSO Topologies

6.2.2.2 Inertia Weight and Constriction

In original PSO, an inertia weight parameter was designed to adjust the influence of the previous particle velocities on the optimization process. By adjusting the value of w, the swarm has a greater tendency to eventually constrict itself down to the area containing the best fitness and explore that area in detail. Similar to the parameter w, standard PSO introduced a new parameter χ known as the constriction factor, which is derived from the existing constants in the velocity update equation:

$$\chi = \frac{2}{|2 - \varphi - \sqrt{\varphi^2 - 4\varphi}|}, \qquad \varphi = c_1 + c_2$$

and the velocity updating formula in standard PSO is

$$V_{id}(t+1) = \chi(V_{id}(t) + c_1 r_1(\tilde{P}_{id}(t) - X_{id}(t)) + c_2 r_2(\hat{P}_{id}(t) - X_{id}(t))) \qquad (6.3)$$

where $\hat{P}$ is no longer the global best but the local best position.

Statistical tests have shown that standard PSO can find better solutions than original PSO, while retaining the simplicity of original PSO. The introduction of standard PSO can give researchers a common grounding to work from. Standard PSO can be used as a means of comparison for future developments and improvements of PSO, and thus prevent unnecessary effort being expended on "reinventing the wheel" on rigorously tested enhancements that are being used at the forefront of the field.

6.2.3 Variable Definition and Initialization

Suppose the fitness value function of the problem is $f(X)$ in the domain $[-r, r]$. The variable definitions are given as follows (notice that every array is one-dimensional):

- Particle position array: X
- Particle velocity array: Y
- Personal best position: $\tilde{P}$
- Local best position: $\hat{P}$
- Fitness value of particles: F
- Personal best fitness value: PF
- Local best fitness value: LF

where the sizes of $X, Y, \tilde{P}$, and $\hat{P}$ are $D * N$; the sizes of F, PF, and LF are N.

6.3 GPU-Based PSO for Single-Objective Optimization

In this section, we will describe the algorithm design of GPU-based PSO (GPU-PSO for short) and its CUDA implementation.

6.3.1 Algorithmic Flow of GPU-PSO

The algorithm presented here is based on the previous works in [213, 214]. The algorithmic flow of GPU-PSO is illustrated in Algorithm 6.1. Here *Iter* is the maximum number of iterations that GPU-PSO runs, which serves as the stop condition for the optimizing process of functions.

6.3.2 Parallelization Methods

The difference between a CPU function and a GPU *kernel* is that the operations of a kernel should be parallelized. So we must design the methods of parallelization carefully for all the subprocesses of GPU-PSO algorithm.

Algorithm 6.1 Algorithmic Flow for GPU-PSO

Initialize the positions and velocities of all particles.
Transfer data from CPU to GPU.

// sub-processes in "for" are done in parallel
for $i = 1$ to *Iter* **do**
    Compute the fitness values of all particles
    Update $\tilde{P}$ of all particles
    Update $\hat{P}$ of all particles
    Update velocities and positions of all particles
end for
Transfer data back to CPU and output.

6.3.2.1 Computation of Fitness Values of Particles

The computation of fitness values is the most important task during the whole search process, where high density of arithmetical computation is required. It should be carefully designed for parallelization so as to improve the overall performance (attention is mainly paid to the running speed) of GPU-PSO.

The algorithm for computing fitness values of all the particles is shown in Algorithm 6.2. From Algorithm 6.2, we can see that the iteration is only applied to dimension index $i = 1, 2, \ldots, D$, while on CPU, it should also be applied to the particle index $j = 1, 2, \ldots, N$. The reason is that the arithmetical operation on all the N data of all the particles in dimension i is done in parallel (synchronously) on GPU.

Algorithm 6.2 Compute Fitness Values

Initialize, set the *"block size"* and *"grid size"*, with the number of threads in a grid equaling to the number of particles(N).

for each dimension i **do**
    Map all threads to the N position values one-to-one
    Load N data from global to shared memory
    Apply arithmetical operations to all N data in parallel
    Store the result of dimension i with $f(X_i)$
end for

Combine $f(X_i)$ $(i = 1, 2 \ldots, D)$ to get the final fitness values $f(X)$ of all particles, store them in array F.

Mapping all the threads to the N data in a one-dimensional array should follow two steps:

• Set the block size to $S_1 \times S_2$ and grid size $T_1 \times T_2$. So the total number of threads in the grid is $S_1 * S_2 * T_1 * T_2$. It must be guaranteed that $S_1 * S_2 * T_1 * T_2 = N$, only in this case can all the data of N particles be loaded and processed synchronously.

- Assuming that the thread with the index (T_x, T_y) in the block whose index is (B_x, B_y), is mapped to the Ith datum in a one-dimensional array, then the relationship between the indexes and I is:

$$I = (B_y * T_2 + B_x) * S_1 * S_2 + T_y * S_2 + T_x \qquad (6.4)$$

In this way, all the threads in a kernel are mapped to N data one-to-one. Then applying an operation to one thread will cause all the N threads to do exactly the same operation synchronously. This is the core mechanism for explaining why GPU can accelerate the computing speed greatly.

6.3.2.2 Update $\tilde{P}$ and $\hat{P}$

After the fitness values are updated, each particle may arrive at a better position $\tilde{P}$ than ever before and a new local best position $\hat{P}$ may be found. So $\tilde{P}$ and $\hat{P}$ (refer to Eq. (6.8)) must be updated according to the current status of the particle swarm. The updating process of $\tilde{P}$ (PF at the same time) can be achieved by Algorithm 6.3.

Algorithm 6.3 Update $\tilde{P}$

Map all the threads to N particles one-to-one.
Transfer all the N data from global to shared memory.

//Do operations to thread i ($i = 1, \ldots, N$) in parallel
if $F(i)$ is better than $PF(i)$ **then**
    $PF(i) = F(i)$
    for each dimension d **do**
        Store the position $X(d * N + i)$ to $\tilde{P}(d * N + i)$
    end for
end if

The updating of $\hat{P}$ (LF at the same time) is similar to that of $\tilde{P}$. Compare a particle's previous $\hat{P}$ to the current $\tilde{P}$ of the right neighbor, left neighbor and its own, respectively, then choose the best one as the new $\hat{P}$ for that particle.

6.3.2.3 Update Velocity and Position

After the personal best and local best positions of all the particles have been updated, the velocities and positions should also be updated according to Eqs. (6.8), (6.7), respectively, by making use of the new information provided by $\tilde{P}$ and $\hat{P}$. This process is conducted dimension by dimension. On the same dimension d ($d = 1, 2, \ldots, D$), the velocity values of all the particles are updated in parallel, using the same technique mentioned in the previous algorithms. What should be paid special attention to is that two random integers P_1 and P_2 should be provided for fetching random numbers from array R, namely the random number "pool."

6.3.2.4 Random Number Generation

During the process of optimization, PSO needs lots of random numbers for velocity updating. The absence of high precision integer arithmetic in current generation GPUs makes random numbers generating on GPU very tricky though it is still possible [99]. In order to focus on the implementation of PSO on GPU, we would rather generate random numbers on CPU and transfer them to GPU. However, the data transportation between GPU and CPU is quite time consuming. If we generate random numbers on CPU and transfer them to GPU during each iteration of PSO, it will greatly slow down the algorithm's running speed due to mountains of data to be transferred. So data transportation between CPU and GPU should be avoided as much as possible.

We solve this problem in this way: M $(M >> D * N)$ random numbers are generated on CPU before the running of PSO algorithm. Then they are transferred to GPU once for ado and stored in an array R on the global memory, serving as a random number "pool." Whenever the velocity updating process is undergone, we just pass two random integer numbers $P_1, P_2 \in [0, M - D * N]$ from CPU to GPU, then $2 * D * N$ numbers can be drawn from array R starting at positions P_1 and P_2, respectively, instead of transferring $2 * D * N$ numbers from CPU to GPU. The running speed can be obviously improved by using this technique.

In the past few years, efficient proposals for generating random numbers on the GPU side have been widely discussed. It will be more effective to use these well-implemented methods for better performance. We will come back to random number generation in Chapter 7 and a detailed discussion will be presented in Chapter 10.

6.3.3 Experimental Results and Discussion

The experimental platform is based on Intel Core 2 Duo 2.20 GHz CPU, 3.0 GB RAM, NVIDIA GeForce 9800GT, and Windows XP. Performance comparisons between GPU-PSO and CPU-PSO are made based on four classical benchmark test functions as shown in Table 6.1.

The variables of f_1, f_2, and f_3 are independent but variables of f_4 are dependent, namely there are related variables such as the ith and $(i+1)$th variable. The optimal solution of all the four functions are 0.

PSO is run both on GPU and CPU, and we call them as GPU-PSO and CPU-PSO, respectively. Now we define *speedup* as the times that GPU-PSO runs faster than CPU-PSO

Table 6.1 Benchmark Test Functions

No.	Name	Equation	Bounds
f_1	Sphere	$\sum_{i=1}^{D} x_i^2$	$(-100, 100)^D$
f_2	Rastrigin	$\sum_{i=1}^{D} [x_i^2 - 10 * \cos(2\pi x_i) + 10]$	$(-10, 10)^D$
f_3	Griewangk	$\frac{1}{4000} \sum_{i=1}^{D} x_i^2 - \prod_{i=1}^{D} \cos(x_i/\sqrt{i}) + 1$	$(-600, 600)^D$
f_4	Rosenbrock	$\sum_{i=1}^{D-1} (100(x_{i+1} - x_i^2)^2 + (x_i - 1)^2)$	$(-10, 10)^D$

$$\gamma = \frac{T_{CPU}}{T_{GPU}}, \tag{6.5}$$

where γ is *speedup*, T_{CPU} and T_{GPU} are the time used by CPU-PSO and GPU-PSO to optimize a function during a specific number of iterations, respectively.

In the following paragraphs, *Iter* is the number of iterations that SPSO runs, D is the dimension, N is the swarm population, namely the number of particles in the swarm; *CPU-Time* and *GPU-Time* are the average time that CPU-PSO and GPU-PSO consumed in the 20 runs, respectively, with second as the unit of time. *CPU-Optima* and *GPU-Optima* stand for the mean final optimized function values of running PSO for 20 times on CPU and GPU, respectively.

The experimental results and analysis are given below.

6.3.3.1 Running Time and Speedup vs. Swarm Population

We run both GPU-PSO and CPU-PSO on f_1, f_2, f_3, and f_4 for 20 times independently, and the results are shown in Tables 6.2–6.5 ($D = 50$, *Iter* = 2000 for f_1 and f_3, *Iter* = 5000 for f_2 and f_4).

6.3.3.2 Optimizing Performance Comparison

GPU-PSO uses a random number "pool" for updating velocity instead of instant random number generation. To some extend it may affect the results. However, seen from the tables above, on all of the four functions, GPU-PSO and CPU-PSO can find optimal solutions of almost the same magnitude, namely the precision of the result given by GPU-PSO is almost the same with CPU-PSO (even better in some cases). So we can say that GPU-PSO is reliable in optimizing functions.

Table 6.2 Results of CPU-PSO and GPU-PSO on f_1 ($D = 50$)

N	CPU Time	GPU Time	Speedup	CPU Optima	GPU Optima
256	3.11	1.17	**2.7**	7.68E−8	5.54E−8
512	6.15	1.25	**4.9**	5.92E−8	4.67E−8
768	9.22	1.46	**6.3**	4.49E−8	3.97E−8
1024	12.4	1.62	**7.7**	3.89E−8	3.94E−8
1280	15.97	1.89	**8.5**	4.17E−8	3.59E−8

Table 6.3 Results of CPU-PSO and GPU-PSO on f_2 ($D = 50$)

N	CPU Time	GPU Time	Speedup	CPU Optima	GPU Optima
256	16.91	3.01	**5.6**	132.10	133.99
512	34.46	3.28	**10.5**	113.64	111.43
768	51.53	3.75	**13.7**	118.62	109.72
1024	70.27	4.12	**17.1**	110.78	106.94
1280	88.61	4.78	**18.5**	108.72	104.11

Table 6.4 Results of CPU-PSO and GPU-PSO on f_3 ($D = 50$)

N	CPU Time	GPU Time	Speedup	CPU Optima	GPU Optima
256	5.94	1.22	**4.9**	1.52E−09	3.87E−08
512	11.86	1.32	**9.0**	1.21E−09	1.18E−08
768	18.05	1.53	**11.8**	9.04E−10	5.96E−09
1024	24.58	1.73	**14.2**	6.87E−10	0
1280	30.85	1.91	**16.2**	6.97E−10	0

Table 6.5 Results of CPU-PSO and GPU-PSO on f_4 ($D = 50$)

N	CPU Time	GPU Time	Speedup	CPU Optima	GPU Optima
256	9.17	3.02	**3.0**	26.09	23.40
512	18.03	3.25	**5.5**	16.21	14.21
768	27.75	3.79	**7.3**	11.62	16.20
1024	37.81	4.20	**9.0**	12.14	10.15
1280	46.62	4.89	**9.5**	6.82	8.88

6.3.3.3 Population Size Setup

When the swarm size grows (from 512 to 1280), the optima of a function found by both CPU-PSO and GPU-PSO are almost of the same magnitude, no obvious precision improvement can be seen. So we can say that a large swarm population is not always necessary. But exceptions may still exist when large swarm population is required in order to obtain better optimizing results, especially in real-world optimization problems.

6.3.3.4 Running Time

Compared with f_1, the fitness evaluation of f_3 is much more complex. f_1 contains only square arithmetic, while f_3 contains square, cosine, and square root arithmetic as well. Similarly we can say that f_2 is much more complex than f_4.

Figs. 6.2 and 6.3 depict how running time of both CPU-PSO and GPU-PSO changes when the swarm size (N) grows. On all of the four functions, the running time of GPU-PSO and CPU-PSO is proportional to the swarm size (N), namely the time increases linearly with N, while keeping the other parameters constant. And when N, D, and *Iter* are fixed, it takes much more time for CPU-PSO to optimize the function with more complex arithmetic than the one with less complex arithmetic.

However, this is no longer true for GPU-PSO in this case. It can be noticed from Fig. 6.2 that two lines which stand for the time consumed by GPU-PSO when optimizing f_1 and f_3, overlap each other, namely it takes almost the same time for GPU-PSO to optimize functions with arithmetic of different complexity. The same phenomenon appears in Fig. 6.3. So it can be concluded that more complex arithmetic a function has, more speed advantages can GPU-PSO gain compared to CPU-PSO.

6.3.3.5 Speedup

As seen from Fig. 6.4, for a certain function, as the swarm size grows, the *speedup* also increases, but it is limited to a specific constant. Furthermore, the line of a function with more complex arithmetic lies above the line of those with less complex arithmetic (f_3 above f_1 and f_2 above f_4), that is to say, optimizing a function with more complex arithmetic by GPU-PSO can reach a relatively higher speedup.

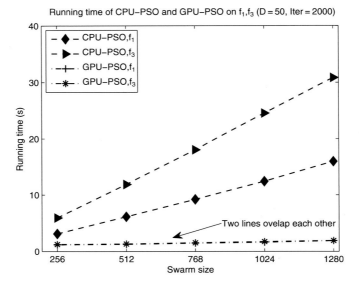

Fig. 6.2 Running Time and Swarm Population (f_1 and f_3)

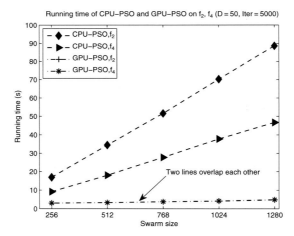

Fig. 6.3 Running Time and Swarm Population (f_2 and f_4)

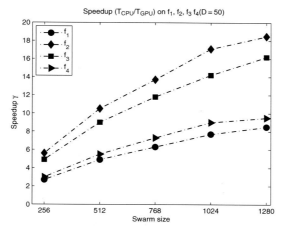

Fig. 6.4 Speedup and Swarm Population

6.3.4 Running Time and Speedup vs. Dimension

Now we fix the swarm size to 50, and vary the dimension of the functions (D). Analysis about the relationship between running time (as well as *Speedup*) and D is given here. We run both GPU-PSO and CPU-PSO on f_1, f_2, and f_3 for 20 times independently, and the results are shown in Tables 6.6–6.9 ($N = 512$, $Iter = 2000$ for f_1 and f_3, $Iter = 5000$ for f_2 and f_4).

From Tables 6.6 to 6.9, we can make the following conclusions.

6.3.4.1 Running Time

As seen from Figs. 6.5 and 6.6, the running time of both GPU-PSO and CPU-PSO increases linearly with the dimension, keeping the other parameters constant. When D, N, and $Iter$ are fixed, functions with more complex arithmetic (f_2 and f_3) need more time than the function with much less complex arithmetic (f_4 and f_1) to be

Table 6.6 Results of CPU-PSO and GPU-PSO on f_1 ($N = 512$)

D	CPU Time	GPU Time	Speedup	CPU Optima	GPU Optima
50	6.90	1.28	**5.4**	5.93E−08	4.67E−08
100	13.22	2.48	**5.3**	0.14	0.13
150	18.67	3.59	**5.2**	24.05	24.69
200	25.48	4.78	**5.3**	350.76	262.98

Table 6.7 Results of CPU-PSO and GPU-PSO on f_2 ($N = 512$)

D	CPU Time	GPU Time	Speedup	CPU Optima	GPU Optima
50	39.29	3.37	**11.7**	113.64	111.43
100	67.61	6.46	**10.5**	407.05	407.13
150	100.05	9.34	**10.7**	848.84	813.50
200	131.41	12.32	**10.7**	1350.94	1315.91

Table 6.8 Results of CPU-PSO and GPU-PSO on f_3 ($N = 512$)

D	CPU Time	GPU Time	Speedup	CPU Optima	GPU Optima
50	13.56	1.37	**9.9**	1.21E−09	1.19E−08
100	24.18	2.53	**9.5**	0.009	0.072
150	41.46	3.80	**10.9**	0.97	1.19
200	54.61	4.95	**11**	4.07	3.54

Table 6.9 Results of CPU-PSO and GPU-PSO on f_4 ($N = 512$)

D	CPU Time	GPU Time	Speedup	CPU Optima	GPU Optima
50	20.12	3.34	**6.0**	16.21	14.21
100	36.57	6.37	**5.7**	154.30	145.45
150	54.57	10.54	**5.2**	425.39	434.12
200	72.51	12.39	**5.9**	1050.18	950.67

optimized by CPU-PSO, while the time is almost the same when optimized by GPU-PSO, just as mentioned in Section 6.3.3.4.

6.3.4.2 Speedup

It can be seen from Fig. 6.7 that the *speedup* remains almost the same when the dimension grows. The reason is, in GPU-PSO, the parallelization can only be applied to swarm size (N), but not to the dimension. Still, the function with more complex arithmetic has a relatively higher speedup under the same conditions.

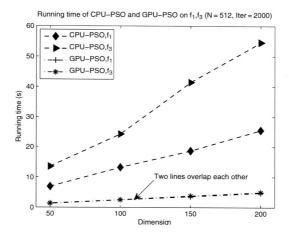

Fig. 6.5 Running Time and Dimension (f_1 and f_3)

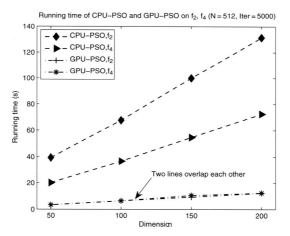

Fig. 6.6 Running Time and Dimension (f_2 and f_4)

6.3.5 Other Characteristics of GPU-PSO

6.3.5.1 Maximum Speedup

In some applications, large swarm size is needed during the optimizing process. In this case, GPU-PSO can greatly benefit the optimization by improving the running speed dramatically. Now we will carry through an experiment to find out how much speedup GPU-PSO can reach. We run GPU-PSO and CPU-PSO on f_2, respectively. Set $D = 50$, $Iter = 5000$, and both GPU-PSO and CPU-PSO are run only

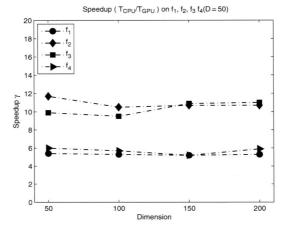

Fig. 6.7 Speedup and Dimension

once (as the time needed for each run is almost the same). The results are shown in Table 6.10.

Table 6.10 GPU-PSO and CPU-PSO on f_2 ($D = 50$)

N	CPU Time	GPU Time	CPU Optima	GPU Optima	Speedup
8192	648.1	25.9	101.49	96.52	**25.02**
16384	2050.3	51.7	83.58	87.56	**39.7**

As shown in Table 6.10, when optimizing f_2, GPU-PSO can reach a *speedup* of almost **40**, when the swarm population size is 16,384. And on the functions more complex than f_2, the speedup may be even greater.

6.3.5.2 High Dimension Application

In some real-world applications such as face recognition and fingerprint recognition, the problem dimension may be very high. Running PSO on CPU to optimize high-dimensional problems can be quite slow, but the speed can be greatly accelerated if running it on GPU. Now we run both GPU-PSO and CPU-PSO on f_2 once ($N = 512$, *Iter* = 5000). The results are given in Table 6.11.

From Table 6.11, we can find out that even when the dimension is as large as 2000, GPU-PSO can run more than 6.5 times faster than GPU-PSO.

Table 6.11 GPU-PSO and CPU-PSO on f_3 ($N = 512$)

D	CPU Time	GPU Time	Speedup
1000	934.5	87.9	**10.6**
2000	2199.7	128.2	**17.2**

6.3.6 Comparison With Texture-PSO

The PSO algorithm was also implemented on GPU in an other way by making use of the texture-rendering of GPU [106]. We call it as *Texture-PSO* for short. This method used the textures on GPU chips to store particle information, and the fitness evaluation, velocity and position updating were done by means of texture rendering. But Texture-PSO has the following disadvantages which make it almost useless when doing real-world optimizations.

- The dimension must be set to a specific number, and it cannot be changed unless redesigning the data structures.
- When the swarm population is small, for example, smaller than 512, the running time of the Texture-PSO may even be longer than corresponding PSO that runs on CPU.
- The functions which can be optimized by Texture-PSO must have completely independent variables as a result of the architecture of GPU textures. So functions like f_4 cannot be optimized by the Texture-PSO.

Instead of using the textures on GPU, we use the global memory to implement GPU-PSO. Global memory is more like memory on CPU than textures do. So GPU-PSO has overcome all the three disadvantages mentioned above:

- The dimension serves as a changeable parameter and it can be set to any reasonable numbers. High-dimensional problems are also solvable by using our GPU-PSO.
- When the swarm population is small, for example, smaller than 512, a remarkable speedup can also be achieved.
- The functions with dependent variables such as f_4 can also be optimized by GPU-PSO.

6.4 GPU-Based PSO for Multiple-Objective Optimization

Multiobjective optimization problems are very common in real-world optimization filed, of which the objectives to be optimized are normally in conflict with respect to each other. As a result, there is no single solution for them. Instead, several solutions with good trade-off among the objectives should be found out. In recent years, multiobjective particle swarm optimization (MOPSO) has become quite popular in the field of multiobjective optimization. However, as a result of the heavy computation task of fitness evaluation and archive maintaining, the execution time of MOPSO for optimizing some difficult problems may be quite long. This section presents a GPU-based parallel PSO for multiobjective problems based on [215]. Experiments on several two objective benchmark test problems are conducted. Compared with a sequential MOPSO based on CPU, our GPU-based parallel MOPSO is much more efficient in reducing the running time than the former, and speedups between 3.74 and 7.92 are reached. And the bigger the size of the swarm is, more nondominated solutions can be found, higher the quality of solutions may be, and bigger speedup can be obtained.

PSO was originally designed to solve single-objective optimization problems, but it can also be extended for multiobjective, resulting in many multiobjective PSO approaches [155].

Parsopoulos and Vrahatis proposed a vector evaluated PSO (VEPSO) approach for multiobjective optimization (only two-objective problems were considered) [144]. The whole swarm consisted of two subswarms. Each subswarm was evaluated according to one of the two objectives but information coming from the other subswarm was used to determine the change of the velocities. Through this technique, the two subswarms purchased their own objective, while at the same time the other one was also under consideration, so a good trade off of the two objectives can be made. Compared with vector evaluated genetic algorithm (VEGA) [166], the performance of VEPSO for multiobjective optimization had an identical performance.

In this section, a modified VEPSO approach for multiobjective optimization is implemented on GPU (GPU-MOPSO). Experiments on four two-objective benchmark test functions are conducted, with the results thoroughly analyzed. Firstly, the performance of our GPU-MOPSO is compared with the corresponding CPU-based serial MOPSO via the comparison of running speed. Secondly, the benefits of implementing MOPSO on GPU are presented.

6.4.1 Multiobjective Optimization

A general multiobjective optimization problem can be described as a vector function $\mathbf{f}$ that maps a tuple of D decision variables to a tuple of M objectives:

$$
\begin{aligned}
min/max \quad & \mathbf{y} = \mathbf{f}(\mathbf{x}) = (f_1(\mathbf{x}), f_2(\mathbf{x}), \ldots, f_M(\mathbf{x})) \\
subject\ to \quad & \mathbf{x} = (x_1, x_2, \ldots, x_D) \in \mathbf{X} \\
& \mathbf{y} = (y_1, y_2, \ldots, y_M) \in \mathbf{Y}
\end{aligned}
$$

where $\mathbf{x}$ is called the decision vector, $\mathbf{X}$ is the parameter space, $\mathbf{y}$ is the objective vector, and $\mathbf{Y}$ is the objective space. The set of solutions of a multiobjective optimization problem consists of all decision vectors for which the corresponding objective vectors cannot be improved in any dimension without degradation in another — these vectors are known as Pareto optimal.

Mathematically, the concept of Pareto optimality can be defined as follows.

Without loss of generality, assume a minimization problem and consider two decision vectors $\mathbf{a}, \mathbf{b} \in \mathbf{X}$. $\mathbf{a}$ is said to dominate $\mathbf{b}$ (written as $\mathbf{a} \prec \mathbf{b}$) iff

$$\forall i \in \{1, 2, \ldots, m\} : f_i(\mathbf{a}) \leqq f_i(\mathbf{b}) \wedge \exists j : f_j(\mathbf{a}) < f_j(\mathbf{b})$$

where $j \in \{1, 2, \ldots, m\}$ as well. Additionally, $\mathbf{a}$ is said to cover $\mathbf{b}$ if $\mathbf{a} \prec \mathbf{b}$ or $f(\mathbf{a}) = f(\mathbf{b})$. All decision vectors which are not dominated by any other decision vector of a given set are called nondominated regarding this set. The decision vectors that are nondominated within the entire search space are denoted as Pareto optimal and constitute the so-called Pareto-optimal set or Pareto-optimal front.

6.4.2 Multiobjective PSO

Assuming that the search space is D-dimensional, the ith particle of the swarm is represented by vector $X_i = (x_{i1}, x_{i2}, \ldots, x_{iD})$ and the best particle in the swarm is denoted by the index g. The best previous position of the ith particle is represented as $P_i = (p_{i1}, p_{i2}, \ldots, p_{iD})$ while the velocity of the ith particle is recorded as $V_i = (v_{i1}, v_{i2}, \ldots, v_{iD})$, and t is the number of current iteration. Following this notation, the particles are manipulated according to the following equations iteratively:

$$v_{id}(t+1) = w \cdot v_{id}(t) + c_1 \cdot r_1 (p_{id}(t) - x_{id}(t))$$
$$+ c_2 \cdot r_2 (p_{gd}(t) - x_{id}(t)) \tag{6.6}$$
$$x_{id}(t+1) = x_{id}(t) + v_{id}(t+1) \tag{6.7}$$

where $d = 1, 2, \ldots, D$; $i = 1, 2, \ldots, N$, N is the size of the population. w is the inertia weight; c_1 and c_2 are two positive constants; r_1 and r_2 are two random numbers within the range [0,1]. Here, w is initially set to 1.0 and linearly decreases to 0.4, $c_1 = c_2 = 2.05$. If x_{id} exceeds the boundary limitation X_{max} or X_{min}, it will be directly set to X_{max} or X_{min}.

In order to solve multiobjective optimization problems, the original PSO has to be modified, as the solution set of a problem consists of different solutions (the Pareto-optimal front) instead of a single one. Given the population-based nature of PSO, it is desirable to produce several (different) nondominated solutions within a single run. The leaders should be carefully chosen among the nondominated solutions found out so far, which are usually stored in an external archive. There are currently over 25 different proposals of MOPSOs reported. A survey of this specialized literature can be found in [155].

In 2002, Parsopoulos et al. proposed a VEPSO approach for multiobjective optimization [144], which might be the first particle swarm approach for multiobjective optimization. They used two subswarms to solve several two-objective problems.

Each subswarm was evaluated with one of the two objectives. Meanwhile, the best particle of the other subswarm was used for the determination of the new velocities of its own particles. The experimental results show that the performance of this approach is as good as VEGA, which was a well-known evolutionary algorithm approach for multiobjective optimization.

They extend their VEPSO approach to multiobjective problems with more than two objectives in 2004 [143]. They used M subswarms to optimize S objectives (M may be bigger than S). Each subswarm optimizes a single objective, and they exchange their best particles through a ring topology. But the performance of this model was only tested on two-objective problems.

Compared with other MOPSO methods, the VEPSO approach has the following promising features:

- As the nondominated solutions found during the evolution process are not responsible for the guidance of the particles in the swarm, they are stored in the archive just for outcome. Strategies which focus on choosing good solutions out of the archive to guide the whole swarm are not necessary, so the implementation of VEPSO is relatively simple.
- It can be parallelized based on various parallel hardware architecture, eg, multicomputer or multiprocessor systems. The running speed of VEPSO can be accelerated.

6.4.3 Vector Evaluated PSO and Its Modification

In VEPSO, the whole swarm consists of two subswarms with the same size. Assume the total swarm size is N, then the population of each subswarm is $N/2$. For each subswarm, Eq. (6.6) (velocity update process) should be adjusted as follows:

$$v_{id}(t+1) = w \cdot v_{id}(t) + c_1 \cdot r_1 (p_{id}(t) - x_{id}(t)) \\ + c_2 \cdot r_2 (p_{gd}^*(t) - x_{id}(t)) \qquad (6.8)$$

where p_{gd}^* is the dth element of the global best particle's position vector coming from the other subswarm. In this way, each subswarm updates the velocities and positions of its particles using Eqs. (6.8), (6.7) corresponding to its own objective, while the other objective is also considered. The nondominated solutions found in each iteration are stored in an external archive, which was built and maintained using the pseudocode provided in [82].

We make a few modifications to VEPSO and propose our GPU-based MOPSO (abr. GPU-MOPSO), for the purpose of reducing the computation task as well as achieving a higher speedup. Firstly, the online performance is considered instead of offline performance, which means there is no need to maintain an external archive. Online performance means that only the nondominated solutions in the final population are considered as the outcome, while offline performance takes the nondominated solutions generated during the entire evolution process into account. The following benefits are brought in by these two modifications.

- Each particle in the swarm is evaluated by only one of the two objectives, which halves the computation task of fitness evaluation, while in VEPSO, each particle must be evaluated using both of the objectives.
- The time-consuming data transportation between GPU and CPU can be greatly reduced, as there is no need to transfer the fitness and position values of each nondominated solution, which reside on GPU, back to CPU, resulting in a higher speedup.

6.4.4 Algorithm for GPU-MOPSO

The GPU-MOPSO can be described by Algorithm 6.4. In this algorithm, $Iter$ is maximum number of iterations. The whole swarm is presented by P. The fitness values of all the N particles are stored in a one-dimensional array F. Steps 5, 6, and 8 are executed in parallel, there are N threads, each one is allocated with one particle to process.

Algorithm 6.4 Algorithm for GPU-MOPSO

1: Set t, the generation counter to 0.
2: Generate N individuals of initial population $P(0)$.
3: Transfer initial data from CPU to GPU.
4: **for** $t = 0$ to $Iter$ **do**
5:      Evaluate the fitness of the ith individual in each subswarm of $P(t)$ with its corresponding objective, store them in $F(t)$.
6:      Update P_i for all particles.
7:      Transfer $F(t)$ back to CPU, find out the indices (g) of the best particle in each subswarm via $F(t)$.
8:      Update velocity and position values of the ith particle, using Eqs. (6.8), (6.7).
9: **end for**
10: Transfer $P(t)$ back to CPU, evaluate each particle using both of the objectives, output the nondominated ones.

6.4.5 Data Organization

As there are N individuals and each one is presented by a D-dimensional vector, we use a one-dimensional array of size $N * D$ on global memory to represent the whole population.

When the concurrent memory accesses by CUDA threads in a half wrap (16 parallel threads) can be coalesced into a single memory transaction, the global memory bandwidth can be improved. In order to fulfill the requirements for coalesced memory accesses, the same variables from all individuals are grouped and form a tile of N values in the global memory. The representation scheme for the swarm is shown in Fig. 6.8.

Fig. 6.8 Representation of N Individuals of D Variables on Global Memory

Generating random numbers on GPU are very tricky though there are several existing approaches [73, 99]. In order to focus on the implementation of MOPSO, we would rather generate random numbers on CPU and transfer them to GPU. For the purpose of saving transferring time, we do it in the following way: Q ($Q >> D*N$) random numbers are generated on CPU before running GPU-MOPSO. Then they are transferred to GPU once for all and stored in an array on the global memory. Each time random numbers are needed during the evolution, pass a random integer (serves as start point) to GPU, and fetch the corresponding number of random numbers from global memory for use. This may impose some negative influence on the performance of GPU-MOPSO, because the numbers are not quite "random."

6.4.6 Fitness Value Evaluation

In step 5 of Algorithm 6.4, the fitness value of each individual is computed. Notice that, it is not necessary to get the complete objective vector for each individual in GPU-MOPSO. The first objective is used to evaluate the individuals of the first subswarm, and just alike for the second one. As there is no interaction among threads, the fitness value evaluation process can be fully parallelized. The fitness values are stored in F, which is an array of size N.

6.4.7 Update of Global Best Particle

This procedure (step 7 in Algorithm 6.4) is performed on CPU, as the minimum (or maximum) fitness values in each subswarm must be found out in array F. Although it is possible to execute it on GPU, it is quite complex to implement and not efficient enough when N is relatively small. We transfer F back to CPU, and the indices (g) of the best particle in each subswarm are found out and recorded.

6.4.8 Update of Velocity and Position

The update of velocity and position for the whole swarm is an essential procedure in GPU-MOPSO and it can be fully parallelized. The position of the global best particle (P_g) of the second subswarm is also responsible for the velocity update of the first subswarm, and vice versa.

6.4.9 Selection of Nondominated Solutions

In the final generation, the nondominated solutions are picked out from the entire swarm, and they are returned as outcome. As there are N individuals, multiple solutions may exist, from which Pareto fronts are constructed.

6.4.10 Experiment and Results Analysis

The benchmark test functions are adopted from [144], which are listed in Table 6.12. Deb et al. [44] give a comprehensive study on how to construct test functions in 2005.

We have also implemented a serial CPU-based MOPSO (abr. CPU-MOPSO) approach corresponding to GPU-MOPSO, just for comparison. All of the experiments are conducted on CUDA^{TM} platform, based on an Intel Core 2 Duo 2.20 GHz CPU, 3.0 GB RAM machine. The display card is NVIDIA GeForce 9800GT, and OS is Windows XP.

Table 6.12 Two-Objective Test Functions

Function	m	Equation	Bounds	D
F1	2	$f_1 = \frac{1}{D} \sum\limits_{i=1}^{D} x_i; f_2 = \frac{1}{D} \sum\limits_{i=1}^{D} (x_i - 2)^2$	$[0,1]$	30
F2	2	$f_1 = x_1; f_2 = g * h; g = 1 + 9.0 \sum\limits_{i=2}^{D} x_i/(D-1);$ $h = 1 - \sqrt{f_1/g}$	$[0,1]$	30
F3	2	As F2, except $h = 1 - \sqrt{f_1/g} - (f_1/g)sin(10\pi * f_1)$	$[0,1]$	30
F4	2	As F2, except $h = 1 - \sqrt[4]{f_1/g} - (f_1/g)^4$	$[0,1]$	30

We set $N = 1024, 2048, 4096, 8192$, respectively. Both GPU-MOPSO and CPU-MOPSO are executed for 30 times to optimize the four test functions with $Iter = 250$. For each function, the average number of nondominated solutions (denoted as No.S) found out by these two approaches, as well as the average running time are recorded. All the results are listed in Tables 6.13–6.16. Several figures (Figs. 6.9, 6.10, and 6.12) are drawn to depict the data in the tables for a more vivid display.

Table 6.13 Results of CPU-MOPSO and GPU-MOPSO on F1

N	CPU-MOPSO		GPU-MOPSO		Speedup
	No.S	Time	No.S	Time	
1024	40	1.01	39	0.21	**4.76**
2048	49	2.03	45	0.33	**6.18**
4096	51	4.38	37	0.62	**7.06**
8192	79	9.40	42	1.19	**7.92**

Table 6.14 Results of CPU-MOPSO and GPU-MOPSO on F2

N	CPU-MOPSO		GPU-MOPSO		Speedup
	No.S	Time	No.S	Time	
1024	22	0.97	24	0.26	**3.74**
2048	41	1.98	30	0.45	**4.36**
4096	95	4.48	147	0.85	**5.23**
8192	171	9.56	106	1.69	**5.65**

Table 6.15 Results of CPU-MOPSO and GPU-MOPSO on F3

N	CPU-MOPSO		GPU-MOPSO		Speedup
	No.S	Time	No.S	Time	
1024	15	0.95	13	0.25	**3.84**
2048	19	1.90	15	0.46	**4.14**
4096	23	3.96	19	0.85	**4.69**
8192	29	9.30	24	1.66	**5.59**

Table 6.16 Results of CPU-MOPSO and GPU-MOPSO on F4

N	CPU-MOPSO		GPU-MOPSO		Speedup
	No.S	Time	No.S	Time	
1024	33	0.99	30	0.26	**3.78**
2048	52	2.02	78	0.47	**4.29**
4096	125	4.60	121	0.86	**5.36**
8192	208	9.71	291	1.80	**5.40**

6.4.11 Running Time and Speedup vs. Swarm Size

Fig. 6.9 shows the relationship between running time and the swarm size (N), when using CPU-MOPSO and GPU-MOPSO to optimize function $F_1 - F_4$, respectively. As N grows in an exponential way, the running time of CPU-MOPSO also grows in the exponential way, while the running time of GPU-MOPSO increases in a linear way.

Fig. 6.10 depicts how speedup changes with N. As N grows, the speedup of the GPU-MOPSO over CPU-MOPSO also increases, running on $F_1 - F_4$. The speedups ranges from 3.74 to 7.92, and when N is bigger than 8192, the speedup is expected to be even larger.

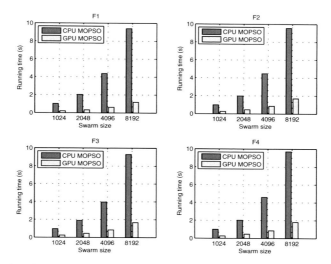

Fig. 6.9 Running Time vs. Swarm Size

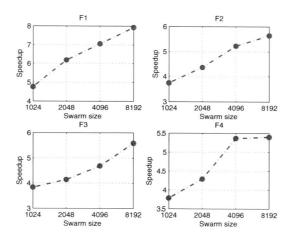

Fig. 6.10 Speedup vs. Swarm Size

6.4.12 Pareto Fronts Found by GPU MOPSO

The Pareto-optimal fronts of $F_1 - F_4$ found out by GPU-MOPSO are shown in Fig. 6.11. Each of them are constructed by the specific run which returns most number of nondominated solutions in the final generation. These fronts are as good as the fronts found by VEPSO [144].

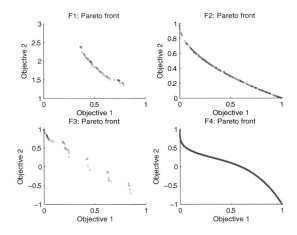

Fig. 6.11 Pareto Fronts Found by GPU MOPSO ($N = 4056$)

6.4.13 Quantity and Quality of Solutions vs. Swarm Size

In single-objective optimization, larger swarm size does not certainly mean a better optimizing results, which was already pointed out by Bratton and Kennedy in [19], and a swarm size of $20 - 100$ was suggested. Consequently, it is not quite necessary to implement PSO on GPU in single-objective optimization, as the GPU-based parallel PSO with a small swarm ($20 - 100$ individuals) runs even slower than serial PSO on CPU.

However, in multiobjective optimization, a larger swarm is more powerful in searching for nondominated solutions. As can be seen from Fig. 6.12, as the swarm size (N) grows, the number of nondominated solutions found out by CPU-MOPSO also increases, when running on all of the four test functions. While in GPU-MOPSO, this rule is also true when running on $F_2 - F_4$, but not so convictive on F_1. The reason may be that the random numbers used by GPU-MOPSO are not quite exactly "random," as explained in Section 6.4.5.

Large swarm size is not only beneficial to finding large quantity number of nondominated solutions, but also helps in improving the quality of them.

The obtained solutions of all 30 runs are evaluated using one established measure, the $\mathscr{C}$ metric [218]. The metric $\mathscr{C}(A,B)$ measures the fraction of members of the Pareto front B that are dominated by members of the Pareto front A. Notice that both the $\mathscr{C}$ metric is neither symmetrical in their arguments.

Here $\mathscr{C}(N_1,N_2)$ denotes the $\mathscr{C}$ values of Pareto fronts returned by the GPU-MOPSO swarm of size N_1 and N_2. The $\mathscr{C}$ values are statistically displayed with matlab boxplots in Fig. 6.13. Each boxplot represents the distribution of the $\mathscr{C}$ values for the ordered pair $(2048, 1024)$ and $(1024, 2048)$, respectively.

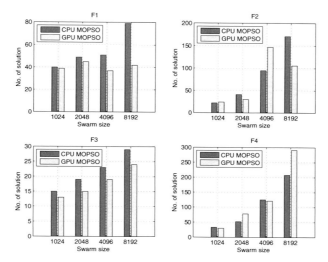

Fig. 6.12 Number of Solutions vs. Swarm Size

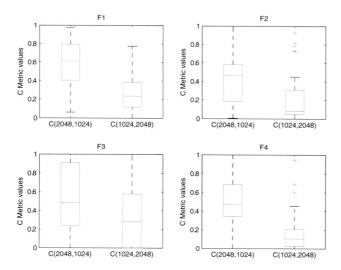

Fig. 6.13 Quality Metric of Nondominated Solutions

Each box of the boxplot has lines at the lower quartile, median, and upper quartile values. The lines that extend from each end of the box are the whiskers, which show the extent of the rest of the data. The outliers that lie beyond the ends of the whiskers are displayed with a red + sign.

As can be seen from Fig. 6.13, the nondominated solutions found out by the swarm of size 2048 dominate a bigger fraction of the solutions obtained by the swarm of size 1024. On the contrary, the fraction is much lower. So it can be concluded that the solutions found out by the swarm with a bigger population are more high quality than those obtained by a small population.

6.5 Remarks

In this section, we brief discuss the key features of GPU-PSO.

For single-objective optimization, GPU-PSO has the following features:

- The running time of GPU-PSO is greatly shortened over CPU-PSO, while maintaining similar optimizing performance. Under certain conditions, the speedup can be as large as nearly $40\times$ on f_2. On other functions with more complex arithmetic, a larger speedup can be expected. On GPU chips that have much more multiprocessors than the GeForce 9800GT used in this paper, the GPU-PSO is expected to run tens of times faster than CPU-PSO.
- The running time and swarm population size take a linear relationship. This is also true for running time and dimension. And it takes almost the same time for GPU-PSO to optimize functions with different arithmetic complexity, while CPU-PSO takes much more time to optimize functions with more complex arithmetic, with the same swarm population, dimension and number of iterations. Furthermore, function with more complex arithmetic has a higher speedup.
- The swarm population can be very large, and the larger the population is, the faster GPU-PSO runs than CPU-PSO. So GPU-PSO can especially benefit optimization with large swarm size.
- High-dimensional problems and functions with dependent variables can also be optimized by GPU-PSO, and noticeable speedup can be reached.
- Because in current common PC, there are GPU chips in the display card, more researchers can make use of our parallel GPU-PSO to solve their practical problems in a quick way.

Because of these features of GPU-PSO, it can be applied to a large scope of practical optimization problems.

For the multiobjective (specifically, only two objectives are considered) PSO has the following promising features:

- Each particle in the swarm is evaluated by only one of the objectives instead of both. Thus the total fitness computation task is halved.
- The Pareto-optimal fronts are constructed by the last generation of the swarm. The maintaining of an external archive for nondominated solutions, which is a complex and quite time-consuming procedure, is not necessary.
- The bigger the size of the swarm is, the more nondominated solutions can be found, the higher their quality are (closer to the true fronts of the problems), and the bigger speedup can be reached by GPU-MOPSO. The speedups range from 3.74 to 7.92, depending on the functions to be optimized and the size of the swarm.

6.6 Summary

In this chapter, detailed GPU-based implementations of PSO for both single- and multiple-objective optimization problems are presented, based on the famous software platform of CUDA from NVIDIA. Compared to the CPU-based PSO, the GPU-based version of PSO has special speed advantages on large-scale and high-dimensional problems which are often happened and widely used in a lot of real-world optimization applications.

Chapter 7
GPU-Based Fireworks Algorithm

Contents

7.1 Introduction

Fireworks algorithm (FWA) is a novel swarm intelligence algorithm under active research [184, 181, 180]. In this chapter, a very efficient FWA variant based on graphics processing units (GPUs), called GPU-FWA for short, is introduced [49]. GPU-FWA modifies the original FWA to suit the particular architecture of the GPU. It does not need special complicated data structure, thus making it easy to implement; meanwhile, it can make full use of the great computing power of GPUs. The key components of GPU-FWA are FWA search, attract-repulse mutation, and implementation which are elaborated in this chapter.

To make the chapter self-contained, a brief introduction to FWA is presented first. Then, we describe GPU-FWA in detail, followed by an empirical comparison of GPU-FWA with FWA and particle swarm optimization (PSO).

7.2 Fireworks Algorithms (FWA)

Inspired by the explosion process of fireworks, FWA was originally proposed by Tan and Zhu for solving optimization problems [185], and modified and greatly improved by Zheng et al. [210, 212] and other researchers [184, 181, 180]. Comparative study shows that FWA is very competitive with respect to real-parameter problems [23]. FWA has been successfully applied to many scientific and engineering problems, such as nonnegative matrix factorization [77], digital filter design [62], parameter optimization [70], document clustering [202], just to name a few. New mechanisms and analyses are actively proposed to further improve the performance of FWA [211, 108].

In this section, the conventional FWA is first summarized and reviewed and then three improved FWAs are briefly described [181, 180].

7.2.1 Conventional FWA

FWA utilizes N D-dimensional parameter vectors x_i^G as a basic population in each generation. Parameter i varied from 1 to N and parameter G stands for the Gth generation. Every individual in the population "explodes" and generates sparks around it. The number of sparks and the amplitude of each individual are determined by certain strategies. Furthermore, a Gaussian explosion is used to generate sparks to keep the diversity of the population. Finally, the algorithm keeps the best individual in the population and selects the rest $N - 1$ individuals based on distance for next generation. More specific strategies in FWA can be described as follows.

7.2.1.1 Explosion Sparks Strategy

The explosion sparks strategy mimics the explosion of fireworks in air and is the core strategy in FWA. When a spark blasts, the spark is vanished and many sparks appear around it. The explosion sparks strategy mimicking this explosion phenomenon is used to produce new individuals by explosion. In this strategy, two parameters need to be determined.

The first one is the number of sparks:

$$s_i = \hat{S} \cdot \frac{y_{max} - f(\mathbf{x}_i) + \xi}{\sum_{i=1}^{N} (y_{max} - f(\mathbf{x}_i)) + N \cdot \xi}, \tag{7.1}$$

where $\hat{S}$ is a parameter controlling the total number of sparks generated by the N fireworks, $y_{max} = max(f(\mathbf{x}_i))\,(i = 1, 2, \ldots, N)$ is the maximum (worst) fitness value of the objective function among the N fireworks, and ξ denotes the machine precision. s_i is rounded to the nearest integer (clamped if beyond a predefined range). (Note that, in the original literature [185] and many following works, the ξ in the denominator is not multiplied by N which will cause the sum of all s_i surpass $\hat{S}$ when the fitness values are very close. The same argue goes for Eq. (7.2) as well.)

The second parameter in this strategy is the amplitude of sparks:

$$A_i = \hat{A} \cdot \left(\frac{f(\mathbf{x}_i) - y_{min} + \xi}{\sum_{i=1}^{N} (f(\mathbf{x}_i) - y_{min}) + N \cdot \xi} + \Delta \right), \tag{7.2}$$

where the predefined $\hat{A}$ denotes the maximum explosion amplitude, and $y_{min} = min(f(\mathbf{x}_i))\,(i = 1, 2, \ldots, N)$, i.e., the minimum (best) value of the objective function among the N fireworks, and ξ , which denotes the machine precision, is utilized to avoid zero division error.

Δ is a small number to guarantee the amplitude is nonzero thus avoid the search process getting stalled. In [210], a minimum amplitude check is conducted instead of using Δ.

Eqs. (7.2), (7.1) guarantee that fireworks with better fitness values generate more sparks within smaller range (see Fig. 7.1). Via this mechanism, more computing resource can be assigned to better space to enhance exploitation, and for the worse space, the search trends to explore.

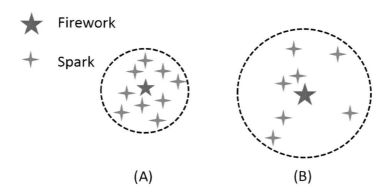

Fig. 7.1 A Firework With Better Fitness Value Can Generate a Larger Population of Sparks Within a Smaller Range and Vice Verse

7.2.1.2 Mapping Strategy

If an individual is close to the boundary, the generated sparks may lie out of the feasible space. Therefore, a mapping method is used to keep sparks inside of the feasible space.

The mapping strategy ensures all the individuals stay in the feasible space. If there are some outlying sparks from the boundary, they will be mapped to their allowable scopes:

$$x_i = x_{min} + |x_i| \% (x_{min} - x_{max}), \qquad (7.3)$$

where x_i represents the positions of any sparks that lie out of bounds, while x_{max} and x_{min} stand for the maximum and minimum boundary of a spark position. The symbol $\%$ stands for the modular arithmetic operation. Aside from the explosion sparks strategy, another way to generate sparks is proposed as Gaussian sparks strategy.

7.2.1.3 Gaussian Sparks Strategy

To keep the diversity of the population, Gaussian sparks strategy is used to generate sparks with Gaussian distribution. Suppose the position of current individual is stated as x_{jk}, the Gaussian explosion sparks are calculated as

$$x_k^j = x_k^j \cdot g, \tag{7.4}$$

where g is a random number drawn in Gaussian distribution:

$$g = Gaussian(1,1). \tag{7.5}$$

The random number g obeys the Gaussian distribution with both mean value and standard deviation are 1. After normal explosions and Gaussian explosions, we consider a proper way to select individuals for next generation. Here, a distance-based selection method is suggested.

7.2.1.4 Selection Strategy

To select the individuals for next generation, the best individual is always kept at first. Then the next $N - 1$ individuals are selected based on their distance to other individuals. The individual that is far from other individuals gets more chance to be selected than those individuals with smaller distances to other individuals. The general distance between two locations is calculated by:

$$R(x_i) = \sum_{j \in K} d(x_i, x_j) = \sum_{j \in K} ||x_i - x_j||, \tag{7.6}$$

where location x_i and x_j $(i \neq j)$ can be any locations and K is the set of all current locations. For the distance measurements, many methods can be used, including Euclidean distance, Manhattan distance, and Angle-based distance. Inspired by the immune density [112], Euclidean distance is used in FWA [185]:

$$d(x_i, x_j) = |f(x_i) - f(x_j)|, \tag{7.7}$$

where $f(x_i)$ is the fitness for location x_i and $d(x_i, x_j)$ represents the distance between two locations. As last, a roulette-wheel method is used to calculate the possibility of selecting the locations.

$$p(x_i) = \frac{R(x_i)}{\sum_{i \in K} R(x_j)}. \tag{7.8}$$

The individuals with larger distance from others have more chance to be selected. In this way, the diversity of a population can be ensured. The flowchart and pseudocode for FWA is stated in Fig. 7.2. Although FWA reaches a great progress at several problems, there are still some places for improvement.

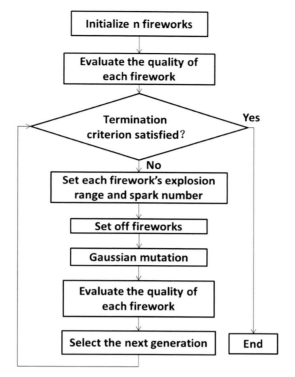

Fig. 7.2 Framework of FWA

7.2.2 Enhanced FWA

To overcome the disadvantages of FWA, many researchers have attempted in different ways to improve it. Zheng et al. [210] proposed an enhanced FWA (EFWA) through improving the conventional FWA in the following five aspects.

7.2.2.1 Minimal Explosion Amplitude Setting

In the explosion process, some explosion amplitude may be closed to zero, which is not conducive to find the global best value. Since the explosion amplitude was closely related to fitness values, two ways to limit the minimum amplitude boundary were proposed. One way is based on a linear function and the other is based on a nonlinear function:

$$A_{min}^i = A_{init} - \frac{A_{init} - A_{final}}{evals\_max} \cdot t. \tag{7.9}$$

$$A_{min}^k(t) = A_{init} - \frac{A_{init} - A_{final}}{evals\_max} \cdot \sqrt{(2 \cdot evals\_max - t) \cdot t}. \tag{7.10}$$

In both formulae, $A_{min}^k(t)$ means the lower boundary for an individual in the kth dimension when the function is evaluated t times. The two new parameters A_{init} and A_{final} stand for the initial and final amplitudes, respectively. The last parameter is the maximum evaluation times, which is expressed as *evals_max*. The schematic diagrams for linear and nonlinear minimal explosion amplitudes are drawn in Fig. 7.3.

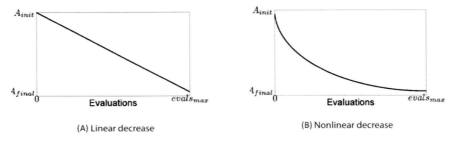

(A) Linear decrease   (B) Nonlinear decrease

Fig. 7.3 Schematic Diagrams of Minimal Amplitude for Linear and Nonlinear Decreases. Obtained From Zheng, S., Janecek, A., Tan, Y.: Enhanced fireworks algorithm. In: Evolutionary Computation (CEC), 2013 IEEE Congress on, pp. 2069–2077 (2013). DOI 10.1109/CEC.2013.6557813

7.2.2.2 Explosion Sparks Strategy

In FWA, the same increment will be added to some selected dimensions of an individual.

As it is shown in Fig. 7.4, the same increment may cause a loss of diversity to a population. Hence, it is necessary to generate different increments and add the increments to each selected dimension for an individual to obtain the diversity of population. In Fig. 7.4, $x_i^j (j = 1, 2, \ldots, D)$ stands for the value in the jth dimension of the ith individual. A_i is the amplitude for that individual x_i.

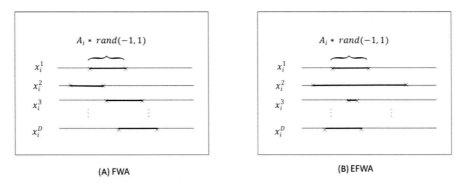

(A) FWA   (B) EFWA

Fig. 7.4 Increment of FWA and EFWA in Each Selected Dimension

7.2.2.3 Gaussian Sparks Strategy

FWA works significantly well on functions that will reach their optimal at the origin of coordinates. For example, the optimal value of a two-dimensional Ackley function lies at the origin of its coordinate. But if the function is shifted, e.g., the optimal value is shifted to $[-70, -55]$, FWA performs badly. Fig. 7.5 shows the location of the Gaussian sparks in FWA. It can be seen that Gaussian sparks can easily find the optimal value at the origin of coordinate when the function is not shifted. But Gaussian sparks work poorly on the shifted function.

To overcome the disadvantage of Gaussian sparks, Zheng et al. [210] used another way to generate Gaussian sparks. Referring the position of the current global best individual, the Gaussian sparks are generated by

$$x_i^k = x_i^k + (x_{best}^k - x_i^k) \cdot g, \tag{7.11}$$

where x_i^k stands for the selected individual to generate Gaussian sparks and x_{best}^k is the best individual the algorithm has found out so far. Parameter g obeys the Gaussian distribution with mean 0 and standard deviation 1.

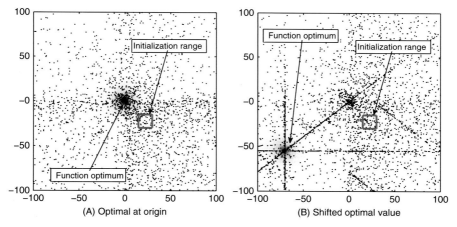

Fig. 7.5 Effect of the Gaussian Sparks. From Zheng, S., Janecek, A., Tan, Y.: Enhanced fireworks algorithm. In: Evolutionary Computation (CEC), 2013 IEEE Congress on, pp. 2069–2077 (2013). DOI 10.1109/CEC.2013.6557813

7.2.2.4 Mapping Strategy

The proposed FWA used modular arithmetic operation to map individuals back into scope. However, modular arithmetic operation is time consuming. Besides, some of the individuals are mapped to a place near the origin, straying from the diversity of population. For example, suppose the solution space varies from -20 to 20. If there is an individual who has a value of -21, then it is mapped to 1 according to the formula suggested in FWA. Hence, a new mapping operator is proposed

$$x_i^k = x_{min}^k + rand(0,1) \cdot (x_{max}^k - x_{min}^k), \qquad (7.12)$$

where x_{min}^k and x_{max}^k are the lower and upper boundary of the solution space.

7.2.2.5 Selection Strategy

The most time-consuming part of conventional FWA lies in the selection process. In the selection strategy of conventional FWA, the distances between individuals need to be calculated. Hence, the computational complexity of selection strategy is much higher than random selection strategy. The selection operation is called elitism random selection (ERS). According to the work of Pei et al. [147], the best individual is always preserved for next generation, while the other $N-1$ individuals are selected randomly. In this way, the running time of FWA is largely decreased and furthermore, the computational complexity is linear with the number of fireworks.

7.3 GPU-Based Fireworks Algorithm

GPU-based fireworks algorithm (GPU-FWA) [49] was proposed for the purpose of achieving the following goals:

- Good quality of solutions. The algorithm can find good solutions, compared to the state-of-the-art algorithms.
- Good scalability. As the problem gets complex, the algorithm can scale in a natural and decent way.
- Ease of implementation and usability, i.e., few control variables to steer the optimization. These variables should also be robust and easy to choose.

To approach these goals, several critical modifications to the FWA are adopted to take benefit of this particular architecture. The pseudocode of GPU-FWA is depicted in Algorithm 7.1.

Like other swarm intelligence algorithms, GPU-FWA is an iterative algorithm. In each iteration, every firework does a local search independently. Then, an information-exchange mechanism is triggered to utilize the heuristic information to guide the search process. The mechanism should make a balance between exploration and exploitation.

As the algorithm is self-descriptive, what is left to be made clear is Algorithms 7.2 and 7.4. Below we will explain these two algorithms in detail, respectively.

Algorithm 7.1 GPU-FWA

1: Initialize n fireworks
2: calculate the fitness value of each fireworks
3: calculate A_i according to Eq. (7.2)
4: **while** termination condition unsatisfied **do**
5:    **for** $i = 1$ to n **do**
6:        Search according to Algorithm 7.2
7:    **end for**
8:    Mutate according to Algorithm 7.4
9:    calculate the fitness values of the new fireworks
10:    update A_i according to Eq. (7.2)
11: **end while**

Algorithm 7.2 FWA Search

1: **for** $i = 1$ to L **do**
2:    generate m sparks according to Algorithm 7.3
3:    evaluate the fitness of each spark
4:    find the best spark with best fitness value, replace it with the current firework if it is better.
5: **end for**

Algorithm 7.3 Sparks Generating I

1: Initialize the spark's location: $\hat{\mathbf{x}}_i = \mathbf{x}_i$;
2: **for** $d = 1$ to D **do**
3:    $r = rand(0,1)$;
4:    **if** $r < \frac{1}{2}$ **then**
5:        $\hat{\mathbf{x}}_{i,d} = \hat{\mathbf{x}}_{i,d} + A_i \cdot rand(-1,1)$;
6:    **end if**
7:    **if** $\hat{\mathbf{x}}_{j,d} > \mathbf{ub}_d$ or $\hat{\mathbf{x}}_{j,d} < \mathbf{lb}_d$ **then**
8:        $\hat{\mathbf{x}}_{j,d} = \mathbf{lb}_d + |\hat{\mathbf{x}}_{j,d} - \mathbf{lb}_d| \bmod (\mathbf{ub}_d - \mathbf{lb}_d)$;
9:    **end if**
10: **end for**

7.3.1 FWA Search

In FWA, each firework generates certain number of sparks to exploit the nearby solution space. Fireworks with better fitness values generate more sparks with a smaller amplitude. This strategy aims to put more computational resources to the more potential position, thus making a balance between exploration and exploitation.

In FWA Search, this strategy is adopted, but in a "greedy" way, i.e., instead of a global selection procedure in FWA, each firework is updated by its current best spark. The mechanism exhibits an enhanced hill-climbing behavior search.

Each firework generates a fixed number of sparks. The exact number (m) of sparks is determined in accordance with the specific GPU hardware architecture. This fixed encoding of firework explosion is more suitable for parallel implementation on the GPUs.

As aforementioned in Chapter 2, within compute unified device architecture (CUDA)-enabled GPU, threads are scheduled by warp, which is nowadays 32 for all the CUDA-enable GPUs. Each warp is assigned certain number of stream processors (SPs). All threads in the same warp execute a common instruction at a time on these SPs. For the older generation Tesla architecture [133], the number is 8, and for Fermi architecture [134] is 16.

To avoid waste of hardware resource, m should be multiple of number of SMs. But, it is unnecessary to pick m too large, as greater m is apt to overexploit a certain position, while a better refined search can be achieved by running more explosions.

So, as a rule of thumb, m should be 16 and 32 on GPUs of the Fermi architecture, and 8 or 16 on the previous generation Tesla architecture. Thus the sparks of each firework can be generated by threads in a single warp, which, as aforementioned, does not need any extra synchronization overhead.

As can seen from Algorithm 7.2, unlike FWA, in GPU-FWA, the fireworks do not exchange information in each explosion procedure, and the number of sparks for each firework generation is fixed.

Such a configuration takes many advantages below.

Firstly, global communications among fireworks need explicit synchronization, which implies a considerable overhead. By letting the algorithm perform a given number of iterations without exchanging information, the running time can be reduced greatly.

Secondly, the number of sparks for each firework to generate is dynamically determined, the computation task must be assigned dynamically through the optimization procedure. As GPUs are inefficient at control operations, the dynamic computation assignment is apt to harm the overall performance of GPUs. By fixing the number of sparks, we can assign each firework to a warp, so that all sparks are synchronized implicitly without extra overhead.

The last but not the least, implemented the explosion in one block of threads, it can fully utilize the shared memory, thus, once the firework position and fitness are loaded from the global memory, no visit to the global memory is needed anymore. The latency of visiting global memory can be reduced greatly.

7.3.2 Attract-Repulse Mutation

While the heuristic information is used to guide local search, other strategies should be taken to keep the diversity of the firework swarm. Keeping a diversity of the swarm is crucial for the success of optimization procedure.

In FWA, a Gaussian mutation is introduced to increase the diversity of the firework swarm. In this mutation procedure, m extra sparks are generated. To generate such a spark, first, a scaling factor g is generated from $G(1, 1)$ (Gaussian distribution with mean 1 and variance 1). For a randomly selected firework, the distance between each corresponding dimension of the firework and the current best firework is

Algorithm 7.4 Attract-Repulse Mutation (AR Mutation)

1: Initialize the new location: $\hat{\mathbf{x}}_i = \mathbf{x}_i$;
2: $s = U(1 - \delta, 1 + \delta)$;
3: **for** $d = 1$ to D **do**
4:      $r = rand(0, 1)$;
5:      **if** $r < \frac{1}{2}$ **then**
6:          $\hat{\mathbf{x}}_{i,d} = \hat{\mathbf{x}}_{i,d} + (\hat{\mathbf{x}}_{i,d} - \mathbf{x}_{best,d}) \cdot s$;
7:      **end if**
8:      **if** $\hat{\mathbf{x}}_{j,d} > x_{UB,d}$ or $\hat{\mathbf{x}}_{j,d} < x_{LB,d}$ **then**
9:          $\hat{\mathbf{x}}_{j,d} = x_{UB,d} + |\hat{\mathbf{x}}_{j,d} - x_{UB,d}| \bmod (x_{UB,d} - x_{UB,d})$;
10:     **end if**
11: **end for**

---

multiplied by g. Thus, the new sparks can be closer to the best firework or further away from it.

Similar to Gaussian mutation, in GPU-FWA, a mechanism called attract-repulse mutation (AR-Mutation) is proposed to achieve this aim in an explicit way, as illustrated by Algorithm 7.4, where $\mathbf{x}_i$ depicts the ith firework, while $\mathbf{x}_{best}$ depicts the firework with the best fitness.

The philosophy behind AR-Mutation, is that, for non-best fireworks, they are either attracted by the best firework to "help" exploit the current best location or repulsed by the best firework to explore more space (see Fig. 7.6). In fact, the choice between "attract" and "repulse" reflects the balance between exploitation and exploration properly.

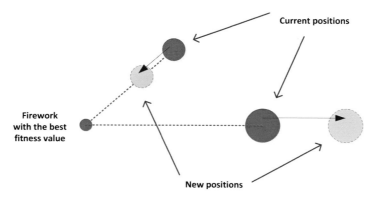

Fig. 7.6 Schematic Diagram of Attract-Repulse Mutation

Despite Gaussian mutation is used in original FWA [185], various random distributions could be taken certainly. As uniform distribution is most straightforward and easiest, so uniform distribution is taken in the proposed algorithm.

To analyze the AR-Mutation mechanism theoretically, the procedure can be simplified to a one-order Markov chain. Given $x_0 = 1$, the next state is generated in Eq. (7.13)

$$x_{t+1} = \alpha_t * x_t, \tag{7.13}$$

where α_t subjects to uniform distribution between a and b, $0 < a < 1$ and $b > 1$.

Then the t-th state can be expressed by the following equation:

$$x_t = \prod_{i=1}^{t} \alpha_i \cdot x_0. \tag{7.14}$$

So the expected position can be calculated as

$$E\left[x_t\right] = E\left[\prod_{i=1}^{t} \alpha_i\right] \cdot x_0 = \prod_{i=1}^{t} E\left[\alpha_i\right] \cdot x_0 = \prod_{i=1}^{t} E\left[\alpha\right] \cdot x_0 = A^t \cdot x_0, \tag{7.15}$$

where $E[\alpha]$ is the expectation of α.

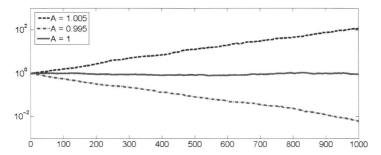

Fig. 7.7 Expected Value of x Under Different Values of A Values

As can be seen from Eq. (7.15), if the expectation of α, i.e., A, is greater than 1, then x is expected to increase exponentially, otherwise, if A less than 1, x is expected to decay exponentially. Fig. 7.7 plots a simulation result, where three traces subject to $U(0.9, 1.11)$ ($A = 1.005$), $U(0.9, 1.1)$ ($A = 1$), and $U(0.9, 1.09)$ ($A = 0.995$), respectively. It is shown from the simulation that, even a small disturbance on $A = 1$, the results tend to diverge to infinite or converge to 0, exponentially.

As for AR-Mutation, it means that fireworks are either "repulsed" to the bounds of feasible range or "attracted" to the current best position. Both conditions lead to prematurity and the loss of diversity.

To make sure that fireworks can "linger" around the search space more steadily, A should take 1. The distribution should be in the form of $s = U(1-\delta, 1+\delta)$, where $\delta \in (0, 1)$.

However, as the search range is limited , so δ should be taken with care, though A is set to 1.

As depicted in Fig. 7.8, from left to right, from top to bottom, δ takes 0.9 to 0.1, respectively. In the simulations, when $x > 100$, x is truncated to 10. x converges to 0 with diverse speeds. As a tendency, greater δ corresponds to faster convergence, and vice versa. But what exact convergence speed is most suitable, is task dependent.

It relies on the landscape of the objective function and how many iterations the algorithm will run.

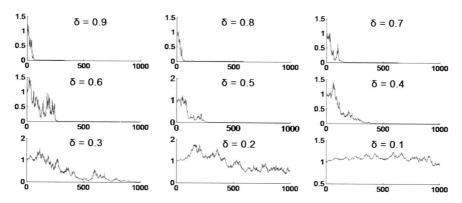

Fig. 7.8 Simulation Results With Different Uniform Distributions

7.3.3 Implementation

The flowchart of GPU-FWA implementation on the platform of CUDA is shown in Fig. 7.9.

7.3.3.1 Thread Assignment

In the FWA search kernel, each firework is assigned to a single warp (i.e., 32 continuous threads). But, not all the threads in the warp are necessary to be used to execute computation. If the number of sparks is set to 16, then we use the former half-warp threads, or if the number is 32, all threads in the warp are used.

Such an implementation brings several advantages. Firstly, since threads in the same warp are synchronized inherently, they will cut down the overhead of inter-spark communications. Secondly, by keeping each firework and their sparks in the same warp, the explosion process takes place in a single block, thus the shared memory can be utilized. As accessing to the shared memory is with much lower latency than global memory, the overall running time can be greatly reduced. Finally, as GPUs automatically dispatch block according to the computing and memory resources, it is easy for the proposed algorithm to extend with the scale of problem.

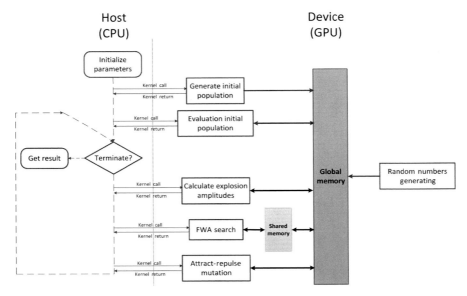

Fig. 7.9 The Flowchart of the GPU-FWA Implementation on CUDA

7.3.3.2 Data Organization

In implementation of GPU-FWA, the position and fitness values of each firework are stored in the global memory, while the data of sparks are stored in the fast-accessed shared memory. For the purpose of coalescing global memory access [136], data are usually organized in an interleaving configuration (i.e., structure of arrays) [215, 158], as in Fig. 7.10. Here, we take the conventional way, i.e., the data of the fireworks and sparks in both global and shared memory are stored in a continuous manner (i.e., array of structures, see Fig. 7.11). In our implementation, each firework occupies a single SM. The threads running on the same SM are up to load the data of a particular firework from global memory, thus data of the same firework should be stored continuously. This organization is also simpler and easier to extend with problem scale than the interleaving pattern.

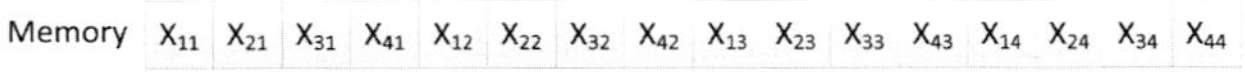

Memory X_{11} X_{21} X_{31} X_{41} X_{12} X_{22} X_{32} X_{42} X_{13} X_{23} X_{33} X_{43} X_{14} X_{24} X_{34} X_{44}

Fig. 7.10 Interleaving Storage

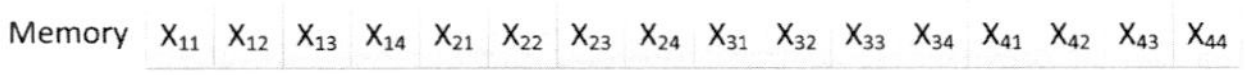

Memory X_{11} X_{12} X_{13} X_{14} X_{21} X_{22} X_{23} X_{24} X_{31} X_{32} X_{33} X_{34} X_{41} X_{42} X_{43} X_{44}

Fig. 7.11 Continuous Storage

7.3.3.3 Random Number Generation

Random numbers play an important role in swarm intelligence algorithms. It is very time consuming to generate tremendous, high-quality random numbers. The performance of the optimization heavily relies on the quality of random numbers (interested readers can refer to Chapter 10 for details). For our implementation, the efficient cuRAND library [137] is used to generate high-quality random numbers on the GPU.

7.3.4 Empirical Analysis

The performance of GPU-FWA can be studied empirically. We compare GPU-FWA with both original FWA [185] and standard PSO [19].

7.3.4.1 Experimental Platform

The experiments were conducted on Windows 7 Professional x64 with 4G DDR3 Memory (1333 MHz) and Intel core I5-2310 (2.9 GHz, 3.1 GHz). The GPU used in the experiments is NVIDIA GeForce GTX 560 Ti with 384 CUDA cores. The CUDA runtime version is 5.0.

PSO is implemented according to [19] with a ring-topology and FWA according to [185] with minor modification as mentioned in Section 7.3.

In all simulations, each function was run 20 times independently. For GPU-FWA, in each running, 1000 iterations were executed. FWA and PSO executed the same number of function evaluations as GPU-FWA.

For GPU-FWA, the parameters are set as: $n = 48$, $L = 30$, $\delta = 0.5$. As in the experimental environment, the GeForce 560 Ti GPU has 12 SMs, the number of fireworks should be the multiplication of 12 and big enough to avoid waste of computational power. 48 is adopted for the comparison of precision, while 72, 96, and 144 are also used when comparing the speedup.

So far, there is no theoretical rule on the criterion of the selection of L and δ. Some experiments are conducted to predetermine them. $L = 30$ and $\delta = 0.5$ performed pretty well compared to various parameter settings ($L = 10, 20, 30, 40, 50$ and $\delta = 0.1 \cdots 0.9$, as the limit of space, the results are omitted here). The total function evaluation times are $48 * 16 * 1000 = 768,000$.

For a fair comparison, all of the three algorithms were tested under the same scale. Here, by saying scale, we mean that the number of function evaluations that can be executed in parallel. For GPU-FWA, the scale in this experiment is 768, so PSO's swarm size is set as the same number. For FWA, as the firework number takes 64, so total spark number is 640 and number of gaussian sparks is 64.

7.3.4.2 Quality of Solutions

Sphere, Hyper-ellipsoid, Schwefel 1.2, Rosenbrock, Rastrigin, Schwefel, Griewangk, and Ackley functions ($f1 \sim f8$) were used as benchmark, see [49] for the detailed configurations. The first three functions are unimodal functions, while others are multimodal functions.

All benchmark functions were optimized in 20 independent trails, and the average results and corresponding standard deviations are listed in Table 7.1.

Under the significance level of 0.01 (observe Table 7.2), it can be seen that GPU-FWA outperforms FWA on $f1 \sim f6$ and f8, it only lost to FWA on f7. PSO outperforms GPU-FWA on unimodal function f2, but fail to GPU-FWA on another unimodal function f3. GPU-FWA can get better results on multimodal functions f4, f5, f6, and f8. In general, as far as the benchmark functions are concerned, we can see that GPU-FWA performs better than both FWA and PSO.

Table 7.1 Precision Comparisons Among GPU-FWA, FWA, and PSO

Fun	GPU-FWA		FWA		PSO	
	Avg.	Std.	Avg.	Std.	Avg.	Std.
f1	**1.31E−09**	1.85E−09	7.41E+00	1.98E+01	3.81E−08	7.42E−07
f2	1.49E−07	6.04E−07	9.91E+01	2.01E+02	**3.52E−11**	1.15E−10
f3	**3.46E+00**	6.75E+01	3.63E+02	7.98E+02	2.34E+04	1.84E+04
f4	**1.92E+01**	3.03E+00	4.01E+02	5.80E+02	1.31E+02	8.68E+02
f5	**7.02E+00**	1.36E+01	2.93E+01	2.92E+00	3.16E+02	1.11E+02
f6	-8.09E+03	2.89E+03	**-1.03E+04**	3.77E+03	-6.49E+03	9.96E+03
f7	1.33E+00	1.78E+01	**7.29E−01**	1.24E+00	1.10E+00	1.18E+00
f8	**3.63E−02**	7.06E−01	7.48E+00	7.12E+00	1.83E+00	1.26E+01

Table 7.2 p-Values of GPU-FWA Against FWA and SPSO

	f1	f2	f3	f4	f5	f6	f7	f8
GPU-FWA vs. FWA	**1.00E−06**	**0.00E+00**	**0.00E+00**	**0.00E+00**	**0.00E+00**	**0.00E+00**	5.16E−01	**0.00E+00**
GPU-FWA vs. PSO	3.46E−01	**1.21E−04**	**0.00E+00**	**2.15E−02**	**0.00E+00**	**6.50E−03**	8.03E−01	**1.21E−02**

7.3.4.3 Speedup vs. Swarm Size

Besides the precision of the solutions, speedup efficiency is another critical factor that has to be considered.

In order to observe the speedups GPU-FWA achieves in comparison with PSO and FWA, a series of experiments were conducted, where n is set, respectively, to $48, 72, 96, 144$ for GPU-FWA. 1000 iterations are run, and the same function evaluation time under the same scale for PSO and FWA.

The running time (in seconds) and speedup with respect to Rosenbrock function is illustrated in Table 7.3. Figs. 7.12 and 7.13 depict the speedup of all the eight benchmark functions with respect to the swarm sizes.

GPU-FWA achieved a speedup as high as $180\times$ with the scale of less than 200, in the meantime, the up-to-date GPU accelerated PSO achieve $200\times$ fold speedup with the scale high up to 10,000 [158]. Therefor, GPU-FWA are more scalable than the conventional GPU-based PSO.

Table 7.3 Running Time and Speedup of Rosenbrock for Three Algorithms

n	FWA(s)	PSO(s)	GPU-FWA(s)	SU(FWA)	SU(PSO)
48	36.420	84.615	0.615	59.2	137.6
72	55.260	78.225	0.624	88.6	125.4
96	65.595	103.485	0.722	90.8	143.3
144	100.005	155.400	0.831	120.3	187.0

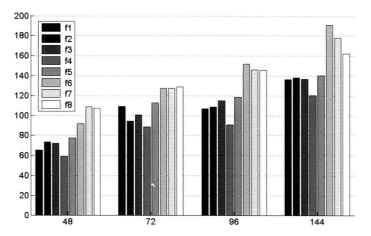

Fig. 7.12 Speedup vs. FWA

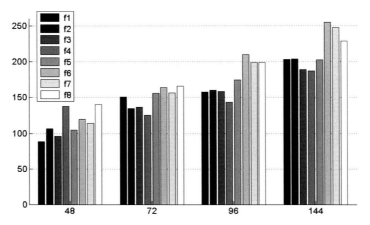

Fig. 7.13 Speedup vs. PSO

7.4 Summary

In this chapter, an efficient GPU-based FWA variant, GPU-FWA was presented. GPU-FWA can fully leverage the great computing power of the GPU architecture, making itself very suitable for parallel computation. It does not need special complicated data structures, thus making it easy to implement. As the problem scale goes large, it can be extended in an easy and natural way. As the new method proposed requires few control variables, thus it is robust as well as easy to use. Tested on a suite of benchmark functions, it is demonstrated that the GPU-FWA outperforms FWA and the popular PSO in the quality of solution. Experimental results obtained a speedup up to $160\times$ and $200\times$ compared to CPU-based FWA and PSO, respectively, on an up-to-date CPU. It is concluded that GPU-FWA is a potential powerful tool for solving large-scale optimization problems on the massively parallel architecture.

Chapter 8
Attract-Repulse Fireworks Algorithm Using Dynamic Parallelism

Contents

8.1 Introduction

Attract-repulse fireworks algorithm (AR-FWA) introduces an efficient adaptive search mechanism (AFW search) and a nonuniform mutation strategy for spark generation. Compared to the state-of-the-art FWA variants, AR-FWA can greatly improve the performance on complicated multimodal problems. Leveraging the cutting-edge dynamic parallelism mechanism provided by compute unified device architecture (CUDA), AR-FWA can be implemented on the graphics processing unit (GPU) easily and efficiently.

This chapter is organized as follows: Section 8.2 discusses the proposed algorithm, AR-FWA. The AFW search and nonuniform mutation are presented in detail. Section 8.3 describes how AR-FWA can be implemented on the GPU using dynamic parallelism. Key kernel codes are also given out in this section. The experiments and analyses are given in Section 8.4. The performance of nonuniform mutation against uniform mutation is studied, as well as AR-FWA against the state-of-the-art FWA variants and the speedup on the basis of extensive experiments.

Algorithm 8.1 AR-FWA

1: Initialize N fireworks
2: **while** terminated conditions not satisfied **do**
3:      Calculate the fitness values of each firework
4:      Calculate s according to Eq. (7.1)
5:      Calculate A according to Eq. (7.2)
6:      **for** $i = 1$ to n **do**
7:          Search according to Algorithm 8.2
8:      **end for**
9:      Mutate according to Algorithm 7.4
10: **end while**

8.2 Attract-Repulse Fireworks Algorithm (AR-FWA)

AR-FWA (AR-FWA) is built on the basis of GPU-FWA in previous chapter and other new developments on FWA. The basic procedure of AR-FWA is depicted in Algorithm 8.1. In the remainder of this section, each component of the AR-FWA will be discussed in detail one by one. Regarding the GPU-based implementation of the proposed AR-FWA will be given in the next section.

8.2.1 Adaptive Firework Search (AFW Search)

In [49], a mechanism called firework search (FW Search) is suggested for efficient local search. In FW search, each firework generates a fixed number of sparks and the exact number of sparks is determined in accordance with the specific GPU hardware. It was argued that, this fixed encoding of firework explosion is more suitable for parallel implementation on GPUs. However, as the GPU architecture has evolved a lot since then, the argument is not necessarily true any more. In AFW search, the number of sparks is determined dynamically according to Eq. (7.1). In Section 8.3, we will see how this can be implemented efficiently using the novel dynamic parallelism mechanism supported by the latest GPUs.

Algorithm 8.2 Adaptive Firework Search (AFW Search)

1: For the kth spark
2: **for** $i = 1$ to L **do**
3:      Generate s_k sparks according to Algorithm 8.3
4:      Evaluate the fitness
5:      Find the best spark, and replace it with the firework if better
6:      **if** firework is updated **then**
7:          $A = A * \alpha$
8:      **else**
9:          $A = A * \beta$
10:     **end if**
11: **end for**

Algorithm 8.3 Spark Generating II

1: Initialize the location: $\hat{\mathbf{x}} = \mathbf{x}$;
2: **for** $i = 1$ to D **do**
3:      $r = uniform(0,1)$;
4:      **if** $r < \frac{1}{2}$ **then**
5:          $\hat{x}_i = \hat{x}_i + A \cdot RNG(\cdot)$;
6:      **end if**
7: **end for**

One of the key parameter in AFW search (as well as FW search in [49]) is the explosion amplitude determined in Eq. (7.2). Recently, the adaptive amplitude control has been actively discussed. Many proposals have been come up with to adjust the amplitude dynamically according to the history information [211, 108]. Among these proposals, Zheng et al. suggested a decent strategy for dynamic search in FWA [211]. In their proposal, the core firework (i.e., the current best firework) uses a dynamic explosion amplitude because the firework is at the currently best position. If the fitness of the best firework is improved, the explosion amplitude increases in order to speedup convergence. On the contrary, if the current position of the best firework is not improved, the explosion amplitude decreases to narrow the search area. It is shown by experiments that using the dynamic strategy, the performance can be greatly improved. Based on this insight, we apply the dynamic strategy for all of the fireworks, instead of only for the core firework.

With all these considerations in mind, we end up with the AFW search. The pseudocode of AFW search is listed in Algorithm 8.1, where $\alpha = 0.9$, $\beta = 1.2$ according to [211].

8.2.2 Nonuniform Mutation

Sparks are generated following Algorithm 8.3. In the conventional FWA, $RNG(\cdot)$ is uniform distribution [49, 211]. To be more general, it can be any distribution that meets the following conditions:

- symmetry with respect to the original;
- distributed very close to 0.

There are many distributions satisfying these conditions. Here, we only discuss two of them, Gaussian distribution and Cauchy distribution.

8.2.2.1 Gaussian Distribution

The probability distribution function (PDF) of Gaussian distribution is illustrated in Eq. (8.1)

$$N(x) = \frac{1}{\sqrt{2\pi}\sigma} e^{-\frac{(x-\mu)^2}{2\sigma^2}}, \tag{8.1}$$

where μ is the expectation and σ is the standard deviation.

8.2.2.2 Cauchy Distribution

The PDF of Cauchy distribution is illustrated in Eq. (8.2)

$$C(x) = \frac{1}{\pi\gamma[1 + (\frac{x-\mu}{\gamma})^2]}, \tag{8.2}$$

where μ is the location parameter which determines the location of the peak of the distribution (the mode of the distribution); γ is the scale parameter, specifying half the width of the PDF at half the maximum height.

Similar to Gaussian distribution, Cauchy distribution has a symmetric "bell shaped" probability density function, however, it is more peaked at the center and has fatter tails than Gaussian distribution.

Fig. 8.1 shows the probability density functions of uniform distribution, the standard Gaussian distribution, and the standard Cauchy distribution. Fig. 8.2 illustrates a 2D simulation results of standard Cauchy distribution ($\mu = 0$, $\gamma = 1$), standard

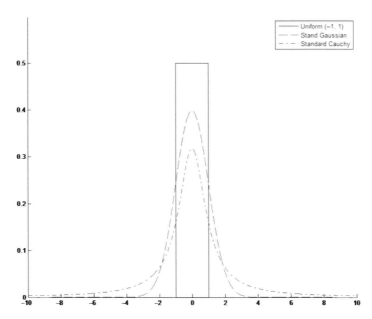

Fig. 8.1 Probability Density Functions of Uniform Distribution, Gaussian Distribution, and Cauchy Distribution

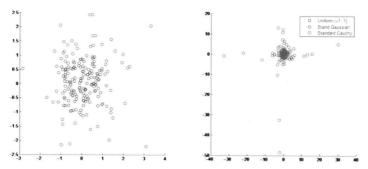

Fig. 8.2 2D Simulation Results of Generating Point From Different Distributions

Gaussian distribution ($\mu = 0$, $\sigma = 1$), and uniform distribution s.t. $[-1, 1]$. In the simulation, up to 100 points are drawn independently from each distribution. As can be seen, the points from uniform distribution are only located between $[-1, 1]$, while Gaussian and Cauchy distributions are more scattered. Most of the points are within the range of 3 σ for Gaussian distribution, and more outliers are generated for Cauchy distribution.

We expect that Gaussian and Cauchy distributions can result in better diversity for the firework swarm, which will be verified by experiments in Section 8.4.

8.3 Implementation

8.3.1 Dynamic Parallelism

Dynamic parallelism in CUDA is supported via an extension to the CUDA programming model that enables a CUDA kernel to create and synchronize new nested work (cf. Fig. 8.3). Basically, a child CUDA kernel can be called from within a parent CUDA kernel and then optionally synchronize on the completion of that child CUDA Kernel. The parent CUDA kernel can consume the output produced from the child CUDA kernel, all without CPU involvement [136].

Dynamic parallelism enjoys many advantages. Firstly, with dynamic parallelism, additional parallelism can be exposed to the GPUs hardware schedulers and load balancers dynamically, adapting in response to data-driven decisions or workloads (cf. Fig. 8.4). Secondly, algorithms and programming patterns that had previously required modifications to eliminate recursion, irregular loop structure, or other constructs that do not fit a flat, single-level of parallelism can be more transparently expressed. Besides, important benefits when new work is invoked within an executing GPU program include removing the burden on the programmer to marshal and transfer the data on which to operate.

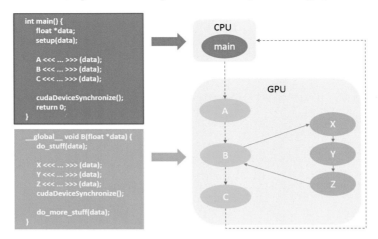

Fig. 8.3 Diagram of Dynamic Parallelism

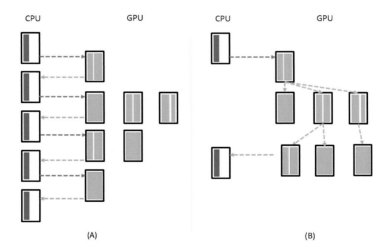

Fig. 8.4 Dynamic Parallelism Allows Allocating Resource in Response to Data-Driven Decisions or Workloads

8.3.2 Framework

AR-FWA is implemented by full GPU parallel model (see Chapter 3), whose framework based on dynamic parallelism is depicted in Fig. 8.5. The implementation relies heavily on dynamic parallel. Different from GPU-FWA, AR-FWA moves the loop to GPU thus releasing CPU from the schedule. The whole optimization procedure is independent from CPU.

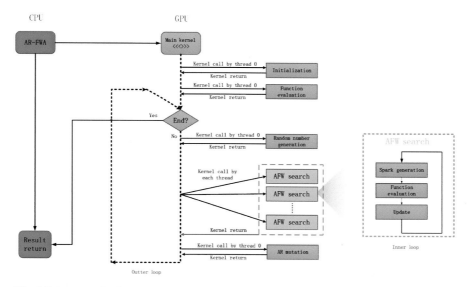

Fig. 8.5 Framework of GPU-Based AR-FWA

In the following subsections, the key components of AR-FWA will be described in detail, respectively.

8.3.3 Random Number Generation

Random number generation is an integral component of FWA, which should be disposed with much care [47].

In [49], random numbers are generated by invoking host API. To avoid the overhead of kernel launch, device API [137] is used in AR-FWA. Another advantage of using device API is that the API calling can be easily integrated with the transformation to get nonuniform distributions. Listing 1 demonstrates how to use cuRAND to get random numbers subject to Cauchy distribution from one single kernel call.

Listing 1 Cauchy Distribution Random Number Generation

```
__global__ void generate_cauchy(int num, float *result,
                                 float mu, float gamma) {
    int tidx = threadIdx.x + blockIdx.x * blockDim.x;
    for (; tidx < num; tidx += blockDim.x * gridDim.x) {
        float r = curand_uniform(&state[blockIdx.x]);
        result[tidx] = mu + gamma * tanf(PI * (r - 0.5f));
    }
}
```

8.3.4 Initialization

All fireworks are initialized randomly within the whole feasible domain. Thus, the implementation can be based on the uniform random number generation and a simple element-wise scale, which can be implemented in a fine-grained manner. To deal with large-scale (high dimension, large population) problems, a grid-stride loops trick can be utilized. For a *D* dimension problem solved by *N* fireworks, the CUDA code snippet is listed in Listing 2.

Listing 2 Initialization

```
__global__
void initialize(float *fireworks, // fireworks to be initialized
                float *rng,        // random number pool
                float upper,       // upper bound for search
                float lower        // lower bound for search
                ) {
   int tidx = threadIdx.x + blockIdx.x * blockDim.x;
   float t;
   for (; tidx < N * D; tidx += blockDim.x * gridDim.x) {
       t = rng[tidx];
       t = lower + (upper - lower) * t;
       fireworks[tidx] = t;
   }
}
```

8.3.5 Reduction

Reduction is a specific kernel in AR-FWA. It is a primitive used by several different kernels instead. Reduction is used to calculate the summation and find the maximum or minimum value of an array. Here, we discuss two methods for efficient reduction operation.

8.3.5.1 Shared Memory-Based Reduction

The procedure of shared memory-based reduction is as Fig. 8.6. In this way, it takes advantage of fast shared memory, and avoids bank conflict.

Listing 3 gives out the code snippet for a summation reduction. The extension to other reductions is obvious and is given by the comment.

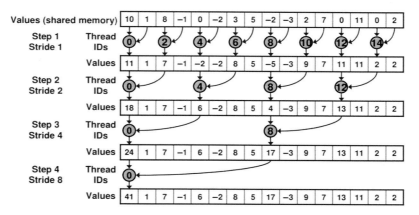

Fig. 8.6 Shared Memory-Based Reduction

Listing 3 Parallel Reduction Based on Shared Memory (Summation)

```
__inline__ __device__
float reduceSum(float *arr, int num) {
    __shared__ float sdata[];

    int tidx = threadIdx.x;
    sdata[tidx] = 0;  // sdata[tidx] = -inf;
    // __syncthreads();

    for (int i = tidx; i < num; i += blockDim.x) {
        sdata[tidx] += arr[i];
        // sdata[tidx] = max(sdata, arr[i]);
    }
    __syncthreads();

    for (int s = blockDim.x / 2; s > 0; s >>= 1) {
        if (tid < s) {
            sdata[tid] += sdata[tid + s];
            // sdata[tid] = max(sdata[tid], sdata[tid + s]);
        }
        __syncthreads();
    }

    return sdata[0];
}
```

8.3.5.2 Shuffle

Shuffle (SHFL) is a new machine instruction introduced in Kepler architecture. The shuffle intrinsics permit exchanging of a variable between threads within the same warp without use of shared memory. The exchange occurs simultaneously for all active threads within the warp, moving 4 bytes of data per thread. Four variants (idx, up, down, and bfly): Refer to [136] B.14 for details.

Compared to shared memory-based reduction, shuffle-based implementation can be faster. Fig. 8.7 compares these two reduction implementations on NVIDIA GTX 970 GPU. As can be seen, when reducing $10M$ data, shuffle can achieve 30–40% improvement under various block sizes.

Code snippet for reduction using shuffle is also given in Listing 4 whose intuition behind can be illustrated in Fig. 8.8. Listing 5 demonstrates how shuffle-based reduction can be operated on the block level. For larger scale problem, a two-path strategy can be used with the help of global memory.

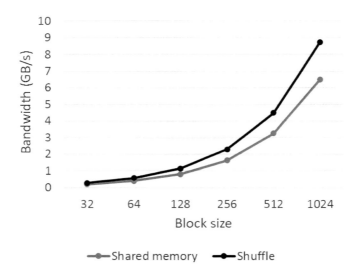

Fig. 8.7 Shared Memory-Based Reduction vs. Shuffle-Based Reduction

Listing 4 Parallel Reduction Using Shuffle (Warp)

```
__inline__ __device__
int warpReduceSum(int val) {
    for (int m = warpSize/2; m > 0; m >>= 1)
        val += __shfl_xor(val, m);
    return val;
}
```

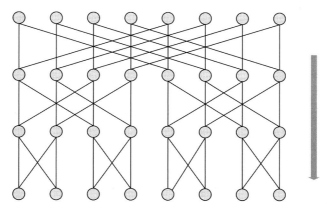

Fig. 8.8 Diagram of Shuffle-Based Reduction

Listing 5 Parallel Reduction Using Shuffle (Block)

```
__inline__ __device__
int blockReduceSum(int val) {
    // Shared memory for 32 partial sums
    static __shared__ int shared[32];
    int lane = threadIdx.x % warpSize;
    int wid = threadIdx.x / warpSize;

    // Each warp performs partial reduction
    val = warpReduceSum(val);

    // Write reduced value to shared memory
    if (lane == 0) shared[wid]=val;

    // Wait for all partial reductions
    __syncthreads();

    // read only if that warp existed
    val = (lane < blockDim.x / warpSize) ?
            shared[lane] : 0;

    // Final reduce within first warp
    if (wid == 0) val = warpReduceSum(val);

    return val;
}
```

8.3.6 AFW Search

Each AFW search is executed by a single kernel which is launched dynamically by the parent thread. The new kernel launches its own child kernel dynamically, for spark generation, objective evaluation, and update.

8.3.7 AR Mutation and Spark Generation

The implementation of AR mutation is very similar to initialization, fine-grained manner, which also draw random numbers from the pool of random numbers. The kernel code is illustrated in Listing 6.

The implementation of spark generation is very similar to that of AR mutation. So we do not list the code here.

Listing 6 AR Mutation

```
__global__ void AR_Mutate(floatX *fireworks,
                          floatX* best_position, floatX *rng) {
    extern __shared__ floatX sdata[];

    int tidx = threadIdx.x;
    fireworks += blockIdx.x * D;
    rng += blockIdx.x * D * 2;

    if (tidx < D) {
        floatX c = best_position[tidx];
        floatX t = fireworks[tidx];

        c += (t - c) * (rng[tidx] * 2 * delta + 1 - delta);
        fireworks[tidx] = rng[tidx + dim] < 0.5 ? c : t;
    }
}
```

8.3.8 Objective Function Evaluation

In the implementation, fine-grained strategy is adopted to parallelize function evaluation [182]. The kernel code is illustrated in Listing 7.

8.3.9 Firework Update

To update the firework using the best spark, the spark with best fitness value should be located. This can be implemented by reduction operation, which we have discussed in the previous section. With the best spark, the update can be conducted in a fine-grained (each thread for a dimension).

Listing 7 Fine-Grained Function Evaluation (Sphere)

```
__inline__ __device__
float evaluate(float *x) {
    extern __shared__ float sdata[];

    int tidx = threadIdx.x;
    sdata[tidx] = 0;

    float tmp;
    for (int i = tidx; i < D; i += blockDim.x) {
        tmp = x[i];
        sdata[tidx] += tmp * tmp;
    }
    __syncthreads();

    for (int s = blockDim.x / 2; s > 0; s >>= 1) {
        if (tidx < s) {
            sdata[tidx] += sdata[tidx + s];
        }
        __syncthreads();
    }

    return sdata[0];
}
```

8.4 Experiments and Analysis

8.4.1 Benchmark Functions

In our experiments, the GPU-based benchmark, cuROB, is used [48]. cuROB is implemented with CUDA and can support any dimension within the limit of hardware. The current release of cuROB includes 37 single-objective real-parameter optimization functions. The test functions fall into four categories: unimodal functions (No. 0–6), basic multimodal functions (No. 7–22), hybrid functions (No. 23–28) and composition functions (No. 29–36). The summary of the suit is listed in Table 12.1. Detailed information for each function is given in Chapter 12.

8.4.2 Algorithm Performance

In the experiments, all algorithms are implemented using the naive parallel model [182] with double precision float operation.

8.4.2.1 Uniform Mutation vs. Nonuniform Mutation

To verify the feasibility of nonuniform mutation, we implement Algorithm 8.3 using uniform distribution over $[-1, 1]$, standard Gaussian distribution and Cauchy distribution, respectively. The test functions are all with dimension of 30 ($D = 30$), and up to $D * 10,000$ function evaluations are conducted for each run. The number of fireworks is $n = 5$, and the number of sparks $s = 150$, $A = 40$, $\Delta = 0.00001$. For AFW search, $L = 100$, $\alpha = 1.2$, $\beta = 0.9$, and for AR mutation $\delta = 0.5$. One hundred fifty-one independent runs are conducted for each test function. The experimental results are listed in Table 8.1.

Via t-test, the comparison results are listed in Table 8.2. Obviously, nonuniform mutation gains no benefit on the simple unimodal problems. However, for the more complicated multimodal problems, both Gaussian and Cauchy distributions improve the performance to some degree. Cauchy (11 better) can achieve more significant improvements compared to Gaussian (9 better).

8.4.2.2 Compared to the State-of-the-Art FWA Variants

In this part, we compare AR-FWA to the-state-of-the-art FWA variants, dynFWA [211] and EFWA [210].

The experimental results are listed in Table 8.3, which is the mean on 151 independent runs with $D * 10,000$ function evaluations. The parameters of dynFWA and EFWA are as in the original paper [210, 211]. Considering the better performance of Cauchy distribution (cf. Section 8.2.2.2), for AR-FWA, Cauchy distribution is adopted. The parameters are the same as in the previous subsection.

Unimodal Functions

The convergence trends on unimodal functions for the three algorithms are depicted in Fig. 8.9. Over all, AR-FWA has slower convergence rate on unimodal functions compared to dynFWA and EFWA.

The t-test results are listed in Table 8.4, and the comparison results are listed in Table 8.5, where $+1$ denotes significantly better, -1 significantly worse, and 0 inconclusive.

AR-FWA is significantly worse on function No. 2–4, and for 2 and 3, the disparity is as mush as an order of magnitude. The result is not surprising. As dynFWA and EFWA select the next generation using the ERS strategy (cf. Chapter 7), population converges to a location quickly due to the high competition pressure. Therefor, dynFWA and EFWA can outperform AF-FWA on unimodal functions.

Despite the poor performance on unimodal functions, we expect AR-FWA can achieve better results for complicated multimodal functions. In the following subsection, we will verify this hypothesis with experiments.

Table 8.1 Results for AR-FWA With Uniform and Nonuniform Mutation

No.	Uniform		Gaussian		Cauchy	
	Mean	Std.	Mean	Std.	Mean	Std.
0	1.00E+02	1.32E−14	1.00E+02	2.26E−14	1.00E+02	3.55E−14
1	1.00E+02	1.93E−13	1.00E+02	4.03E−12	1.00E+02	5.25E−07
2	5.28E+05	2.14E+05	5.42E+05	2.44E+05	1.03E+06	4.35E+05
3	8.97E+02	4.14E+02	8.02E+02	4.01E+02	3.09E+03	1.55E+03
4	6.97E+03	7.67E+03	7.21E+03	6.87E+03	9.86E+03	8.37E+03
5	1.00E+02	2.13E−05	1.00E+02	2.60E−05	1.00E+02	5.41E−05
6	1.01E+02	1.04E+00	1.01E+02	1.40E+00	1.02E+02	2.20E+00
7	1.00E+02	5.46E−01	1.00E+02	5.12E−01	1.00E+02	4.04E−01
8	1.10E+02	2.17E+00	1.09E+02	2.16E+00	1.11E+02	2.43E+00
9	1.00E+02	2.57E−03	1.00E+02	3.38E−03	1.00E+02	4.34E−03
10	1.84E+02	1.48E+01	1.73E+02	1.36E+01	1.05E+02	3.00E+00
11	1.86E+02	1.43E+01	1.77E+02	1.17E+01	1.82E+02	1.37E+01
12	1.28E+02	6.62E+00	1.17E+02	4.44E+00	1.16E+02	4.40E+00
13	1.05E+02	1.27E+00	1.05E+02	1.46E+00	1.06E+02	1.62E+00
14	1.19E+02	2.65E+00	1.19E+02	2.81E+00	1.22E+02	2.62E+00
15	2.48E+03	3.41E+02	2.14E+03	3.27E+02	2.65E+02	1.16E+02
16	2.54E+03	3.60E+02	2.35E+03	3.37E+02	2.50E+03	3.79E+02
17	1.00E+02	7.02E−02	1.00E+02	7.43E−02	1.00E+02	8.98E−02
18	1.30E+02	4.79E−01	1.30E+02	4.76E−01	1.30E+02	6.71E−01
19	1.20E+02	6.36E−04	1.20E+02	1.47E−04	1.20E+02	4.06E−04
20	1.00E+02	6.26E−02	1.00E+02	5.70E−02	1.00E+02	6.28E−02
21	1.00E+02	6.13E−02	1.00E+02	3.73E−02	1.00E+02	9.74E−02
22	1.11E+02	4.68E−01	1.11E+02	3.92E−01	1.10E+02	3.82E−01
23	4.62E+04	1.70E+04	4.59E+04	1.47E+04	3.84E+04	1.25E+04
24	4.10E+04	8.01E+03	4.14E+04	9.11E+03	7.94E+03	5.78E+03
25	1.16E+02	6.86E+00	1.19E+02	1.84E+01	1.17E+02	1.83E+01
26	7.53E+03	5.31E+03	7.58E+03	4.87E+03	5.57E+03	3.04E+03
27	2.57E+04	1.03E+04	2.70E+04	1.12E+04	3.55E+04	3.29E+04
28	1.22E+02	5.45E−01	1.22E+02	5.71E−01	1.21E+02	6.48E−01
29	3.76E+02	2.58E−06	3.76E+02	2.84E−06	3.76E+02	2.41E−02
30	4.17E+02	1.80E+01	4.07E+02	1.47E+01	4.05E+02	1.44E+01
31	3.23E+02	4.82E+00	3.24E+02	4.04E+00	3.22E+02	3.48E+00
32	2.01E+02	5.75E−02	2.01E+02	5.46E−02	2.01E+02	6.68E−02
33	4.62E+02	4.41E+00	4.61E+02	4.72E+00	4.63E+02	4.46E+00
34	1.62E+03	1.52E+02	1.49E+03	1.36E+02	1.30E+03	1.12E+02
35	2.42E+07	2.55E+06	2.31E+07	2.40E+06	1.90E+07	3.81E+05
36	5.05E+06	1.04E+06	4.39E+06	7.46E+05	3.02E+06	3.18E+05

Table 8.2 Performance Comparison Between Uniform and Gaussian and Cauchy Distributions (Better/Inconclusive/Worse)

	Unimodal	Basic Multimodal	Hybrid	Composition	Summary
Uniform vs. Gaussian	3/3/1	2/6/8	3/2/1	3/3/2	11/14/12
Uniform vs. Cauchy	3/4/0	3/8/5	1/1/4	2/0/5	9/14/14

Table 8.3 Optimization Results of AR-FWA, dynFWA, and EFWA

ID	AR-FWA		dynFWA		EFWA	
	Mean	Std.	Mean	Std.	Mean	Std.
0	1.000E+02	3.551E−14	1.000E+02	7.965E−14	1.000E+02	3.764E−04
1	1.000E+02	5.250E−07	1.000E+02	2.282E−13	1.004E+02	1.378E−01
2	1.034E+06	4.351E+05	8.128E+05	3.858E+05	7.552E+05	2.803E+05
3	3.092E+03	1.555E+03	6.621E+02	3.104E+02	1.005E+02	2.011E−01
4	9.860E+03	8.371E+03	9.365E+03	1.112E+04	4.814E+03	4.843E+03
5	1.000E+02	5.413E−05	1.000E+02	1.479E−05	1.000E+02	9.879E−05
6	1.018E+02	2.198E+00	1.070E+02	1.060E+01	1.092E+02	9.949E+00
7	1.002E+02	4.039E−01	1.109E+02	3.725E+00	1.023E+02	1.825E+00
8	1.110E+02	2.434E+00	1.291E+02	4.527E+00	1.330E+02	3.489E+00
9	1.000E+02	4.340E−03	1.000E+02	1.243E−02	1.000E+02	1.287E−02
10	1.045E+02	3.000E+00	2.682E+02	4.835E+01	2.689E+02	3.461E+01
11	1.823E+02	1.374E+01	3.243E+02	4.638E+01	3.115E+02	4.713E+01
12	1.155E+02	4.404E+00	1.632E+02	9.136E+00	1.634E+02	9.270E+00
13	1.060E+02	1.615E+00	1.179E+02	1.315E+01	1.170E+02	5.887E+00
14	1.223E+02	2.625E+00	1.285E+02	2.327E+01	1.418E+02	3.055E+01
15	2.648E+02	1.162E+02	2.332E+03	6.405E+02	3.226E+03	6.073E+02
16	2.500E+03	3.794E+02	4.184E+03	6.845E+02	4.424E+03	6.520E+02
17	1.002E+02	8.980E−02	1.006E+02	2.719E−01	1.004E+02	2.221E−01
18	1.301E+02	6.709E−01	1.300E+02	2.794E−13	1.300E+02	8.733E−04
19	1.200E+02	4.057E−04	1.200E+02	1.480E−04	1.200E+02	4.465E−04
20	1.004E+02	6.281E−02	1.006E+02	1.443E−01	1.005E+02	1.326E−01
21	1.002E+02	9.736E−02	1.005E+02	2.860E−01	1.003E+02	1.140E−01
22	1.104E+02	3.820E−01	1.117E+02	5.439E−01	1.121E+02	5.059E−01
23	3.836E+04	1.246E+04	8.773E+04	5.074E+04	4.546E+04	1.677E+04
24	7.937E+03	5.784E+03	6.564E+03	8.112E+03	4.564E+03	5.273E+03
25	1.171E+02	1.834E+01	8.852E+02	2.876E+03	5.610E+02	1.540E+03
26	5.568E+03	3.038E+03	2.912E+04	3.473E+04	6.446E+03	9.266E+03
27	3.548E+04	3.289E+04	7.684E+04	9.194E+04	2.835E+04	2.076E+04
28	1.213E+02	6.476E−01	2.647E+02	1.866E+02	1.328E+02	4.867E+01
29	3.764E+02	2.410E−02	3.768E+02	4.146E+00	3.764E+02	7.962E−04
30	4.048E+02	1.443E+01	6.162E+02	8.352E+01	7.539E+02	9.603E+01
31	3.222E+02	3.483E+00	3.401E+02	2.623E+01	3.684E+02	1.768E+01
32	2.014E+02	6.678E−02	2.115E+02	5.037E+01	2.032E+02	2.299E+01
33	4.634E+02	4.461E+00	5.045E+02	1.996E+01	5.181E+02	1.375E+01
34	1.304E+03	1.120E+02	1.154E+03	8.460E+02	3.569E+03	6.951E+02
35	1.897E+07	3.813E+05	2.257E+02	5.844E+02	1.409E+07	9.768E+06
36	3.016E+06	3.181E+05	1.889E+03	3.020E+03	2.573E+03	2.263E+03

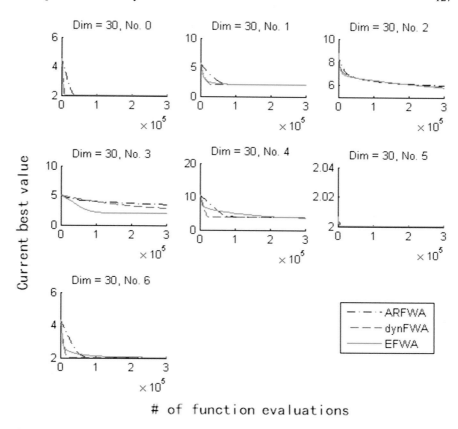

Fig. 8.9 Convergence Trends for AR-FWA, dynFWA, and EFWA on Unimodal Functions

Basic Multimodal Functions

Similar to the analysis of unimodal functions of above, the t-test and comparison results are listed in Tables 8.6 and 8.7, respectively. Out of the 18 functions, AR-FWA outperforms dynFWA on 13 functions and only 1 function not statistically significant. AR-FWA outperforms EFWA on 11 functions and 4 not statistically

Table 8.4 p-Values of t-Test (AF-FWA vs. dynFWA and AR-FWA vs. EFWA on Unimodal Functions)

	0	1	2	3	4	5	6
dynFWA	1.00E+00	1.55E−109	1.00E−06	1.43E−96	4.70E−06	1.85E−10	1.50E−52
EFWA	3.07E−02	8.30E−03	2.45E−54	4.09E−53	9.04E−19	4.38E−26	6.89E−16

Table 8.5 Performance Comparison Between AR-FWA and dynFWA & AR-FWA and EFWA on Unimodal Functions (Better/Inconclusive/Worse)

	0	1	2	3	4	5	6
dynFWA	0	−1	−1	−1	−1	−1	+1
EFWA	+1	+1	−1	−1	−1	+1	+1

Table 8.6 p-Values of t-Test (AF-FWA vs. dynFWA and AR-FWA vs. EFWA on Multimodal Functions)

	7	8	9	10	11	12	13	14
dynFWA	3.08E−70	6.64E−1	6.33E−10	3.58E−53	9.48E−131	1.61E−08	7.39E−17	6.70E−108
EFWA	4.24E−72	2.77E−101	7.4E−26	4.05E−05	9.25E−2	2.51E−07	1.20E−3	4.8E−4
	15	16	17	18	19	20	21	22
dynFWA	3.46E−34	1.15E−130	9.09E−176	8.37E−19	1.05E−16	5.11E−126	5.73E−165	9.00E−111
EFWA	4.29E−15	2.71E−1	3.9303E−07	2.55E−2	1.33E−18	4.1132E−3	2.17E−1	1.52E−1

Table 8.7 Performance Comparison Between AR-FWA and dynFWA & AR-FWA and EFWA on Basic Multimodal Functions (Better/Inconclusive/Worse)

	7	8	9	10	11	12	13	14
dynFWA	+1	0	+1	+1	+1	+1	+1	+1
EFWA	+1	+1	+1	+1	0	+1	+1	+1
	15	16	17	18	19	20	21	22
dynFWA	+1	+1	+1	−1	−1	+1	+1	+1
EFWA	+1	0	+1	−1	+1	+1	0	0

significant. Obviously, AR-FWA can achieve better performance than dynFWA and EFWA over the basic multimodal functions.

Hybrid Functions

Hybrid functions are more complicated than basic multimodal functions, thus can simulate the complicated real-world scenarios better. The results on hybrid functions are listed in Tables 8.8 and 8.9, respectively. Out of the six hybrid functions, AR-FWA outperforms dynFWA on five of them, and get worse result on one of them. AR-FWA outperforms EFWA on three functions, worse on two, and one inconclusive. Overall, AF-FWA performs better than EFWA and dynFWA for hybrid functions.

Table 8.8 p-Values of t-Test (AF-FWA vs. dynFWA and AR-FWA vs. EFWA on Hybrid Functions)

	23	24	25	26	27	28
dynFWA	1.97E−99	3.08E−164	2.50E−163	6.21E−24	2.05E−64	1.28E−03
EFWA	4.53E−94	5.80E−133	4.00E−15	7.80E−97	1.43E−02	3.19E−01

Table 8.9 Performance Comparison Between AR-FWA and dynFWA & AR-FWA and EFWA on Hybrid Functions (Better/Inconclusive/Worse)

	23	24	25	26	27	28
dynFWA	+1	−1	+1	+1	+1	+1
EFWA	+1	−1	+1	+1	−1	0

Composition Functions

Composition functions are more complicated than basic multimodal and hybrid functions. The results on composition functions are listed in Tables 8.10 and 8.11. Out of the eight composition functions, AR-FWA outperforms dynFWA on five of them, get worse result on three of them. AR-FWA outperforms EFWA on five functions, worse on three. At least AF-FWA performs no worse than dynFWA and EFWA.

All comparison results are summarized in Table 8.12. AR-FWA is worse than dynFWA and EFWA on unimodal functions, but outperforms the other two algorithms on multimodal and complicated functions generally.

Table 8.10 p-Values of t-Test (AF-FWA vs. dynFWA and AR-FWA vs. EFWA on Composition Functions)

	29	30	31	32	33	34	35	36
dynFWA	9.95E−14	3.15E−119	2.03E−166	4.60E−80	2.66E−96	2.60E−48	1.33E−20	2.77E−02
EFWA	5.84E−74	1.13E−138	3.22E−02	1.23E−120	0.00E+00	3.02E−09	2.74E−251	2.91E−251

Table 8.11 Performance Comparison Between AR-FWA and dynFWA & AR-FWA and EFWA on Composition Functions (Better/Inconclusive/Worse)

	29	30	31	32	33	34	35	36
dynFWA	+1	+1	+1	+1	+1	−1	−1	−1
EFWA	−1	+1	+1	+1	+1	+1	−1	−1

Table 8.12 Summary of Comparison Results

	Better	Inconclusive	Worse
AR-FWA vs. dynFWA	24	2	11
AR-FWA vs. EFWA	23	5	9

8.4.3 Parallel Performance

In this part, we study the parallel performance of the GPU-based implementation of AR-FWA. All experiments were conducted on a personal computer running Windows 7 x64 with 8 GB DDR3 memory and Intel core I5-2310 and NVIDIA GeForce GTX 970 GPU. The programs are compiled with VS 2013 with CUDA 6.5. Single precision float number is adopted by both CPU and GPU implementations.

In practice, the speedup is closely related with the characteristics of the objective function. Here, we use Sphere function as benchmark for evaluating the speedup under different conditions. In the experiments, the total number of sparks ($\hat{S}$) are set to 20-fold of the number of fireworks (n).

8.4.3.1 Speedup Against Population Size

Fig. 8.10 illustrates the speedup achieved by GPU-based AR-FWA with respect to its CPU-based counterpart, under various population sizes. In this experiment, the dimension of the test function is set to 30 ($D = 30$).

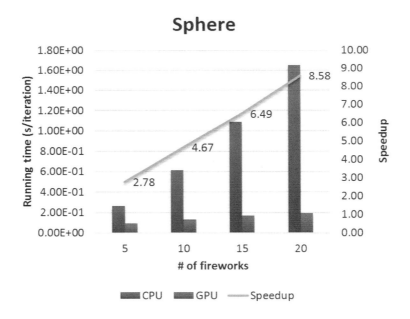

Fig. 8.10 Speedup With Different Population Sizes ($D = 30$)

Even with small population ($n = 5$), the GPU-based version can achieve up to $3\times$ speedup. As the population size goes larger, the speedup become more significant ($\sim 9\times$ with $n = 20$).

8.4.3.2 Speedup Against Parallelism

Besides the population size, parallelism of the objective function is one of the key factors impacting the overall speedup. In our implementation, the objective function is parallelized in a fine-grained way. Therefore, by controlling the dimension, we can alter the parallelism of the test function. Fig. 8.11 compares the speedups under various dimensions. Similar to the impact of population size, the speedup is increasingly larger along with the dimensions. With high parallelism, AR-FWA can achieve approximately $40\times$ speedup.

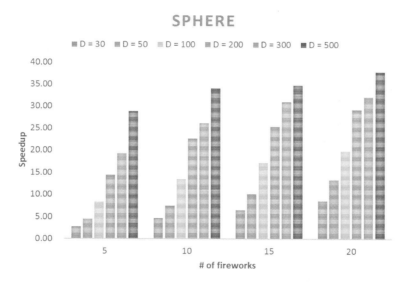

Fig. 8.11 Speedup With Different Dimensions

8.5 Summary

In this chapter, an efficient FWA variant, AR-FWA, was discussed. AR-FWA leveraged the recently developed techniques from both FWA study and GPU computing, ending up with an AFW search mechanism and a novel nonuniform mutation strategy. Compared to the state-of-the-art FWA variants, dynFWA and EFWA,

AR-FWA can improve the performance greatly on the complicated multimodal functions. AR-FWA relies heavily on the cutting-edge CUDA techniques, e.g., dynamic parallelism, shuffle instruction, etc. Compared to the CPU-based implementation, the GPU-based AR-FWA can achieve significant speedup under different population sizes and objective function parallelism.

Chapter 9
Other Typical Swarm Intelligence Algorithms Based on GPUs

Contents

9.1 GPU-Based Genetic Algorithm

9.1.1 Genetic Algorithm

Genetic algorithm (GA) was first developed by John Holland [71] in 1975 for solving optimization problems. The key idea of GA is inspired from natural evolution of species, which includes the conceptions and operations of mutation, crossover, and selection. GA has been widely used to solve the optimization problems in both discrete and continuous domains.

9.1.1.1 Basic Concepts of Genetic Algorithm

Assume $\{f(x)|f:X \rightarrow R, X \in R^d\}$ is the optimization function that only the value of $f(x)$ is computable, the general target is to find the global minima

$$x = \arg\min \ f(x), \ x \in X. \tag{9.1}$$

In GA, however, the search is not directly done in the space of X, the vector x is often regarded as the "phenotype" and then encoded by the "genotype" — a string or vector c of length l using a mapping function

$$\{x = z(c)|z : C \rightarrow X\}. \tag{9.2}$$

Thus, the optimization problem is converted and becomes finding

$$x = \arg\min \ f(z(c)), \ c \in C. \tag{9.3}$$

GA is a population-based algorithm, n individuals are grouped together to simulate the evolution of a biotic population. The string c used as the "genotype" of each individual is usually referred to as "chromosome" in the GA literature.

Another concept of "fitness function" is also derived from natural evolution. Once an individual has a better solution of the optimization problem, the fitness value is higher, which indicates its chromosome is more adapted to the environment. In addition, the fitness function $y(c)$ is usually defined as $\{y(c) = h(f(z(c))) | h : R \to R^+\}$, where h is a monotonic function and only has positive values.

9.1.1.2 Operators of Genetic Algorithm

Assume there are parents $c1$ and $c2$ and their offsprings $c3$ and $c4$. Each of the parents' chromosome is consisted of four variables

$$c1 = (g_1 \ g_2 \ g_3 \ g_4), \ c2 = (d_1 \ d_2 \ d_3 \ d_4). \tag{9.4}$$

The operator of crossover means that the chromosomes of the offsprings are the combination of their parents' [56]. First of all, the positions to separate the parents' chromosomes are decided, which is usually called m-point crossover if there is m cross-points. Then each chromosome is separated into $m + 1$ pieces. Finally the offsprings' chromosome is produced by combining the corresponding pieces of their parents. For instance, for a 2-point crossover with cross-points 1 and 3, the offsprings would be

$$c3 = (g_1 \ d_2 \ d_3 \ g_4), \ c2 = (d_1 \ g_2 \ g_3 \ d_4). \tag{9.5}$$

The mutation operator simply denotes the sudden change of some points in the chromosome, which significantly increases the diversity of the population. For instance, a mutation happens after crossover in $c3$ upon point 2 may be

$$c3 : (g_1 \ d_2 \ d_3 \ g_4) \to (g_1 \ m_2 \ d_3 \ g_4), \tag{9.6}$$

where m_2 is the inversion of d_2.

After the crossover and mutation, sufficient offsprings are created. In order to keep the population size, the selection operator is employed. In natural evolution, only individuals with higher adaptability survive. Analogously, a new generation is selected according to their fitness values. Among several strategies, roulette-wheel selection (RWS) is a commonly used implementation. In RWS, the selection probability of each individual is easily computed by

$$p(c_i) = \frac{y(c_i)}{\sum_j y(c_j)}, \tag{9.7}$$

where c_i indicates the chromosome of the ith individual, $y(.)$ is the fitness function. Then the new population is randomly sampled from the discrete probability distribution of p.

9.1.1.3 Pseudocode for Genetic Algorithm

The pseudocode of GA is illustrated by Algorithm 9.1

Algorithm 9.1 Genetic Algorithm

Randomly create the initial population P^0
set $i = 0$
while Convergence not meet OR $i \leq maxIteration$ **do**
    set $i = i + 1$
    if Crossover condition satisfied **then**
        Randomly select parent chromosome
        Randomly choose crossover positions according to m-point crossover
        Do crossover, create offsprings
    end if
    if Mutation condition satisfied **then**
        Randomly select individuals to mutation
        Randomly choose mutation positions
        Do mutation
    end if
    Compute the fitness values
    Select P^i using roulette-wheel selection
end while
Return the best individual

9.1.2 GPU Implementation of GA

Although GA is very effective in solving many practical problems, the execution time can become a limiting factor for some large problems, because a lot of candidate solutions must be evaluated in GA. However, the most time-consuming part of GA — fitness evaluation and mutation can be computed independently for each individual. In this section, we will introduce the common parallel GA model based on GPU.

Firstly, let us introduce the parallel traits of GPUs. A GPU usually consists of multiprocessors which are capable of performing lightweight tasks in parallel. In order to maintain the data consistency, threads in the same multiprocessor can be synchronized easily by using barriers. However, it is hard to perform synchronization between multiprocessors. The memory of GPU is divided into two levels, i.e., main memory and on-chip memory. The size of on-chip memory is a limitation for parallel threads in multiprocessors.

The GPU implementation of GA begins with population initialization on the CPU side. After transferring the chromosomes and GA's parameters to the GPU main memory, the population is distributed to several groups, where individuals in one local group share the same on-chip memory.

9.1.2.1 Crossover

Crossover, basically, is a memory-banded operator. It can be conducted in two phases. Firstly, for every individual, select another individual randomly and store the selected individual properly into shared memory. Secondly, according to the random numbers which are generated prehand, the crossover operation is conducted. Each individual can be assigned to a single thread or a single thread block depending on the scale of the problem and the parallel model adopted. The procedure of crossover is demonstrated in Fig. 9.1.

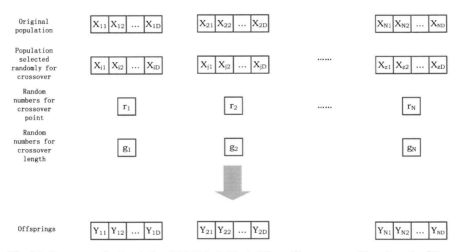

Fig. 9.1 Crossover of a Population With N Individuals Whose Chromosomes Have Length of D

9.1.2.2 Mutation

As illustrated in Fig. 9.2, mutation is a point-wise operator. The parallel uniform RNG in each thread generates the number r_i and g_i for the ith individual. Then r_i is compared with the mutation probability to decide whether the mutation operation is performed or not. g_i stands for the mutation position for the ith individual.

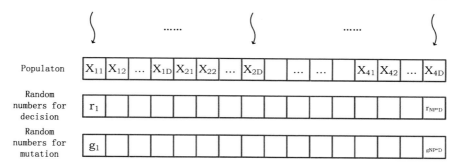

Fig. 9.2 Mutation of a Population With N Individuals Whose Chromosomes Have Length of D

9.1.2.3 Roulette-Wheel Selection

To conduct the selection process based on roulette-wheel, the probability weights should be calculated based on the fitness values of each individual. The probability weights (a vector of numbers between 0 and 1) can be preprocessed by prefix-sum, which is of linear complexity, i.e., $O(N)$. The real selection can be conducted in a straightforward way, or more efficiently can be conducted with the help segment tree, whose time complexity is $log(N)$ instead of $O(N)$.

As N is not very large in any real-world scenario (say, less than 100, maybe 1000 in some case), we may prefer to do the selection on the CPU side. However, the GPU-based implementation will be discussed when to introduce the path construction procedure in ant colony optimization (ACO).

For the whole GPU implementation of GA, readers can refer to [150]. Some recent applications of GPU-based GA are described in [79, 171].

9.2 GPU-Based Differential Evolution

9.2.1 Differential Evolution

Similar to GA[151], differential evolution(DE) also used the operators named crossover, mutation, and selection, but with less model parameters than GA. DE is named after its "mutation with difference vector" operation which is proved to bring significant diversity to the population. DE has become one of the most successful algorithms in continuous domain in recent years [39].

The definition of basic concepts are same as in Section 9.1.1.1 except that DE is mainly used in continuous optimization problems. Fortunately, in DE, the domain of the function X is directly used as the chromosome space of each individual, or, vector in DE literature. If we denote the generations of DE by $G = 0, 1, 2 \ldots$ and the ith vector of the Gth generation is defined as

$$X_{i,G} = \{X_{i,1,G}, X_{i,2,G}, \ldots, X_{i,d,G}\}, i = 1, 2, \ldots, N, \tag{9.8}$$

where N denotes the number of population in each generation and d is the dimension of the optimization problem.

9.2.1.1 Operators of Differential Evolution

Mutation operators is generally regarded as a random disturbance term of the individual chromosome, such that it can escape from the local area. These mutations are turned to lasting diversity during the evolution process. In DE algorithm, the ith of the N mutant vector, which is also called the donor vector, created after mutation operator is denoted by $V_{i,G}, i = 1, 2, \ldots, N$. In order to perform the mutation operator, for each mutant vector $V_{i,G}$, three distinct parent vectors $X_{r(i,1),G}$, $X_{r(i,2),G}$, and $X_{r(i,3),G}$ are sampled from the current population X_G, where the index $r(i, 1)$, $r(i, 2)$, and $r(i, 3)$ are integers randomly generated from the interval $[1, N]$. Then, a donor vector is created by one parent plus the difference between the other two parents, and the difference is usually scaled by a factor F, i.e.,

$$V_{i,G} = X_{r(i,1),G} + F \times (X_{r(i,2),G} - X_{r(i,3),G}). \tag{9.9}$$

The offspring of the current generation in DE is also called the trial vector in DE literature, which is created after the crossover operator. We use $U_{i,j,G}$ to denote the jth dimension of the ith trial vector and another control parameter CR means the crossover rate of DE. Thus each trail vector is the combination of the current generation and the donor vectors

$$\textit{For each } j \textit{ and } i, \ U_{i,j,G} = \begin{cases} V_{i,j,G} & \textit{if } rand[0, 1] \leq CR \\ X_{i,j,G} & \textit{else} \end{cases} \tag{9.10}$$

Selection operator in DE uses the simplest strategy: pairwise comparison is employed between the current generation and the trial vectors to get better solutions as the next generation

$$\textit{For each } i \in [1, N], \ X_{i,G+1} = \begin{cases} X_{i,G} & \textit{if } fit(X_{i,G}) \geq fit(U_{i,G}) \\ U_{i,G} & \textit{else} \end{cases} \tag{9.11}$$

9.2.1.2 Pseudocode for Differential Evolution

Algorithm 9.2 Differential Evolution Algorithm

Randomly create the initial population X_0
set $i = 0$
while Convergence not meet OR $i \leq maxIteration$ **do**
   set $i = i + 1$
   Perform mutation and create donor vectors V_G
   $V_{i,G} = X_{r(i,1),G} + F \times (X_{r(i,2),G} - X_{r(i,3),G})$
   Perform crossover and create trial vectors U_G
   For each j and i, $U_{i,j,G} = \begin{cases} V_{i,j,G} & if\ rand[0,1] \leq CR \\ X_{i,j,G} & else \end{cases}$
   Select the next generation X_{G+1}
   For each $i \in [1,N]$, $X_{i,G+1} = \begin{cases} X_{i,G} & if\ fit(X_{i,G}) \geq fit(U_{i,G}) \\ U_{i,G} & else \end{cases}$
end while
Return the best individual

9.2.2 GPU Implementation

With the knowledge of GPU implementation of GA, only the crossover operator needs further description. The GPU-based implementation of this procedure is illustrated in Fig. 9.3.

Firstly, three individuals are selected randomly. In order to guarantee that three individuals are different, the random numbers may be generated for several times, which might be problematic for GPU. To tackle this issue, Veronese and Krohling [195]) generate the random numbers on the CPU side then transfer them to the GPU side. Secondly, the real crossover operator can be conducted in a straightforward way.

The whole implementation details for GPU-based DE can be found in [195, 97].

9.3 GPU-Based Ant Colony Optimization

9.3.1 Ant Colony Optimization

ACO [52] is another nature heuristic algorithm which is an analog of the method ants searching the shortest path between its nest and the food. When the ants move along a path, a material called "pheromone" is perceived and then left on it as information transmission among ants. Once a path has more pheromone than the others, the ants

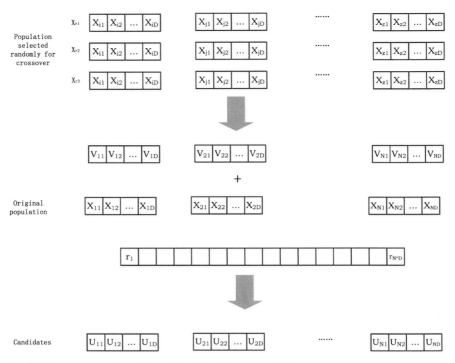

Fig. 9.3 Crossover of a Population With N Individuals and D Parameters

are more likely to be guided to this path, which in turn leads to the greater concentration of the pheromone on this path. So the ant colony composed of a large number of ants will show a information positive feedback phenomenon: a path through the more the ants, the greater the probability of others to choose the path.

ACO is mainly used to solve hard combinatorial optimization problems, such as the famous traveling salesman problem (TSP) problem. We define a n-city TSP problem in the graph $G = (V, E)$, the distance between city i and j is denoted by $d_{i,j}$, w denotes a solution of TSP, which is a sequence of the n cities: $w = \{w_1, w_2, \ldots, w_n\}$, with $w_{n+1} = w_1$. So the optimization function is given by

$$f(w) = \sum_{l=1}^{n} d_{w_l, w_{l+1}} \tag{9.12}$$

In the artificial ant system, a group of m ants is used to construct the solution of a TSP. These ants move along the neighboring city and choose the path according to the probability given by the concentration of pheromone. At the same time, the ant left pheromone on the path and the pheromone update is implemented.

9.3.1.1 Operations for Ant Colony Optimization

In the operation of solution construction, each ant randomly choose a city as its starting point. A history path vector is maintained to record the cities have been through. Each new city in the path is randomly chosen by the following probability distribution [50]

$$P_{i,j}^k(t) = \begin{cases} \dfrac{[\tau_{ij}(t)]^\alpha \times [\eta_{ij}]^\beta}{\sum_{k \, in \, allowed_k} [\tau_{ik}(t)]^\alpha \times [\eta_{ik}]^\beta} & if \ j \in allowed_k, \\ 0 & else. \end{cases} \tag{9.13}$$

where i, j denotes the start and the end of the path. η_{ij} is a heuristic value called the heuristic information, which is usually calculate by $\eta_{ij} = \frac{1}{d_{ij}}$. The $allowed_k$ means the cities not visited. α and β are two parameters keeping the balance between the influence of the pheromone and the heuristic information. $\tau_{ij}(t)$ is the concentration of the pheromone on path form city i to j at time t.

Another important operation of ACO is the update of the pheromone, which is usually initialized as a constant value

$$\tau_{ij} = C \tag{9.14}$$

In the process of ACO, the pheromone update is determined by two aspects. One is called pheromone evaporation, which means the concentration of the pheromone decreases over time. The other is called pheromone reinforcement, which refers to that the pheromone is increased when a ant goes through a path. Thus, the update of the pheromone is combined with these two terms

$$\tau_{ij}(t) = (1 - \rho)\tau_{ij} + \sum_{k=1}^{m} \Delta \tau_{ij}^k, \tag{9.15}$$

where $\rho \in (0, 1]$ is the parameter denoting the evaporation rate. $\Delta \tau_{ij}^k$ means the pheromone perceived by the kth ant on the path from city i to j.

If C_k stands for the total length of this path, then $\Delta \tau_{ij}^k$ is usually calculated as

$$\Delta \tau_{ij}^k = \begin{cases} (C_k)^{-1} & if \ k-th \ ant \ goes \ through \ (i,j), \\ 0 & else. \end{cases} \tag{9.16}$$

9.3.1.2 Pseudocode for Ant Colony Optimization

See "Algorithm 9.3.1.2 9.3 Ant Colony Optimization for TSP."

Algorithm 9.3 Ant Colony Optimization for TSP

---

set initial pheromone value $\tau_{ij} = C$
set $i = 0$
while Convergence not meet OR $i \leq maxIteration$ **do**
    set $i = i + 1$
    for each ant k **do**
        Randomly choose an initial city
        for $i = 1$ to n **do**
            choose next city j with

$$P_{i,j}^k(t) = \begin{cases} \dfrac{[\tau_{ij}(t)]^\alpha \times [\eta_{ij}]^\beta}{\sum_{kinallowed_k}[\tau_{ik}(t)]^\alpha \times [\eta_{ik}]^\beta} & if\ j \in allowed_k \\ \\ 0 & else \end{cases}$$

        end for
    end for
    for each edge **do**
        Update the pheromone value with

$$\Delta \tau_{ij}^k = \begin{cases} (C_k)^{-1} & if\ k-th\ ant\ goes\ through\ (i,j), \\ \\ 0 & else. \end{cases}$$

    end for
end while
Return the result

9.3.2 GPU Implementation of ACO

9.3.2.1 Path Construction

The path construction in ACO is inherently parallel. The key to efficiently parallelize the construction process is how to select the next unvisited city which is classically implemented via roulette-wheel selection. Many proposals have been reported to address this issue.

Cecilia et al. [33] observed the existence of redundant computation and thread divergences in such task-parallel approach used by [31]. A fine-grained data-parallel approach was used to enhance construction performance for solving the TSP. A new method called I-Roulette (independent roulette) was proposed to replicate the classic roulette wheel while improving GPU parallelism. Details on this proposal can be found in [32, 34].

Here we describe the method proposed by Dawson and Stewart [41], which is an improvement of the work in [33].

The proposed parallel implementation of roulette-wheel selection algorithm is named double-spin roulette (DS-Roulette). DS-Roulette, in effect, is a two-phase prefix-sum-based implementation of roulette-wheel selection by leveraging the fast shared memory. The method is illustrated in Fig. 9.4.

In the first phase, each thread within the subblock checks if the city it represents has previously been visited in the current tour. This valid city is stored in shared memory and is known as the Tabu value. A warp-level poll is then executed to determine if any valid cities remain in the subblock. If valid cities remain then each

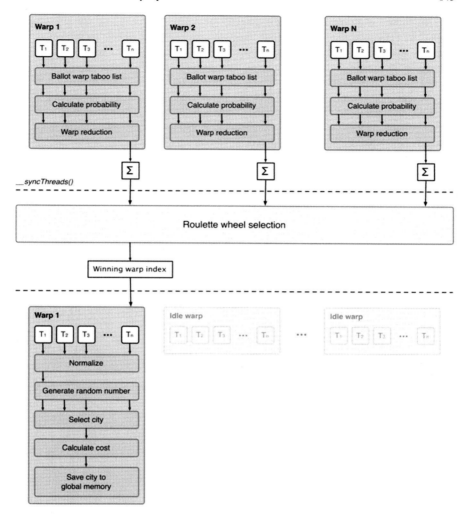

Fig. 9.4 Path Construction With Roulette-Wheel Selection [41]

thread retrieves the respective probability from the choice info array and multiplies the probability by the associated Tabu value. A warp reduction is performed on the probabilities to calculate the subblock probability. Once the probability is calculated, the subblocks then tile to ensure complete coverage of all cities within the tour. At the end of phase 1, the results are a list of subblock probabilities.

Phase 2 performs roulette-wheel selection on this set of probabilities to chose a specific subblock from which the next city to be visited will be chosen.

In the final phase of DS-Roulette, using the block value calculated in the previous phase, the first 32 threads load, from shared memory, the probabilities calculated by the winning subblock in phase 1.

Each thread then loads the total probability of the subblock and the probabilities are normalized. As each thread is accessing the same 32-bit value from shared memory, the value is broadcast to each thread eliminating bank conflicts and serialization. A single random number is then generated and each thread checks if the number is within their range thus completing the second spin of the roulette wheel. The winning thread then saves the next city to shared memory and global memory, and updates the total tour cost. After n^2 iterations, the tour cost is saved to global memory using an atomic max operator. This value is subsequently used at the pheromone update stage.

Uchida et al. [191] described a group of implementation strategies for path construction. Different from [33], only one random number is needed and a straightforward roulette-wheel based on prefix-sum is adopted for city selection. A compressed mechanism was proposed to remove the visited cities before prefix-sum. To avoid performing prefix-sum for every selection (as the case of the former two methods and [41]), stochastic trial was proposed. In this proposal, before path construction starts, the prefix sums for each city are calculated. When selecting city, regular roulette-wheel selection is performed until an unvisited city is picked out. Finally, a hybrid method of the three methods was proposed for better performance.

As roulette-wheel selection is widely used for other population-based heuristic algorithms, so the proposed techniques might be also used in the areas like GA and ABC [129].

9.3.2.2 Pheromone Update

Pheromone update includes two tasks, i.e., pheromone evaporation and pheromone deposition.

Pheromone evaporation, in essence, is a procedure of vector update thus easy to handle. However, as different ants may try to deposit pheromone onto the same edge at the same time, pheromone deposition is of problematic.

Pheromone deposition can be directly implemented by using atomic instructions to prevent race conditions when accessing the pheromone matrix [33]. Though usage of atomic operations seems to diminish the performance, experimental results in [33, 34] showed that the naïve atomic instruction-based parallel implementation outperforms the proposed more complicated, atomic-free technique.

Another implementation based on atomic operation was proposed by Uchida et al. [191]. A special data structure was introduced for presenting the constructed path. With this structure, pheromone update for each city can perform indecently. In this design, the atomic operations happen in shared memory instead of in the global memory as the case of [33].

Cecilia et al. [33] proposed a scatter to gather transformations technique to perform pheromone deposition without atomic operations, at the cost of drastically increasing the number of accesses to device memory ($O(n^4)$ in comparison with $O(n^2)$ in the atomic-instruction implementation). The configuration launches routine for the pheromone update kernel sets as many threads as there are, cells are in the pheromone matrix (n^2), and equally distributes these threads among thread blocks. Each thread is now in charge of checking whether the cell represented by it has been visited by any ant, i.e., each thread accesses device memory to check that information. Therefore, this proposal performs the computation without usage of atomic operations at the cost of drastically increasing the number of accessing the device memory. Experimental results in [33, 34] also showed that this implementation is significantly inefficient ($\sim$10-fold slower) than the atomic operation-based implementation.

9.3.2.3 Local Search

Local search is an optional component for ACO. This mechanism can improve the solution quality greatly at the cost of enormous computation time. As each solution has being improved independently of others, so this step is very suitable for task parallel. Tsutsui and Fujimoto proposed an ACO variant (cAS) with Tabu search [188, 190] and 2-opt search [189] as local search component, respectively. A technique called move-cost adjusted thread assignment (MATA) was introduced for further accelerating the computing cost in the process of local search at the cost of extra memory space.

9.4 Summary

There are increasing number of swarm intelligence algorithms (SIAs) out there. We cannot include all of them in this book due to a limited space. In this chapter, only some specific implementation techniques for three popular SIAs of GA, DE, and ACO are introduced for instances. We believe that with the knowledge in this chapter as well as the previous chapters, readers can implement, optimize, and analyze other algorithms they met very well.

Chapter 10
GPU-Based Random Number Generators

Contents

10.1 Introduction

A key component of swarm intelligence algorithms (SIAs) is the random number generator (RNG) which provide random numbers to drive the stochastic search process. RNG plays a key role in driving the search process. Much effort is devoted to develop efficient RNGs with good statistical properties, and many highly optimized libraries are ready to use for generating random numbers fast on both CPUs and other hardware platforms such as GPUs.

According to the source of randomness, RNGs fall into three categories [73]: true random number generators (TRNGs), quasirandom number generators (QRNGs), and pseudorandom number generators (PRNGs).

TRNGs utilize physical sources of randomness to provide truly unpredictable numbers. These generators are usually slow and unrepeatable, and usually need the support of specialist hardware [3]. So TRNGs hardly used in the field of stochastic optimization. QRNGs are designed to evenly fill an n-dimensional space with points. Though quite useful, they are not widely used in the domain of optimization. PRNGs are used to generate pseudorandom sequences of numbers that satisfy most of the statistical properties of a truly random sequence but is generated by a deterministic algorithm. PRNGs are the most widely used RNGs of the three groups, and provided by almost all programming languages. There also exist many well-optimized PRNGs with open access. As this chapter discusses PRNGs, we will use random numbers and pseudorandom numbers alternatively henceforth.

Random numbers can obey various distributions, such as uniform, normal, and Cauchy distributions. Of all the distributions, uniform distribution is the most important one. Not only uniform random numbers are widely used in many different domains, but they are used as the base generators for generating random numbers subject to other distributions. Many methods, like transformation methods and rejection methods, can be used to convert uniformly distributed numbers to ones with specific nonuniform distributions [3, 156].

10.2 Uniform Random Number Generators

RNGs for generating uniform distribution random numbers can be classified into two groups, according to the basic arithmetic operations utilized: RNGs based on modular arithmetic and RNGs based on binary arithmetic.

10.2.1 Modular Arithmetic-Based RNGs

RNGs of this type yield sequences of random numbers by means of linear recurrence modulo m, where m is a large integer.

10.2.1.1 Linear Congruential Generator (LCG)

LCG is one of the best-known RNGs. LCG is defined by the following recurrence relation:

$$x_i = a \cdot x_{i-1} + c \quad \mod m, \tag{10.1}$$

where x is the sequence of the generated random numbers and $m > 0$, $0 < a < m$, and $0 \leq c, x_0 < m$. If uniform distribution on $[0, 1)$ is need, then use $u = \frac{x}{m}$ as the output sequence.

For LCG, a, c, and m should be carefully chosen to make sure that maximum period can be obtained [93]. LCG can be easily implemented on computer hardware which can provide modulo arithmetic by storage-bit truncation. RNG using LCG is shipped with C library (rand()) as well as many other languages such as Java (java.lang.Random). LCG has a relatively short period (at most 2^{32} for 32-bit integer) compared to other more complicated ones.

A special case of LCG is when $c = 0$, which presents a class of multiplicative congruential generators (MCG) [102]. Multiple carefully selected MCGs can be combined into more complicated algorithms such as Wichmann–Hill generator [186].

10.2.1.2 Multiple Recursive Generator (MRG)

MRG is a derivative of LCG and can achieve much longer period. An MRG of order k is defined as follows:

$$x_i = (a_1 \cdot x_{i-1} + a_2 \cdot x_{i-2} + \cdots + a_k \cdot x_{i-k}) \mod m. \tag{10.2}$$

The recurrence has maximal period length $m^k - 1$, if tuple $(a_1, \ldots, a_k)$ has certain properties [93].

10.2.1.3 Combined Multiple Recursive Generator (CMR)

CMR combines multiple MRGs and can obtain better statistical properties and longer periods compared to a single MRG. A well-known implementation of CMR, CMR32k3a [101], combines two MRGs:

$$
\begin{aligned}
x_i &= a_{11} \cdot x_{i-1} + a_{12} \cdot x_{i-2} + x_{13} \cdot x_{i-3} \mod m_1, \\
y_i &= a_{21} \cdot y_{i-1} + a_{22} \cdot y_{i-2} + x_{23} \cdot y_{i-3} \mod m_2, \\
z_i &= x_i - y_i \mod m_1,
\end{aligned}
\tag{10.3}
$$

where z forms the required sequence.

10.2.2 Binary Arithmetic-Based RNGs

RNGs of this type are defined directly in terms of bit strings and sequences. As computers are fast for binary arithmetic operations, binary arithmetic-based RNGs can be more efficient than modulo arithmetic-based ones.

10.2.2.1 Xorshift

Xorshift [116] produces random numbers by means of repeated use of bit-wise exclusive-or (xor, $\oplus$) and shift ($\ll$ for left and $\gg$ for right) operations.

A xorshift with four seeds (x, y, z, w) can be implemented as follows:

$$
\begin{aligned}
t &= (x \oplus (x_i \ll a)) \\
x &= y \\
y &= z \\
z &= w \\
w &= (w \oplus (w \gg b)) \oplus (t \oplus (t \gg c))
\end{aligned}
\tag{10.4}
$$

where w forms the required sequence.

With a carefully selected tuple (a, b, c), the generated sequence can have a period as long as $2^{128} - 1$.

10.2.2.2 Generalized Feedback Shift Register (GFSR)

Generalized feedback shift register (GFSR) [105], also known as linear feedback shift register (LFSR), can be used as another RNG. GFSR consecutively generates numbers based on previous states. It has several different implementations, e.g., Fibonacci LFSRs and Galois LFSRs. Taking Fibonacci LFSR as an example, given a 16-bit register state x and $(0, 2, 3, 5)$ as taps which are the bit positions that affect the next state, next number generates as follows:

$$
\begin{aligned}
z &= ((x \gg 0) \wedge (x \gg 2) \wedge (x \gg 3) \wedge (x \gg 5)) \& 1, \\
x &= (x \gg 1) | (z \gg 15),
\end{aligned}
\tag{10.5}
$$

where sequence x gives the required numbers.

10.2.2.3 Mersenne Twister (MT)

MT [117] is one of the most widely respected RNGs, it is a twisted GFSR. The underlying algorithm of MT is as follows:

- Set r w-bit numbers $(x_i, i = 1, 2, \ldots, r)$ randomly as initial values.
- Let

$$
A = \begin{pmatrix} 0 & I_{w-1} \\ a_w & a_{w-1} \cdots a_1 \end{pmatrix},
\tag{10.6}
$$

where I_{w-1} is the $(w-1) \times (w-1)$ identity matrix and $a_i, i = 1, \ldots, w$ take values of either 0 or 1. Define

$$
x_{i+r} = \left(x_{i+s} \oplus \left(x_i^{(w:(l+1))} | x_{i+1}^{(l:1)} \right) A \right),
\tag{10.7}
$$

where $x_i^{(w:(l+1))} | x_{i+1}^{(l:1)}$ indicates the concatenation of the most significant (upper) $w - l$ bits of x_i and the least significant l bits of x_{i+1}.

- Perform the following operations sequentially:

$$
\begin{aligned}
z &= x_{i+r} \oplus (x_{i+r} \gg t_1) \\
z &= z \oplus ((z \ll t_2) \,\&\, m_1) \\
z &= z \oplus ((z \ll t_3) \,\&\, m_2) \\
z &= z \oplus (x \gg t_4) \\
u_{i+r} &= z/(2^w - 1),
\end{aligned}
\tag{10.8}
$$

where t_1, t_2, t_3, and t_4 are integers and m_1 and m_2 are bit-masks and "&" is a bit-wise and operation.

$u_{i+r}, i = 1, 2, \ldots$, form the required sequence on interval $(0, 1]$.

With proper parameter values, MT can generate sequence with a period as long as $2^{19,937}$ and extremely good statistical properties [117]. Strategies for selecting good initial values are studied in [164] while Saito and Matsumoto [165] proposed an efficient implementation for fast execution on GPUs.

10.3 Random Numbers With Nonuniform Distributions

Various transformation techniques can be applied to generate nonuniform distributions from a source of uniformly distributed random numbers. Some basic techniques are briefly described below [156].

10.3.1 Inverse Transformation

The cumulative distribution function (CDF) of variate X is defined as follows:

$$
F(x) = P(X \le x)
$$

Any CDF is defined on the whole real axis and is monotonically increasing, where

$$
F(-\infty) = 0, F(+\infty) = 1
$$

In the case of continuous distribution, the CDF $F(x)$ is continuous too. Assuming the CDF steadily increases, the following single-valued inverse function should exist:

$$
x = F^{-1}(u), 0 \le u \le 1
$$

It can be proved that if U is a variate with a uniform distribution on the interval $(0, 1)$, then the variate X is of $F(x)$ distribution:

$$
X = F^{-1}(U) = G(U)
$$

Thus, the inverse transformation method can be implemented as follows:

1. Generate a uniformly distributed random number meeting the requirements: $0 \leq u \leq 1$.
2. Assume $x = G(u)$ as a random number of the distribution $F(x)$.

This approach suffers a drawback that $G(u)$ often has no closed form, while numerical solution to the following equation is excessively time consuming:

$$F(x) - u = 0$$

Example: Consider a one-dimension distribution with probability $p(X = x) = x/2, 0 \leq x \leq 2$, the CDF is given by

$$F(x) = \int_0^x p(X = x)dx = \frac{1}{4}x^2,$$

with $F(0) = 0$ and $F(2) = 1$. For denoting $F(x)$ by variable u, we have

$$x = 2\sqrt{u}$$

If we sample u from $[0, 1]$ uniform distribution, the corresponding set x forms the required nonuniform distribution.

10.3.2 Acceptance/Rejection

For some distributions, it is easier to compute the probability density function (for continuous distributions) and the probability mass function (for discrete distributions) than operate the CDFs and their inverses. In these cases, methods based on the use of density (mass) functions will be more efficient.

Suppose to generate random numbers x with distribution density $f(x)$. Apart from the variate X, consider the variate Y with the density $g(x)$, which has a fast method of random number generation and the constant c such that

$$f(x) \leq cg(x), -\infty < x < +\infty$$

Random numbers x with the distribution $F(x)$ can be generated as follows:

1. Generate a random number y with the distribution density $g(x)$.
2. Generate a random number u (independent of y) that is uniformly distributed over the interval $(0, 1)$.
3. If $u \leq f(y)/cg(y)$, accept y as a random number x with the distribution $F(x)$. Otherwise, go back to step 1.

Example: If we want to generate numbers based on a nonuniform distribution, e.g., Gaussian distribution with $N(0, 1)$, we can adopt acceptance/rejection method (though not usually). Here, we set $g(x)$ be an uniform distribution in interval $[-2, 2]$ and hence

$$g(x) = 1/4, -2 \leq x \leq 2.$$

Because the maximal marginal probability of $N(0,1)$ is $1/\sqrt{2\pi}$ with input equaling to zero, setting c bing $2\sqrt{2/\pi}$ satisfies the requirement, i.e., $f(x) \leq cg(x)$. Then we can sample random numbers following aforementioned steps.

10.3.3 Mixture of Distributions

You can split the initial distribution into several simpler distributions

$$F(x) = \sum_{i=1}^{k} p_i F_i(x), \sum_{i=1}^{k} p_i = 1$$

In this case, random numbers for each of the distributions $F_i(x)$ are easy to generate. An appropriate algorithm may be as follows:

1. Generate a random number i with the probability p_i.
2. Generate a random number y (independent of i) with the distribution $F_i(x)$.
3. Accept y as a random number x with the distribution $F(x)$.

Example: Consider sampling from Gaussian mixture model:

$$p(x) = \sum_{i=1}^{k} \alpha_i N(u_i, \Sigma_i), \sum_{i=1}^{k} \alpha_i = 1,$$

a simple and practical way is to firstly select a single Gaussian distribution based on weight with probability $p(z = j) = \alpha_j$ and then generate a number from this single distribution $p(x|z = j) = N(u_j, \Sigma_j)$. Because the following equation exists, i.e.,

$$p(x) = \sum_{j} p(z = j) p(x|z = j),$$

so, the generated numbers obey the distribution of defined Gaussian mixture model.

10.3.4 Special Properties

Special properties of distributions can be utilized to generate random numbers efficiently. For example, based on the 2D inverse transformation known as the Box–Muller method [18], normally distributed random numbers can be generated from uniform random numbers:

$$x_1 = \sqrt{-2\ln(u_1)}\sin(2\pi u_2)$$

$$x_2 = \sqrt{-2\ln(u_1)}\cos(2\pi u_2)$$

where u_i is a sequence of uniformly distributed numbers while x_i makes the required number sequence subject to normal distribution.

10.4 Measurements of Randomness

The most important factor of assessing RNGs is to measure their randomness. This can be conducted by theoretical analysis or through statistical test.

10.4.1 Theoretical Analysis

Theoretical research provides the basis for better understanding of generator properties. The results obtained through theoretical testing refer to a basic generator used over the entire period. The most important figures of merit for this task are discrepancy and the spectral test, and a newcomer, the weighted spectral test. By theoretical evaluation, bad generators can be rejected immediately.

Discrepancy is a statistical measurement of equidistribution. The discrepancy D_N for a random number set $\{s1, s2, s3, \ldots\}$ with respect to the interval $[a, b]$ is defined as

$$D_N = \sup_{a \leq c \leq d \leq d} | \frac{|\{s_1, s_2, \ldots, s_N\} \bigcap [c, d]|}{N} - \frac{d-c}{b-a} |$$

A sequence is more uniform distributed if the discrepancy D_N tends to zero as N grows into infinity.

Spectral test is devised to study of the properties of LCGs, so it cannot be applied to measure the performance of other RNGs. The theory behind it is quite complicated. A detailed description of these theoretical analyses are out of the scope of this book, readers can refer to [93, 3, 100] for details. But note should be taken that none of these figures of merit can guarantee the performance of the generator in the real applications.

10.4.2 Statistical Test

Theoretical support for RNGs is not enough. Theoretical assessment of RNGs cannot guarantee good performance of the samples in numerical practice. So empirical evidence is indispensable, as it ensures that the remaining generators are of acceptable quality by testing a generator over a small fraction of the period actually used.

Some important tests are serial test, overlapping serial test, run test, just to name a few. The most exciting development in the field of statistical testing in the last few years has been the publication of the TESTU01 [103], which comprises many practically statistical tests that have been designed.

TESTU01 is a software library, implemented in C language. It not only has several types of RNGs, but also comprises a great number of empirical statistical testings of uniform RNGs. The test can be applied to predefined RNGs in library, user-defined generators or random numbers recorded in file stream.

10.5 Impact of Random Numbers on Performance of SIAs

In order to discuss the impact of RNGs on the performance of swarm intelligence algorithms, we empirically compared 13 widely used RNGs with uniform distribution based on both CPUs and GPUs, with respect to algorithm efficiency as well as their impact on particle swarm optimization. Two strategies were adopted to conduct the comparison among multiple RNGs for multiple objectives. The experiments were conducted on well-known benchmark functions of diverse landscapes, and were run on the GPU for the purpose of acceleration. The results show that RNGs have very different efficiencies in terms of speed, and GPU-based RNGs can be much faster than their CPU-based counterparts if properly utilized.

10.5.1 Background

As aforementioned, the performance of RNGs can be analyzed theoretically using criteria such as period and lattice structure [93, 3], or by systematic statistical test [103]. However, none of these analyses are relevant directly to RNGs' impact on optimization algorithms like PSO.

It is interesting to ask how RNGs can effect these stochastic search methods. Clerc [37] replaced the conventional RNGs with a short length list of numbers (i.e., a RNG with a very short period) and empirically studied the performance of PSO. The experiments showed that, at least for the moment, there is no sure way to build a "good" list for high performance. Thus, RNGs with certain degree of randomness are necessary for the success of stochastic search.

Bastos-Filho et al. [12, 13] studied the impact of the quality of CPU- and GPU-based RNGs on the performance of PSO. The experiments showed that PSO needs RNGs with minimum quality and no significative improvements were achieved when comparing high quality RNGs to medium quality RNGs. Only LCG [93] and Xorshift algorithms [116] were compared for CPUs, and only one method for generating random numbers in an ad hoc manner on GPUs was adopted for comparing GPUs.

In general, RNGs shipped with math libraries of programming languages or other specific random libraries are used when implementing intelligent optimization algorithms. These RNGs generate random numbers of very diverse qualities with different efficiencies. A comparative study on the impact of these popular RNGs will be helpful when implementing intelligent optimization algorithms for solving optimization problems.

Following the work by Ding and Tan [47], we selected 13 widely used, highly optimized uniformly distributed RNGs and applied them to PSO for empirically comparing their impact on the optimization performance. Nine well-known benchmark functions were implemented for the sake of comparison. All the experiments were conducted on the GPU for fast execution. Two novel strategies, league scoring strategy and lose-rank strategy, were introduced to conduct a systematic comparison on these RNGs' performance. Though the work is limited to the impact on PSO, other intelligent optimization algorithms can also be studied in the proposed framework.

10.5.2 Experimental Setup

In this part, we describe our experimental environment and parameter settings in detail.

10.5.2.1 Testbed

We conducted the experiments on a PC running 64-bit Windows 7 Professional with 8 GB DDR3 Memory and Intel Core I5-2310 (@2.9 GHz 3.1 GHz). The GPU used for implementing PSO in the experiments is NVIDIA GeForce GTX 560 Ti with 384 CUDA cores. The program was implemented with C and compiled with Visual Studio 2010 and CUDA 5.5.

10.5.2.2 Particle Swarm Optimization

A standard PSO algorithms [19] with ring topology was adopted in our experiments. Velocity vectors and position vectors are updated with Eqs. (10.9), (10.10), where in Eq. (10.9), $\omega = 1/(2\log(2)) \approx 0.721$, $c_1 = c_2 = 0.5 + log(2) \approx 1.193$, and r_1, r_2 are random numbers derived from uniform distribution on interval $(0, 1)$ The swarm size was fixed to 50 for all experiments, and 10,000 iterations was performed for each optimization run

$$v_{id} = \omega \cdot v_{id} + c_1 r_1 (p_{id} - x_{id}) + c_2 r_2 (p_{gd} - x_{id}) \qquad (10.9)$$

$$\mathbf{x}_i = \mathbf{x}_i + \mathbf{v}_i \qquad (10.10)$$

The PSO algorithm was implemented on the GPU with CUDA based on the work by Zhou and Tan [213]. The generation process of random numbers was replaced by RNGs under test.

Table 10.1 Random Number Generators Tested

No.	Algorithm	Description	Note
1	xorshift	Implemented using the xorshift algorithm [116], created with generator type CU-RAND_RNG_PSEUDO_XORWOW	CURAND with CUDA Toolkit 5.5
2	xorshift	Same algorithm as 1, faster but probably statistically weaker, set ordering to CU-RAND_ORDERING_PSEUDO_SEEDED	
3	Combined multiple recursive	Implemented using the combined multiple recursive algorithm [101], created with generator type CURAND_RNG_PSEUDO_MRG32K3A	
4	Mersenne twister	Implemented using the mersenne twister algorithm with parameters customized for operation on the GPU [165], created with generator type CU-RAND_RNG_PSEUDO_MTGP32	
5	Multiplicative congruential	Implemented using the 31-bit multiplicative congruential algorithm [102], create with parameter VSL_BRNG_MCG31	MKL 11.1
6	Generalized feedback shift register	Implemented using the 32-bit generalized feedback shift register algorithms, create with parameter VSL_BRNG_R250 [91]	
7	Combined multiple recursive	Implemented using combined multiple recursive algorithm [101], create with parameter VSL_BRNG_MRG32K3A	
8	Multiplicative congruential	Implemented using the 59-bit multiplicative congruential algorithm from NAG Numerical Libraries [186], create with parameter VSL_BRNG_MCG59	
9	Wichmann–Hill	Implemented using the Wichmann–Hill algorithm from NAG Numerical Libraries [186], create with parameter VSL_BRNG_WH	
10	Mersenne twister	Implemented using the mersenne twister algorithm MT19937 [117], create with parameter VSL_BRNG_MT19937	
11	Mersenne twister	Implemented using the mersenne twister algorithms MT2203 [118] with a set of 6024 configurations. Parameters of the generators provide mutual independence of the corresponding sequences., create with parameter VSL_BRNG_MT2203	
12	Mersenne twister	Implemented using the SIMD-oriented fast mersenne twister algorithm SFMT19937 [164], create with parameter VSL_BRNG_SFMT19937	
13	Linear congruential	Implementing using linear congruential algorithm with $a = 1103515245$, $c = 12345$, $m = 2^{32}$, only high 16 bits are used as output	MS Visual Studio C library rand()

10.5.2.3 RNGs Used for Comparison

Besides functions provided by programming languages, many libraries with well-implemented RNGs are available, such as AMD's ACML [6] and Boost Random Number Library [1] targeted at CPUs and specific implementations [73, 164, 99] for GPU platform.

Among all these candidates, Math Kernel Library (MKL) [76] (for CPU) and CURAND [137] (for GPU) were selected for the experiments by considering the following reasons: (1) RNGs provided by the two libraries cover the most popular RNG algorithms and (2) both MKL and CURAND are well-optimized for our hardware platform (I5 CPU and GeForce 560 Ti GPU), so a fair comparison of efficiency can be expected. So experiments with these two libraries are broadly covered in terms of types of RNGs and present a fair comparison in terms of time efficiency.

As LCG is widely shipped by standard library of various programming language, we added a RNG with LCG (C's rand()). The RNGs used in the experiments are listed in Table 10.1.

10.5.2.4 Benchmark Functions

Nine benchmark functions were implemented on the GPU with float numbers of single precision. All these functions are minimizing problems while $f_1 \sim f_3$ are unimodal function while the left are multimodal functions.

The search space are all limited within $[-10.0, 10.0]^D$, where D is the dimension which could be $10, 30, 50, 100$ in the experiments. The optimum points were shifted to 1.0^D if some where else, and bias values were added to each function to make sure the minimal values are 100 for all functions, with the only except of Weierstrass function. Weierstrass function was implemented just as Eq. (12.9) and no effort was made to move the optima point or adjust the minimal value. The formulae of the used benchmark functions are listed as follows:

Sphere Function:

$$f_1 = \sum_{i=1}^{D} \mathbf{x}_i^2. \tag{10.11}$$

High Conditioned Elliptic Function:

$$f_2 = \sum_{i=1}^{D} (10^6)^{\frac{i-1}{D-1}} \mathbf{x}_i^2. \tag{10.12}$$

Discus Function:

$$f_3 = 10^6 \cdot \mathbf{x}_1^2 + \sum_{i=2}^{D} \mathbf{x}_i^2. \tag{10.13}$$

Rosenbrock Function:

$$f_4 = \sum_{i=1}^{D-1} \left(100 \cdot \left(\mathbf{x}_{i+1} - \mathbf{x}_i^2 \right)^2 + (1 - \mathbf{x}_i)^2 \right). \tag{10.14}$$

Ackley Function:

$$f_5 = -20 \cdot \exp(-0.2 \cdot \sqrt{\frac{1}{D} \sum_{i=1}^{D} \mathbf{x}_i^2}) - \exp(\frac{1}{D} \sum_{i=1}^{D} \cos(2\pi \cdot \mathbf{x}_i)). \tag{10.15}$$

Weierstrass Function:

$$f_6 = \sum_{i=1}^{D} (\sum_{k=0}^{20} [0.5^k \cos(2\pi \cdot 3^k (x_i + 0.5))]). \tag{10.16}$$

Schaffer's F7 Function:

$$f_7 = (\frac{1}{D-1} \sum_{i=1}^{D-1} (\sqrt{\mathbf{y}_i} + \sqrt{\mathbf{y}_i} \sin^2(50 \cdot \mathbf{y}_i^{0.2})))^2. \tag{10.17}$$

where $\mathbf{y}_i = \sqrt{\mathbf{x}_i^2 + \mathbf{x}_{i+1}^2}$

Griewank Function:

$$f_8 = \sum_{i=1}^{D} \frac{\mathbf{x}_i^2}{4000} - \prod_{i=1}^{D} \cos(\frac{\mathbf{x}_i}{\sqrt{i}}) + 1. \tag{10.18}$$

Rastrigin Function:

$$f_9 = \sum_{i=1}^{D} (\mathbf{x}_i^2 - 10\cos(2\pi \cdot \mathbf{x}_i) + 10). \qquad (10.19)$$

10.5.3 Results and Analysis

This section presents the experimental results. Both efficiency of RNGs and solution quality of PSO using each RNG are described and analyzed.

10.5.3.1 RNGs Efficiency

We ran each RNG program to generate random numbers in batch of different sizes, and test the speed. The results are presented in Table 10.2.

In general, RNGs based on both CPUs and GPUs achieve better performance by generating batches of random numbers, and GPUs need larger batch size to get peek performance than CPUs. In the condition of large batch size, CURAND can be several to tens of fold faster than MKL for the same algorithms.

Modulo arithmetic-based RNGs are less efficient than binary arithmetic ones, just as aforementioned. Combined Multiple Recursive algorithm (No. 7) and Wichmann–Hill algorithm (No. 9) presents the slowest RNGs, followed by Multiplicative Congruential (No. 8). As a comparison, mersenne twister algorithm presents the fastest RNGs. CPU-based SFMT19937 (No. 12) can be one order of magnitude faster than

Table 10.2 RNG Efficiency Comparison Under Different Batch Size (# of Random Numbers per Nanosecond)

	GPU				CPU								C
	CURAND				MKL								
Batch Size	1	2	3	4	5	6	7	8	9	10	11	12	13
1	0.3	0.3	0.3	0.3	17.5	17.3	14.8	15.9	7.8	15.2	14.7	15.2	
10	2.7	2.6	1.9	2.6	95.2	116.3	54.6	109.9	56.8	93.5	87.7	129.9	
20	4.8	4.9	3.2	5.1	144.9	166.7	67.1	192.3	79.4	181.8	161.3	227.3	
50	10.9	11.0	7.2	12.8	294.1	227.3	112.4	285.7	120.5	344.8	294.1	454.5	
100	21.1	21.6	14.2	25.8	400.0	263.2	138.9	357.1	142.9	434.8	384.6	714.3	
200	41.7	43.7	28.9	49.8	555.6	285.7	156.3	416.7	158.7	500.0	555.6	1111.1	
500	104.2	114.9	76.9	125.0	625.0	416.7	178.6	454.5	166.7	625.0	666.7	1428.6	
1000	200.0	243.9	163.9	232.6	666.7	555.6	185.2	454.5	172.4	666.7	769.2	1111.1	
2000	312.5	476.2	344.8	434.8	666.7	666.7	188.7	454.5	172.4	714.3	769.2	1250.0	
5000	500.0	1250.0	1000.0	909.1	769.2	769.2	192.3	476.2	172.4	833.3	833.3	1428.6	
10,000	588.2	2500.0	1428.6	1250.0	714.3	833.3	192.3	476.2	175.4	833.3	833.3	1428.6	36.5
20,000	666.7	3333.3	1666.7	1666.7	714.3	833.3	192.3	476.2	175.4	769.2	769.2	1428.6	
50,000	769.2	10,000.0	2500.0	3333.3	769.2	833.3	192.3	476.2	175.4	769.2	769.2	1428.6	
100,000	714.3	10,000.0	2500.0	5000.0	714.3	833.3	192.3	476.2	175.4	769.2	769.2	1428.6	
200,000	714.3	10,000.0	2500.0	10,000.0	714.3	714.3	192.3	476.2	175.4	769.2	769.2	1666.7	

CPU-based CMR32K3A (No. 7) while the GPU version (No. 4) can be fivefold faster than the CPU implementation. Considering the good statistical property of MT [117, 164, 118], it makes the best RNG of all the RNGs concerned.

10.5.3.2 Solution Quality

In all experiments, 150 independent trials were performed for each function on each dimension, where 10,000 iterations were executed for each trial. One hundred fifty integer numbers were randomly generated from uniform distribution as seeds for each trail, and all RNGs shared the same 150 seeds. All particles were initialized randomly within the whole feasible search space and the initialization was shared by all RNGs (to be exactly, RNG No. 10 was used for the purpose of initialization).

The results (average values and standard deviations) are listed in Table 10.3.

For a particular function, the solution quality can be compared between any two RNGs with statistical test. But there is no direct way to compare a groups of RNGs (13 in our experiments).

League Scoring Strategy

In order to compare the results in a systematic and quantitative way, a league scoring strategy was adopted here. The results for two different RNGs, say A and B, on the same function of the same dimension are compared with $p = 0.05$ using rank-sum test. The scoring rules are illustrated in Table 10.5. If A is better than B (i.e., $A < B$ assuming minimum problems), then A scores a points while B scores b points. On the contrary, if B is better than A, then B scored a points while A scores b points. Otherwise, it is a tie so each scores c points. a, b, and c satisfy the relation of $b < c < a$.

The scores calculated by the method shown in Table 10.5, is presented in Table 10.4, where $a = 2$, $b = 0$, $c = 1$. For each row in the table, a maximum value can be picked out.

Observing Table 10.4 and the corresponding Radar Map (Fig. 10.1), almost all cells were 14. Intuitively, it seems no significant disparity among all these RNGs. To analyze the performance in a more quantitative manner, the total scores were calculated (see the last row in Table 10.4). At most 16 points gap was observed among all the 13 RNGs. It is a very narrow gap considering that it is the total difference after $12 * 36 = 432$ rounds of "competitions."

To make a detailed observation about if disparity exits for particular dimension or specific function, the scores were aggregated by dimension and by function, respectively. Figs. 10.2 and 10.3 illustrate the aggregated results. No significant disparity was observed for these two conditions.

As the last comment on league score strategy, we shall take notice that the score-based comparison depend on the selection of scoring rules which determine to what degree a win is awarded and a lose is penalized. However, since what we encounter here is in effect a multiobjective comparison, there is no trivial optimal strategy

Table 10.3 Results for Benchmark Functions

Function	D	1	2	3	4	5	6	7	8	9	10	11	12	13
Shpere	10	1.00E+02 (0.00E+00)	1.00E+02 (0.00E+00)	1.00E+02 (0.00E+00)	1.00E+02 (0.00E+00)	1.00E+02 (0.00E+00)	1.00E+02 (0.00E+00)	1.00E+02 (0.00E+00)	1.00E+02 (0.00E+00)	1.00E+02 (0.00E+00)	1.00E+02 (0.00E+00)	1.00E+02 (0.00E+00)	1.00E+02 (0.00E+00)	1.00E+02 (0.00E+00)
	30	1.00E+02 (1.19E-03)	1.00E+02 (8.29E-04)	1.00E+02 (8.40E-04)	1.00E+02 (1.00E-03)	1.00E+02 (6.48E-04)	1.00E+02 (9.33E-04)	1.00E+02 (1.42E-03)	1.00E+02 (7.47E-04)	1.00E+02 (5.83E-04)	1.00E+02 (3.71E-04)	1.00E+02 (5.67E-04)	1.00E+02 (9.30E-04)	1.00E+02 (1.18E-03)
	50	1.02E+02 (2.06E-01)	1.01E+02 (2.82E-01)	1.01E+02 (2.71E-01)	1.01E+02 (2.56E-01)	1.01E+02 (2.59E-01)	1.01E+02 (2.22E-01)	1.02E+02 (2.51E-01)	1.02E+02 (2.52E-01)	1.01E+02 (2.45E-01)	1.01E+02 (2.40E-01)	1.01E+02 (3.28E-01)	1.01E+02 (2.38E-01)	1.01E+02 (2.89E-01)
	100	1.68E+02 (3.71E-03)	1.68E+02 (5.03E-03)	1.68E+02 (6.59E-03)	1.68E+02 (9.43E-03)	1.68E+02 (6.46E-03)	1.68E+02 (3.88E-03)	1.68E+02 (5.46E-03)	1.68E+02 (6.03E-03)	1.68E+02 (5.74E-03)	1.68E+02 (1.06E-02)	1.68E+02 (6.64E-03)	1.68E+02 (5.82E-03)	1.68E+02 (5.55E-03)
Elliptic	10	1.00E+02 (0.00E+00)	1.00E+02 (0.00E+00)	1.00E+02 (0.00E+00)	1.00E+02 (0.00E+00)	1.00E+02 (0.00E+00)	1.00E+02 (0.00E+00)	1.00E+02 (0.00E+00)	1.00E+02 (0.00E+00)	1.00E+02 (0.00E+00)	1.00E+02 (0.00E+00)	1.00E+02 (0.00E+00)	1.00E+02 (0.00E+00)	1.00E+02 (0.00E+00)
	30	1.00E+02 (1.11E-05)	1.00E+02 (1.13E-05)	1.00E+02 (4.20E-05)	1.00E+02 (1.34E-05)	1.00E+02 (1.26E-05)	1.00E+02 (2.74E-05)	1.00E+02 (1.56E-05)	1.00E+02 (2.09E-05)	1.00E+02 (1.55E-05)	1.00E+02 (1.39E-05)	1.00E+02 (1.18E-05)	1.00E+02 (1.49E-05)	1.00E+02 (1.31E-05)
	50	1.09E+02 (1.57E+00)	1.09E+02 (1.69E+00)	1.08E+02 (1.75E+00)	1.08E+02 (1.44E+00)	1.08E+02 (1.52E+00)	1.08E+02 (1.35E+00)	1.08E+02 (1.47E+00)	1.08E+02 (1.82E+00)	1.08E+02 (1.36E+00)	1.08E+02 (1.46E+00)	1.08E+02 (1.74E+00)	1.08E+02 (1.30E+00)	1.09E+02 (1.43E+00)
	100	4.46E+02 (1.02E-02)	4.46E+02 (1.07E-02)	4.46E+02 (1.02E-02)	4.46E+02 (1.14E-02)	4.46E+02 (8.95E-03)	4.46E+02 (2.39E-02)	4.46E+02 (7.79E-03)	4.46E+02 (1.38E-02)	4.46E+02 (1.06E-02)	4.46E+02 (9.73E-03)	4.46E+02 (9.27E-03)	4.46E+02 (5.59E-03)	4.46E+02 (6.89E-03)
Discus	10	1.00E+02 (0.00E+00)	1.00E+02 (0.00E+00)	1.00E+02 (0.00E+00)	1.00E+02 (0.00E+00)	1.00E+02 (0.00E+00)	1.00E+02 (0.00E+00)	1.00E+02 (0.00E+00)	1.00E+02 (0.00E+00)	1.00E+02 (0.00E+00)	1.00E+02 (0.00E+00)	1.00E+02 (0.00E+00)	1.00E+02 (0.00E+00)	1.00E+02 (0.00E+00)
	30	1.00E+02 (3.88E-06)	1.00E+02 (6.91E-06)	1.00E+02 (5.93E-06)	1.00E+02 (5.84E-06)	1.00E+02 (7.92E-06)	1.00E+02 (5.37E-06)	1.00E+02 (3.93E-06)	1.00E+02 (5.96E-06)	1.00E+02 (6.52E-06)	1.00E+02 (6.62E-06)	1.00E+02 (7.35E-06)	1.00E+02 (6.24E-06)	1.00E+02 (6.01E-06)
	50	1.01E+02 (3.13E-01)	1.01E+02 (2.62E-01)	1.01E+02 (2.94E-01)	1.01E+02 (2.59E-01)	1.01E+02 (2.99E-01)	1.01E+02 (2.22E-01)	1.01E+02 (2.69E-01)	1.01E+02 (2.67E-01)	1.01E+02 (3.15E-01)	1.02E+02 (3.21E-01)	1.01E+02 (2.58E-01)	1.01E+02 (2.88E-01)	1.01E+02 (3.04E-01)
	100	1.68E+02 (1.13E-02)	1.68E+02 (5.76E-03)	1.68E+02 (1.01E-02)	1.68E+02 (6.42E-03)	1.68E+02 (5.09E-03)	1.68E+02 (7.81E-03)	1.68E+02 (5.41E-03)	1.68E+02 (7.07E-03)	1.68E+02 (6.15E-03)	1.68E+02 (8.30E-03)	1.68E+02 (1.02E-02)	1.68E+02 (4.76E-03)	1.68E+02 (6.64E-03)
Rosenbrock	10	1.05E+02 (1.27E+00)	1.05E+02 (1.79E+00)	1.05E+02 (1.54E+00)	1.05E+02 (1.60E+00)	1.05E+02 (1.47E+00)	1.06E+02 (1.20E+00)	1.05E+02 (1.88E+00)	1.05E+02 (1.55E+00)	1.05E+02 (1.84E+00)	1.05E+02 (1.65E+00)	1.05E+02 (1.63E+00)	1.05E+02 (1.29E+00)	1.05E+02 (1.88E+00)
	30	1.27E+02 (2.15E-01)	1.27E+02 (3.11E-01)	1.27E+02 (2.50E-01)	1.27E+02 (2.02E-01)	1.27E+02 (3.04E-01)	1.27E+02 (2.27E-01)	1.27E+02 (2.58E-01)	1.27E+02 (1.79E-01)	1.27E+02 (2.44E-01)	1.27E+02 (2.59E-01)	1.27E+02 (2.42E-01)	1.27E+02 (2.27E-01)	1.27E+02 (4.07E-01)
	50	7.54E+03 (2.00E+02)	7.61E+03 (3.03E+02)	7.58E+03 (2.03E+02)	7.57E+03 (1.86E+02)	7.65E+03 (1.86E+02)	7.60E+03 (2.07E+02)	7.57E+03 (2.16E+02)	7.54E+03 (2.22E+02)	7.58E+03 (1.97E+02)	7.59E+03 (2.47E+02)	7.61E+03 (2.59E+02)	7.57E+03 (1.99E+02)	7.57E+03 (2.25E+02)
	100	2.60E+04 (8.03E+02)	2.60E+04 (5.85E+02)	2.62E+04 (5.23E+02)	2.58E+04 (6.94E+02)	2.59E+04 (6.16E+02)	2.61E+04 (4.65E+02)	2.60E+04 (7.11E+02)	2.60E+04 (6.54E+02)	2.60E+04 (4.73E+02)	2.58E+04 (6.85E+02)	2.58E+04 (7.48E+02)	2.60E+04 (6.34E+02)	2.59E+04 (4.84E+02)
Ackley	10	1.00E+02 (2.16E-06)	1.00E+02 (3.31E-06)	1.00E+02 (3.48E-06)	1.00E+02 (3.88E-06)	1.00E+02 (2.96E-06)	1.00E+02 (6.75E-06)	1.00E+02 (3.07E-06)	1.00E+02 (4.17E-06)	1.00E+02 (3.05E-06)	1.00E+02 (6.34E-06)	1.00E+02 (2.74E-06)	1.00E+02 (2.82E-06)	1.00E+02 (4.27E-06)
	30	1.00E+02 (3.65E-02)	1.00E+02 (4.75E-02)	1.00E+02 (4.11E-02)	1.00E+02 (2.89E-02)	1.00E+02 (3.25E-02)	1.00E+02 (2.35E-02)	1.00E+02 (2.36E-02)	1.00E+02 (6.79E-02)	1.00E+02 (3.01E-02)	1.00E+02 (4.28E-02)	1.00E+02 (3.48E-02)	1.00E+02 (3.41E-02)	1.00E+02 (3.47E-02)
	50	1.16E+02 (9.11E-02)	1.16E+02 (8.76E-02)	1.16E+02 (8.13E-02)	1.16E+02 (9.58E-02)	1.16E+02 (6.69E-02)	1.16E+02 (9.67E-02)	1.16E+02 (7.95E-02)	1.16E+02 (1.16E-01)	1.16E+02 (8.20E-02)	1.16E+02 (8.14E-02)	1.16E+02 (7.89E-02)	1.16E+02 (9.40E-02)	1.16E+02 (9.84E-02)
	100	1.17E+02 (5.15E+01)	1.17E+02 (5.15E+01)	1.17E+02 (5.15E+01)	1.17E+02 (5.15E+01)	1.17E+02 (5.15E+01)	1.17E+02 (5.15E+01)	1.17E+02 (5.15E+01)	1.17E+02 (5.15E+01)	1.17E+02 (5.15E+01)	1.17E+02 (5.15E+01)	1.17E+02 (5.15E+01)	1.17E+02 (5.15E+01)	1.17E+02 (5.15E+01)
Weierstrass	10	-2.00E+01 (3.70E-02)	-2.00E+01 (4.20E-02)	-2.00E+01 (9.90E-03)	-2.00E+01 (9.01E-02)	-2.00E+01 (1.24E-02)	-2.00E+01 (6.43E-02)	-2.00E+01 (5.78E-02)	-2.00E+01 (2.06E-02)	-2.00E+01 (5.77E-02)	-2.00E+01 (4.83E-02)	-2.00E+01 (1.08E-02)	-2.00E+01 (1.42E-01)	-2.00E+01 (6.41E-02)
	30	-5.82E+01 (4.43E+00)	-5.91E+01 (3.24E+00)	-5.93E+01 (2.87E+00)	-5.80E+01 (4.49E+00)	-5.94E+01 (2.12E+00)	-5.94E+01 (2.15E+00)	-5.98E+01 (1.48E+00)	-5.92E+01 (2.74E+00)	-5.77E+01 (4.95E+00)	-5.80E+01 (5.33E+00)	-5.90E+01 (3.53E+00)	-5.91E+01 (3.44E+00)	-5.84E+01 (3.89E+00)
	50	-1.00E+02 (2.88E-14)	-1.00E+02 (2.88E-14)	-1.00E+02 (2.88E-14)	-1.00E+02 (2.88E-14)	-1.00E+02 (2.88E-14)	-1.00E+02 (2.88E-14)	-1.00E+02 (2.88E-14)	-1.00E+02 (2.88E-14)	-1.00E+02 (2.88E-14)	-1.00E+02 (2.88E-14)	-1.00E+02 (2.88E-14)	-1.00E+02 (2.88E-14)	-1.00E+02 (2.88E-14)
	100	-2.00E+02 (2.88E-14)	-2.00E+02 (2.88E-14)	-2.00E+02 (2.88E-14)	-2.00E+02 (2.88E-14)	-2.00E+02 (2.88E-14)	-2.00E+02 (2.88E-14)	-2.00E+02 (2.88E-14)	-2.00E+02 (2.88E-14)	-2.00E+02 (2.88E-14)	-2.00E+02 (2.88E-14)	-2.00E+02 (2.88E-14)	-2.00E+02 (2.88E-14)	-2.00E+02 (2.88E-14)
Schaffer's F7	10	1.00E+02 (3.65E-03)	1.00E+02 (8.14E-03)	1.00E+02 (1.16E-02)	1.00E+02 (4.98E-03)	1.00E+02 (7.53E-03)	1.00E+02 (7.99E-03)	1.00E+02 (1.76E-02)	1.00E+02 (7.04E-03)	1.00E+02 (8.09E-03)	1.00E+02 (6.30E-03)	1.00E+02 (6.00E-03)	1.00E+02 (1.01E-02)	1.00E+02 (9.48E-03)
	30	1.01E+02 (1.79E-01)	1.01E+02 (1.98E-01)	1.01E+02 (1.38E-01)	1.01E+02 (1.73E-01)	1.01E+02 (2.07E-01)	1.01E+02 (1.59E-01)	1.01E+02 (1.83E-01)	1.01E+02 (1.65E-01)	1.01E+02 (1.45E-01)	1.01E+02 (1.46E-01)	1.01E+02 (1.85E-01)	1.01E+02 (1.79E-01)	1.01E+02 (1.88E-01)
	50	1.02E+02 (2.96E-01)	1.02E+02 (2.83E-01)	1.02E+02 (2.88E-01)	1.02E+02 (2.36E-01)	1.02E+02 (2.87E-01)	1.02E+02 (2.67E-01)	1.02E+02 (2.30E-01)	1.02E+02 (2.90E-01)	1.02E+02 (2.16E-01)	1.02E+02 (2.31E-01)	1.02E+02 (2.62E-01)	1.02E+02 (2.84E-01)	1.02E+02 (2.80E-01)
	100	1.44E+02 (2.09E-01)	1.44E+02 (1.92E-01)	1.44E+02 (2.37E-01)	1.44E+02 (2.10E-01)	1.44E+02 (1.68E-01)	1.44E+02 (1.82E-01)	1.44E+02 (2.43E-01)	1.44E+02 (2.03E-01)	1.44E+02 (1.78E-01)	1.44E+02 (2.52E-01)	1.44E+02 (1.76E-01)	1.44E+02 (2.55E-01)	1.44E+02 (2.03E-01)
Griewank	10	1.00E+02 (8.61E-03)	1.00E+02 (9.61E-03)	1.00E+02 (7.99E-03)	1.00E+02 (8.46E-03)	1.00E+02 (9.49E-03)	1.00E+02 (1.10E-02)	1.00E+02 (1.05E-02)	1.00E+02 (9.42E-03)	1.00E+02 (8.29E-03)	1.00E+02 (8.53E-03)	1.00E+02 (9.19E-03)	1.00E+02 (8.37E-03)	1.00E+02 (1.09E-02)
	30	1.00E+02 (4.29E-02)	1.00E+02 (5.48E-02)	1.00E+02 (5.47E-02)	1.00E+02 (4.25E-02)	1.00E+02 (4.89E-02)	1.00E+02 (4.80E-02)	1.00E+02 (5.32E-02)	1.00E+02 (5.69E-02)	1.00E+02 (4.88E-02)	1.00E+02 (4.71E-02)	1.00E+02 (5.07E-02)	1.00E+02 (5.04E-02)	1.00E+02 (5.66E-02)
	50	1.00E+02 (6.98E-02)	1.00E+02 (6.96E-02)	1.00E+02 (7.92E-02)	1.00E+02 (7.45E-02)	1.00E+02 (8.14E-02)	1.00E+02 (1.03E-01)	1.00E+02 (8.11E-02)	1.00E+02 (7.20E-02)	1.00E+02 (7.74E-02)	1.00E+02 (9.55E-02)	1.00E+02 (8.30E-02)	1.00E+02 (9.03E-02)	1.00E+02 (8.22E-02)
	100	1.03E+02 (1.49E-02)	1.03E+02 (1.24E-02)	1.03E+02 (1.39E-02)	1.03E+02 (1.33E-02)	1.03E+02 (1.38E-02)	1.03E+02 (1.68E-02)	1.03E+02 (1.70E-02)	1.03E+02 (1.62E-02)	1.03E+02 (1.37E-02)	1.03E+02 (1.41E-02)	1.03E+02 (1.12E-02)	1.03E+02 (1.50E-02)	1.03E+02 (1.85E-02)
Rastrigin	10	1.03E+02 (1.20E+00)	1.03E+02 (1.57E+00)	1.03E+02 (1.22E+00)	1.03E+02 (1.82E+00)	1.03E+02 (1.94E+00)	1.03E+02 (1.87E+00)	1.03E+02 (1.60E+00)	1.03E+02 (1.78E+00)	1.03E+02 (2.03E+00)	1.03E+02 (2.20E+00)	1.03E+02 (1.74E+00)	1.03E+02 (1.95E+00)	1.04E+02 (1.67E+00)
	30	1.30E+02 (5.51E-01)	1.29E+02 (8.14E-01)	1.30E+02 (4.64E-01)	1.29E+02 (7.81E-01)	1.30E+02 (6.14E-01)	1.30E+02 (9.05E-01)	1.30E+02 (7.41E-01)	1.29E+02 (8.75E-01)	1.29E+02 (7.41E-01)	1.30E+02 (5.28E-01)	1.30E+02 (4.96E-01)	1.30E+02 (7.24E-01)	1.30E+02 (6.15E-01)
	50	3.80E+02 (2.90E+01)	3.88E+02 (2.78E+01)	3.86E+02 (2.27E+01)	3.80E+02 (2.48E+01)	3.76E+02 (3.04E+01)	3.85E+02 (2.92E+01)	3.83E+02 (1.85E+01)	3.86E+02 (2.81E+01)	3.93E+02 (2.47E+01)	4.00E+02 (3.08E+01)	3.87E+02 (2.64E+01)	3.85E+02 (2.64E+01)	3.89E+02 (2.44E+01)
	100	9.12E+03 (6.59E+01)	9.14E+03 (5.06E+01)	9.13E+03 (5.99E+01)	9.13E+03 (5.44E+01)	9.12E+03 (5.90E+01)	9.14E+03 (5.85E+01)	9.12E+03 (6.05E+01)	9.11E+03 (6.10E+01)	9.12E+03 (6.10E+01)	9.12E+03 (7.26E+01)	9.13E+03 (5.97E+01)	9.12E+03 (5.62E+01)	9.12E+03 (5.94E+01)

without further knowledge. But the conclusion holds for common scoring rules, such as $a = 3$, $b = 0$, $c = 1$ and $a = 1$, $b = -1$, $c = 0$.

Lose-Rank Strategy

In order to avoid determining the rational scoring rules, a new criterion named "lose-rank" is proposed to compare the performance of multiple RNGs.

Table 10.4 Scores Achieved by RNGs for Each Function

Function	D	GPU				CPU								C
		CURAND				MKL								
		1	2	3	4	5	6	7	8	9	10	11	12	13
Sphere	10	14	14	14	14	14	14	14	14	14	14	14	14	14
	30	14	14	13	14	14	15	14	14	14	14	14	14	14
	50	14	14	14	14	14	14	14	14	14	14	14	14	14
	100	14	14	14	14	12	14	16	14	14	16	12	14	14
Elliptic	10	14	14	14	14	14	14	14	14	14	14	14	14	14
	30	14	14	14	14	14	14	14	14	14	14	14	14	14
	50	14	14	14	14	14	14	14	14	14	14	14	14	14
	100	14	14	14	15	14	14	11	15	14	14	15	14	14
Discus	10	14	14	14	14	14	14	14	14	14	14	14	14	14
	30	14	14	14	14	14	14	14	14	14	14	14	14	14
	50	14	14	14	14	14	14	14	14	14	14	14	14	14
	100	14	14	14	14	14	14	14	14	14	14	14	14	14
Ronsenbrock	10	14	14	14	15	13	10	14	15	14	14	15	13	17
	30	14	14	14	14	14	15	14	13	14	14	14	14	14
	50	15	14	14	14	12	14	14	14	14	14	14	14	15
	100	14	11	11	19	14	11	11	12	14	18	14	13	20
Ackley	10	14	14	12	15	14	14	14	15	14	14	14	14	14
	30	14	14	14	14	14	14	14	14	14	14	14	14	14
	50	14	14	14	14	14	14	14	14	14	14	14	14	14
	100	14	14	14	14	14	14	14	14	14	14	14	14	14
Weierstrass	10	14	14	14	14	14	14	14	14	14	14	14	14	14
	30	13	14	14	14	13	14	17	14	14	13	14	14	14
	50	14	14	14	14	14	14	14	14	14	14	14	14	14
	100	14	14	14	14	14	14	14	14	14	14	14	14	14
Schaffers F7	10	14	14	14	14	14	14	14	14	14	14	14	14	14
	30	14	14	14	14	14	14	14	14	14	14	14	14	14
	50	14	14	14	14	14	14	14	14	14	14	14	14	14
	100	14	14	14	14	14	14	14	14	14	14	14	14	14
Griewank	10	15	15	15	14	14	15	9	15	14	14	14	14	14
	30	14	14	14	14	14	14	14	14	14	14	14	14	14
	50	14	14	14	14	14	14	14	14	14	14	14	14	14
	100	14	14	14	14	14	14	14	14	14	14	14	14	14
Rastrigin	10	14	14	14	14	14	14	14	14	14	14	14	14	14
	30	14	14	14	15	14	13	14	14	14	14	14	14	14
	50	14	14	14	14	14	14	14	14	14	14	14	14	14
	100	14	14	14	14	14	14	14	14	15	13	14	14	14
Total		505	502	500	512	498	499	498	505	505	508	504	502	514

Table 10.5 Scoring Rules for Quality Comparison

Condition	Score of A	Score of B
$A < B$	$+a$	$+b$
$A > B$	$+b$	$+a$
Otherwise	$+c$	$+c$

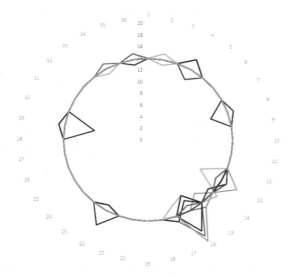

Fig. 10.1 Scores of All RNGs for Each Function

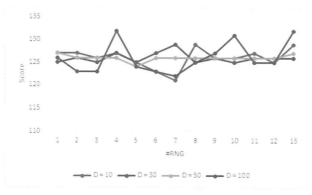

Fig. 10.2 Scores Aggregated by Dimension

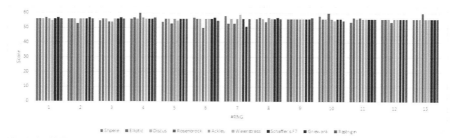

Fig. 10.3 Scores Aggregated by Function

Table 10.6 Average Lose-Rank Values

	1	2	3	4	5	6	7	8	9	10	11	12	13
Lose-rank	1.0	0.6	0.8	1.6	0.4	1.1	0.9	1.4	0.9	0.9	1.0	0.5	1.3

Lose-rank can be calculated as follows: For A certain RNG, say R1, set its lose-rank to 0. R1 compares its solutions for a function with those of all other RNGs' one after another. If R1 statistically worse than some RNG, then add 1 to its lose-rank. In this way, we can calculate all RNGs' lose-ranks for all functions.

The idea of the lose-rank is that if some RNG performs significantly worse in terms of solution quality, then it will has a relative large value of lose-rank.

The average lose-rank on all functions is listed in Table 10.6. The maximum lose-rank is about 1.6 (No. 4), which means any RNG, at its worst, is worse than less than 2 other RNGs. Considering each RNGs has 12 "rivals," it is a relatively minor lose-rank. The minimum lose-rank is around 0.4 (No. 5), which means that any RNG, at its best, will lose to some RNGs for certain functions. (Note No. 13 is among one of the worst in accordance with lose-rank criterion while it achieved the highest score under league scoring criterion.)

The average lose-rank on each dimension and each function type is presented in Figs. 10.4 and 10.5, respectively. For a certain RNG, the lose-ranks can be lower or higher, but the fluctuation follows no remarkable pattern, and very high lose-ranks were observed rarely.

It turns out, based on all these observations, that there exits no significant bad RNG, and there is no outright good one either. There is no strong reason to prefer any RNG to others as far as its impact on solution quality concerned.

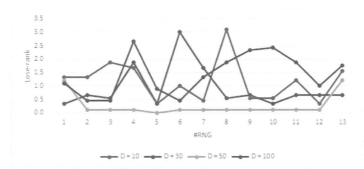

Fig. 10.4 Lose-Rank Average on Dimension

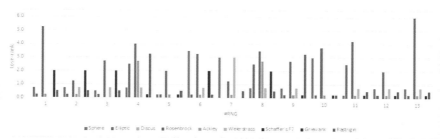

Fig. 10.5 Lose-Rank Averaged on Function

10.6 Summary

This chapter introduces how to generate random numbers with various distributions.

Though different RNGs have various statistical strength, no significant disparity was observed in PSO in the experiments. Even the most common LCG performs very well, despite the fact that random number sequences generated by LCG are of lower quality in terms of randomness compared to other more complicated RNGs. As the 13 RNGs under research widely cover high quality RNGs provided by many programming languages and math libraries, this conclusion is applicable in most common situations involving PSO. However, no statistically significant disparity in solution quality was observed.

As a result, it is reasonable to utilize the most efficient algorithms for random number generation. In general, both CPU- and GPU-based RNGs can achieve best performance when generating blocks of random numbers that are as large as possible. Fewer calls to generate many random numbers are more efficient than many calls generating only a few random numbers. GPU-based RNGs can be several folds or even one order of magnitude faster than their CPU-based counterparts, and Mersenne Twister algorithm presents the most efficient RNG.

Only PSO using uniformly distributed RNGs was discussed in this chapter, however, the two proposed strategies can be extended to compare any stochastic optimization algorithm on any real-world optimization problems as well as benchmarks. RNGs for nonuniform distributions can also be studied in the same framework.

Chapter 11
Applications

Contents

11.1 Image Processing

Image processing is any form of signal processing for which the input is an image, such as a photograph or video frame, and the output of image processing may be either an image or a set of characteristics or parameters related to the image. Most image processing techniques involve treating the image as a two-dimensional signal and applying standard signal-processing techniques to it.

11.1.1 Image Segmentation

Image segmentation is the process of partitioning an image into multiple segments. Image segmentation is typically used to locate objects and boundaries in images. Fig. 11.1 presents the segmenting result of a femur image. It shows the outer surface

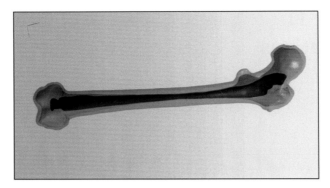

Fig. 11.1 Model of a Segmented Femur

(red), the surface between compact bone and spongy bone (green) and the surface of the bone marrow (blue).

Kristiadi et al. [94] proposed using PSO to segment color images. The testing applied an example of an image segmentation to demonstrate PSO method to find best clusters of image segmentation. The results showed that PSO run 170% faster when it used GPU in parallel mode other than that used CPU alone, for number of particles 100. This speedup is growing as the number of particles gets higher.

11.1.2 Edge Detection

Dawson and Stewart [42] presented the first parallel implementation of an ant colony optimization (ACO)-based edge detection algorithm on the GPU. The proposed implementation is able to match the quality of edge maps produced by the sequential implementation and executed up to $150\times$ faster. This approach yields the best result and speedups of around $150\times$ against an optimized sequential counterpart.

11.1.3 Registration

Image registration is the process of transforming different sets of data into one coordinate system. Data may be multiple photographs, data from different sensors, times, depths, or viewpoints [20]. Image registration is often used in medical and satellite imagery to align images from different camera sources. Fig. 11.2 demonstrates the use of registration to align and connect adjacent images into a single panoramic image.

A high-performance PSO powered by the GPU for ground control point-based nonlinear registration of airborne push-broom imagery was introduced by

Fig. 11.2 Registering Aerial Photos Using Point Mapping

Reguera-Salgado and Martin-Herrero [153]. In this approach, PSO is used to find the best match between the projected pixels and a number of ground control points, compensating any systematic errors in the navigation data used for the generation of the orthoimage. The speedup achieved by GPU allows using evolutionary methods in feasible time, enabling hundreds of repeated approximations during rectification, in contrast to classical geocorrection methods.

11.1.4 Watermarking

Watermarking is presented when a pattern is inserted in an image, video or audio file, it helps to copyright the information in the files. Cano and Rodríguez [29] utilized PSO for determining the best place for inserting watermark into images. The objective of optimization is to find the best frequency band set to insert the watermark within the image. Different frequency bands are tested through the iterations of the algorithm finding out the best solution. At the end of the execution, the application has the results of the watermarked image and a matrix with the whole best positions (frequency bands) for inserting the complete watermark.

11.2 Computer Vision

Computer vision is a field that includes methods for acquiring, processing, analyzing, and understanding images in order to produce numerical or symbolic information. A theme in the development of this field has been to duplicate the abilities of human vision by electronically perceiving and understanding an image. Subdomains of computer vision include object detection, video tracking, object pose estimation, motion estimation, and image restoration.

11.2.1 Object Detection

Object detection deals with detecting instances of semantic objects of a certain class (such as humans, buildings, or cars) in digital images and videos. Object detection has applications in many areas of computer vision, including image retrieval, face detection (see Fig. 11.3) and video surveillance.

Fig. 11.3 Face Detection Is a Classic Example of Objection Detection

Road sign detection is a major goal of intelligent driving assistance systems. Mussi et al. [124] presented a road sign detection system based on both sign shape and color, which applies the PSO method for object detection. Remarkably, a single fitness function can be used both to detect a sign belonging to a certain category and, at the same time, to estimate its actual position with respect to the camera reference frame. To speedup execution time, the proposed algorithm fully exploited the parallelism offered by GPU. The effectiveness of the approach has been assessed on a synthetic video sequence, which has been successfully processed in real time at full frame rate.

A similar work was presented by Ugolotti et al. [192, 193], who proposed to tackle object detection problem by using PSO and DE. The authors used a model-based approach in which a prototype of the sign to be detected is transformed and matched to the image using evolutionary techniques. It was reported that the GPU-accelerated system was tested over two real sequences taken from a camera mounted on-board a car and was able to correctly detect and classify around 70% of the signs at 17.5 fps, a similar result in shorter time, compared to the best results obtained on the same sequences so far.

11.2.2 Video Tracking

Video tracking is the process of locating a moving object (or multiple objects) over time (observe Fig. 11.4). Video tracking is an active research topic in the computer vision community and is a prerequisite for many tasks, such as human-computer interaction, security and surveillance, video communication and compression, augmented reality, traffic control, medical imaging, and video editing. The challenge is to track the object irrespective of scale, rotation, perspective projection, occlusions, changes of appearance, and illumination. However, it should be fast enough to maintain transparent interaction with the user.

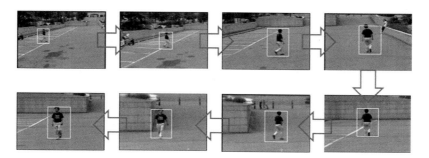

Fig. 11.4 Object Tracking by Using a Camera

Recently, PSO is used to achieve video tracking by searching for the best match of the predefined object model in the image. In PSO, each particle in the swarm represents a candidate solution to the optimization problem. The most time-consuming operation in PSO-based object tracking is evaluation of the fitness function. Since multiple candidate solutions are evaluated in each iteration, PSO-based tracking algorithms are computationally demanding for real-time applications.

To reduce the running time, Rymut and Kwolek [161] developed a GPU implementation of the tracking using PSO with adaptive appearance models. Experimental results showed that the GPU implementation of the algorithm exhibits a more than 40-fold speedup against the CPU implementation. As a result, the tracking algorithm can be run in real-time (at frame-rates exceeding 60 fps).

More specifically, GPU-accelerated PSO, combined with other techniques, has been successfully applied to human body tracking problems. Zhang and Seah [208] proposed tracking the body pose in 3D space by using 3D data reconstructed at every frame. The authors parallelized the PSO-based stochastic search algorithm and 3D distance transform (DT) computation of the pose estimation method on GPU. The GPU implementation largely accelerates the pose tracking process, making our system capable of tracking full body movements in an interactive rate.

For more detailed, other swarm intelligence-based body tracking methods powered by GPU are given in [127, 163, 162].

11.3 Machine Learning

Machine learning is the science of getting computers to act without being explicitly programmed [119]. Machine learning tasks are typically classified into three broad categories, supervised learning (e.g., classification), unsupervised learning (e.g., clustering), and reinforcement learning.

11.3.1 Classification

The goal of classification is to be able to accurately assign a class to a given data point in an automated way and according to some number of the data points characteristics.

Weiss [200] proposed an ACO variant (ACOMinerGPU) for training rule-based classifier. Results indicate that the ACOMinerGPU algorithm is markedly faster than the sequential algorithm on which it is based, and is able to produce classification rules which are competitive with those generated by traditional methods.

Plates et al. [149] used a GPU-accelerated PSO for classifying documents.

Cano et al. [28] presented a parallelization approach of an existing multiobjective ant programming model for classification. The proposed GPU model can scale efficiently to larger datasets and to multiple GPU devices, which allows the expansion of its applicability to significantly more complicated data sets, previously unmanageable by the original algorithm in reasonable time.

11.3.2 Clustering

Clustering is the task of grouping a set of objects in such a way that objects in the same group (called a cluster) are more similar (in some sense or another) to each other than to those in other groups (clusters).

Weiss [201] presented a SIA (ClusterFlockGPU) for cluster analysis, whose salient feature in ClusterFlockGPU is that the number of clusters does not need to be known at runtime. Implemented by the massively parallel GPU, the time complexity of this proposal was significantly reduced to nearly $O(n)$, thus well-suited for large-scale datasets.

11.4 Parameter Optimization

Tasks from different domains can be transformed down to the optimization of parameters.

Inversion is a critical and challenging task in geophysical research. Geophysical inversion can be formulated as an optimization problem to find the best parameters whose forward synthesis data most fit the observed data. The inverse problems are usually highly nonlinear, multimodal as well as ill-posed, so conventional optimization algorithms cannot handle it very efficiently. SIAs are widely applied to inverse problems and achieve great success. Datta et al. [40] used GPU-powered PSO to invert self-potential, magnetic, and resistivity data. According to the experiments,

GPU implemented algorithms in the geophysical domain can show rich benefits of reduced computing time and accurate results at the same time.

Support vector machine (SVM) has shown great advantages in various machine learning tasks, such as text classification, handwriting recognition, image classification, and bioinformatics. SVM's good performance relies on the choices of kernel functions and slack variables. That is to say, to optimize the SVM algorithm, the optimization of the two parameters play a very important role. Zhang et al. [205] applied OpenCL-based ACO to find a well hyperparameters for SVM. Through the GPU-powered ACO, satisfactory parameters of SVM can be found and the convergence accuracy can be guaranteed more than 85% according to experimental results.

Latin hypercube designs (LHDs) are widely used in many applications. As the number of design points or factors becomes large, the total number of LHDs grows exponentially. The large number of feasible designs makes the search for optimal LHDs being a difficult discrete optimization problem. Chen et al. [36] proposed a PSO variant (LaPSO) for LHD which is accelerated by GPU. According to extensive comparisons, the proposed LaPSO is more stable than existing approaches and is capable of greatly improving the known results.

The electromagnetic modeling of antennas and radio frequency devices has become increasingly challenging as the applications demand intricate and complex designs, such as fine features embedded in electrically large structures or integrated systems. The design stage is further challenged by the need to find an optimal solution, which results in a numerically intensive problem. To tackle such challenging design and optimizations, Kilic et al. [89] presented a multi-GPU implementation of PSO, and then demonstrated the acceleration achieved by the GPUs in designing a variety of radio frequency structures such as reconfigurable patch antennas and antireflective surfaces.

11.5 Miscellaneous

11.5.1 Economic Domain

It is a critical and complicated task to price the options in the market. Swarm intelligence algorithms have been proposed for option pricing, which provide same or better results for simple options than that of numerical techniques at much less computational cost (time) [169]. Sharma et al. [169, 170] proposed an improved PSO (called NPSO) model to price complex chooser option. They implemented the NPSO model on the GPU platform and achieved a great speedup. The same method was also used for portfolio management.

11.5.2 Vehicle Navigation

Bura and Boryczka [22] described an OpenCL-based implementation of ACO and its application in vehicle navigation. Experiments on real-world data showed that proposed algorithm enjoys better performance and can give the results as good as previous methods.

11.5.3 Library

Nashed et al. [130] presented an open source library of GPU-based meta-heuristics called libCudaOptimize which implemented some meta-heuristics for continuous optimization including PSO, DE, scatter search (SS), and Solis&Wets local search. This library allows users to apply these meta-heuristics directly to their own fitness function, in this case the optimization of fitness function is due to the users. Also, users are allowed to extend libCudaOptimize by implementing their own parallel optimization techniques. Meta-heuristic optimization is abstracted to three-phased procedure: step, update, and fitness evaluation or to extend it by implementing their own parallel optimization techniques.

11.6 Case Study: CUDA-Based PSO for Road Sign Detection

In this section, we present a real-world application using GPU-based SIA, say, PSO to be specific. As will be seen, GPU-based PSO can accomplish the road sign detection task in real time.

11.6.1 Problem

Automatic traffic sign detection is a very significant issue for traffic security. Mussi et al. [124] presented an PSO-based method for road sign detection problem. Different from color-based or gray-scale-based method, the algorithm does not require the preprocessing for input image and has advantages against color unbalance. The efficiency of PSO is guaranteed by the modern parallel device, i.e., NVIDIA general-purpose graphic process unit and the fundamental platform — CUDA is used for algorithm implementation.

The road sign detection is an computer-vision domain task. During driving, one needs to take every road sign in consideration. However, one will probably miss some signs sometimes. This remains a problem for researcher to detect these signs automatically and give the information to drivers. The goal to the solution is making this procedure faster and more precise. The PSO-based method give an improvement to this vision detection task. In the following, we briefly describe this model and illustrate how PSO can be implemented by GPGPU.

11.6.2 Model

In this method the number of road sign categories is assumed to be limited and the road sign templates are predefined. It makes sense since real-world road signs are less variant comparing to other visual category. As the image is taken by the camera as two-dimension format its shape and size will definitely change after projection. The algorithm is to find the best corresponding geometry transformation. Precisely, (1) at first the image is taken by camera at each frame. (2) Then according to the given geometry transformation parameters we can obtain the corresponding pixels in the image. (3) The fitness is computed comparing these pixels and predefined template. These three steps form the framework for the evolution procedure in PSO algorithm. The parameters to be optimized is the geometry transformation matrixes.

First of all, we briefly give the framework of PSO algorithm. After that the fitness function is manually defined. Given the fitness function, the PSO algorithm will gradually evolve toward better geometry transformation. At last, we simply illustrate the CUDA implementation for the PSO.

11.6.2.1 PSO

Here we simply recall the PSO algorithm. The standard PSO algorithm is a kind of practical optimization method for continuous optimization problems. The swarm consists of multiple particles. Each of them represents a candidate solution, i.e., each of them is typically a numerical vector. During execution the algorithm iteratively updates particles in both velocity and position. The update formulation is

$$V_i(t) = wV_i(t-1) + C_1R_1[X_{ib}(t-1) - X_i(t-1)] + C_2R_2[X_{igb}(t-1) - X_i(t-1)]$$

$$X_i(t) = X_i(t-1) + V_i(t)$$

where, as aforementioned, the X_{ib} is the current individual best while X_{igb} is the global best.

11.6.2.2 Fitness Function

The fitness function is an essential component for evolutionary algorithm. It defines what solution is supposed to be obtained. In this problem, as declared in previous, we aim to find the best geometry transformation solution for the given image and specific road sign. This fitness function bases on the projection pixels, i.e., the pixels on the projection of predefined template (one template for one type of road sign). To get the projection pixels we need geometry transformation whose matrix is to be optimized

$$p_i = A(R_eP_i + t_e)$$

where the p_i is the 2D projection of 3D P_i (the pixels of road sign template), R_e is the rotation matrix, and t_e is the translation vector.

Note that P_i consists three sets of pixels for certain type of sign class, particularly denoted as P_1, P_2, P_3. Each set has 16 pixels. The fitness function is defined according to following assumptions:

- Histograms computed on the first two sets of points be as different as possible, hypothesizing that, in case the sign had been detected, the background color nearby the sign would differ significantly from the band.

- The histogram of the points in the band be as different as possible from the one computed on the inner area of the sign.
- Histograms resemble as much as possible the reference histograms computed for the band surrounding the sign.

Hence the fitness function is defined as

$$f = \frac{k_0(1 - S_{1,2}) + k_1(1 - S_{2,3}) + k_2 S_{1,ref})}{k_0 + k_1 + k_2}$$

$$S_{x,y} = \frac{g(H_x^H, H_y^H) + g(H_x^S, H_y^S) + g(H_x^V, H_y^V)}{3}$$

$$g(H_x, H_y) = \sum_{b=1}^{N_{bin}} \sqrt{H_1(b)H_2(b)}$$

$$H_x^c(b) = \frac{1}{n} \sum_{i=1}^{n} \theta(I_c(p_I^x) - b)$$

where $c \in H, S, V$ specifies the color channel, $x \in 1, 2, 3$ identifies the set of points, $b \in [1, N_{bin}]$, (N_{bin} being the number of bins in the histogram), n represents the number of points in the set (sixteen in our case), the function $\theta(n)$ returns 1 when n = 0 and zero otherwise and, finally, $I_c(p) : R_2 \xrightarrow{R}$ maps the intensity of channel c at pixel location p to a certain bin index. The term $\frac{1}{n}$ is used to normalize the histogram.

Moreover, three additional histograms, denoted as H_c^{ref}, are used as reference histograms for the band surrounding all three sign models taken into consideration. The Bhattacharyya coefficient, which offers an estimate of the amount of overlap between two statistical samples, is then used to compare the histograms. The Bhattacharyya coefficient returns a real value between 0 (when there is no overlap at all between the two histograms) and 1 (when the two histograms are identical). Finally the fitness function is given.

11.6.3 Implementing PSO Within CUDA

Real-world problem demands high detection frequency. Standard PSO is time consuming, however, GPU provides an easy solution for it. The PSO implementation in CUDA utilizes classical ring topology which provides a very compromise between efficiency, quality, and easiness.

11.6.3.1 Position Update

The key element in PSO is its update process. At each iteration, PSO gradually changes individual's position via stochastic velocity. In terms of CUDA-implemented

PSO each particle uses one block and each thread is used for updating of each dimension. In the beginning, the particle's current position, personal best velocity, and local best information are integrated and then the update equations are applied.

11.6.3.2 Fitness Function

As the fitness function uses a lot of matrix calculations, the fitness in each block can be easily paralleled. One thread is responsible for one dimension calculation.

11.6.3.3 Best Updates

Standard PSO needs global best to obtain the velocity of each individual which needs to be stored in global memory. However, the global memory is really slow to be accessed. To avoid the use of global device memory, the classical ring topology method is adopted here. Firstly, each thread loads in shared memory both the current and the best fitness values of its corresponding particle, to update the personal best. Next, the current local best fitness value is found by computing the best fitness of each particles neighborhood (including the particle and the neighboring one on both sides of the ring), comparing it to the best value found so far and updating it.

11.7 Summary

In this chapter, we take a quick review of some real-world applications of GPU-based SIAs. The flexibility of SIAs make them suitable for various problems which may be hard even infeasible for conventional methods. In the meantime, the enormous computational power of GPU render SIAs feasible for some time-consuming tasks which is impractical for them before. In the case study part, we simply illustrated the CUDA-based PSO for road sign detection problem. After defining the fitness function, PSO can be easily applied. To speedup processing, the algorithmic implementation fully exploited the parallel computing capabilities offered by modern GPUs. Since the framework of CUDA-based PSO is universal, the method can also be easily modified to tackle other complex real-world problem as well.

Chapter 12
A CUDA-Based Test Suit

Contents

12.1 Overview

Proposed algorithms are usually tested on benchmark for comparing both performance and efficiency. However, as it can be a very tedious task to select and implement test functions rigorously. Thanks to graphics processing units' (GPUs) massive parallelism, a GPU-based optimization function suit will be beneficial to test and compare various optimization algorithms.

Based on the well-known CPU-based benchmarks presented in [58, 110, 109], a compute unified device architecture (CUDA)-based real parameter optimization benchmark, called cuROB, was proposed in [48]. Thanks to the great computing power of GPUs, cuROB has been of great help for optimization related tasks [47].

In the current release of cuROB, a set of single-objective real-parameter optimization functions are defined and implemented. It is a great start, as research on the single-objective optimization algorithms is the basis of the research on more complex optimization algorithms such as constrained optimization algorithms, multiobjective optimizations algorithms, and so forth.

In cuROB, the test functions are selected according to the following criteria: (1) the functions should be scalable in dimension so that algorithms can be tested under various complexities; (2) the expressions of the functions should be with good parallelism, thus efficient implementation is possible on GPUs; (3) the functions should be comprehensible such that algorithm behaviors can be analyzed in the topological context; (4) last but most important, the test suit should cover functions of various properties in order to get a systematic evaluation of the optimization algorithms.

The source code and a sample can be freely download from https://github.com/DingKe/cuROB.

12.1.1 Symbol Conventions and Definitions

Symbols and definitions used in this book are described as follows. By default, all vectors refer to column vectors which are depicted by lowercase letter and typeset in bold.

- $[\cdot]$ indicates the nearest integer value
- $\lfloor \cdot \rfloor$ indicates the largest integer less than or equal to
- $\mathbf{x}_i$ denotes ith element of vector $\mathbf{x}$
- $f(\cdot)$, $g(\cdot)$ and $G(\cdot)$ denote multivariable functions
- f_{opt} denotes optimal (minimal) value of function f

- $\mathbf{x}^{opt}$ denotes optimal solution vector, such that $f(\mathbf{x}^{opt}) = f_{opt}$
- $\mathbf{R}$ denotes normalized orthogonal matrix for rotation
- D denotes dimension
- $\mathbf{1} = (1, \ldots, 1)^T$ denotes all one vector

12.1.2 General Setup

The general setup of the test suit is presented as follows:

- **Dimensions:** The test suit is scalable in terms of dimension. Within the hardware limit, any dimension $D \geq 2$ works. However, to construct a real hybrid function, D should be at least 10.
- **Search Space:** All functions are defined and can be evaluated over $\mathscr{R}^D$, while the actual search domain is given as $[-100, 100]^D$.
- f_{opt}: All functions, by definition, have a minimal value of 0, a bias (f_{opt}) can be added to each function. The selection can be arbitrary, f_{opt} for each function in the test suit is listed in Table 12.1.
- $\mathbf{x}^{opt}$: The optimum point of each function is located at original, which is randomly distributed in $[-70, 70]^D$, and is selected as the new optimum.
- **Rotation Matrix:** To derive nonseparable functions from separable ones, the search space is rotated by a normalized orthogonal matrix $\mathbf{R}$. For a given function in one dimension, a different $\mathbf{R}$ is used. Variables are divided into three (almost) equal-sized subcomponents randomly. The rotation matrix for each subcomponent is generated from standard normally distributed entries by Gram–Schmidt orthonormalization. Then, these matrices consist of the $\mathbf{R}$ actually used.

12.1.3 CUDA Interface and Implementation

A simple description of the interface and implementation is given below. For detail, see the source code and its accompanied readme file.

12.1.3.1 Interface

Only benchmark.h needs to be included to access the test functions, and the CUDA file benchmark.cu needs be compiled and linked. Before the compiling start, two macro, DIM and *MAX_CONCURRENCY* should be modified accordingly. *DIM* defines the dimension of the test suit to be used while *MAX_CONCURRENCY* defines the number of function evaluations which can be invoked concurrently. As memory needed to be pre-allocated, *MAX_CONCURRENCY* should not exceed the hardware limit.

Host interface function *initialize ()* accomplish all initialization tasks, so must be called before any test function can be evaluated. Allocated resource is released by host interface function *dispose ()*.

Both double precision (DP) and single precision (SP) are supported through *func_evaluate ()* and *func_evaluatef()* respectively. Take note that device pointers should be passed to these two functions. For the convenience of CPU code, C interfaces are provided, with *h_func_evaluate ()* for DP and *h_func_evaluatef()* for SP. (In fact, they are just wrappers of the GPU interfaces.)

12.1.3.2 Efficiency Considerations

When configuration of the suit, some should be taken care for the sake of efficiency. It is better to evaluate a batch of vectors. Dimensions of fold of 32 (the warp size) can more efficient. For example, dimension of 96 is much more efficient than 100, even though 100 is just little greater than 96.

12.1.4 Test Suite Summary

The whole of the test functions fall into four categories: unimodal functions, basic multimodal functions, hybrid functions, and composition functions. The summary of the suit is listed in Table 12.1. Detailed information of each function will be given in the following sections.

12.2 Speedup and Baseline Results

With different hardware, various speedups can be achieved. Thirty functions are the same as CEC'14 benchmark. We test the cuROB's speedup with these 30 functions under the following settings: Windows 7 SP1 x64 running on Intel i5-2310 CPU with NVIDIA 560 Ti, the CUDA version is 5.5. Fifty evaluations were performed concurrently and repeated 1000 runs. The evaluation data were generated randomly from uniform distribution.

The speedups with respect to different dimensions are listed in Tables 12.2 (SP) and 12.3 (DP). Notice that the corresponding dimensions of cuROB are 10, 32, 64, and 96, respectively, and the numbers are the same in Table 12.1.

Fig. 12.1 demonstrates the overall speedup for each dimension. On average, cuROB is never slower than its CPU-base CEC'14 benchmark, and speedup of one order of magnitude can be achieved when dimension becomes high. SP is more efficient than DP as far as execution time is concerned.

Some preliminary results on standard particle swarm optimization (PSO) are also presented in Table 12.4 as a performance baseline. PSO runs 10 independently for 64 dimension. In each trail, 640,000 function evaluations are conducted.

Table 12.1 Summary of cuROB's Test Functions

Category	No.	Function Name	ID	Description
Unimodal Functions	0	Rotated Sphere	SPHERE	Optimum easy to track
	1	Rotated Ellipsoid	ELLIPSOID	
	2	Rotated Elliptic	ELLIPTIC	
	3	Rotated Discus	DISCUS	Optimum hard to track
	4	Rotated Bent Cigar	CIGAR	
	5	Rotated Different Powers	POWERS	
	6	Rotated Sharp Valley	SHARPV	
Basic Multimodal Functions	7	Rotated Step	STEP	With adepuate global structure
	8	Rotated Weierstrass	WEIERSTRASS	
	9	Rotated Griewank	GRIEWANK	
	10	Rastrigin	RARSTRIGIN_U	
	11	Rotated Rastrigin	RARSTRIGIN	
	12	Rotated Schaffer's F7	SCHAFFERSF7	
	13	Rotated Expanded Griewank plus Rosenbrock	GRIE_ROSEN	
	14	Rotated Rosenbrock	ROSENBROCK	
	15	Modified Schwefel	SCHWEFEL_U	
	16	Rotated Modified Schwefel	SCHWEFEL	With weak global structure
	17	Rotated Katsuura	KATSUURA	
	18	Rotated Lunacek bi-Rastrigin	LUNACEK	
	19	Rotated Ackley	ACKLEY	
	20	Rotated HappyCat	HAPPYCAT	
	21	Rotated HGBat	HGBAT	
	22	Rotated Expanded Schaffer's F6	SCHAFFERSF6	
Hybrid Functions	23	Hybrid Function 1	HYBRID1	With different properties for different variables subcomponents
	24	Hybrid Function 2	HYBRID2	
	25	Hybrid Function 3	HYBRID3	
	26	Hybrid Function 4	HYBRID4	
	27	Hybrid Function 5	HYBRID5	
	28	Hybrid Function 6	HYBRID6	
Composition Functions	29	Composition Function 1	COMPOSITION1	Properties similar to particular subfunction when approaching the corresponding optimum
	30	Composition Function 2	COMPOSITION2	
	31	Composition Function 3	COMPOSITION3	
	32	Composition Function 4	COMPOSITION4	
	33	Composition Function 5	COMPOSITION5	
	34	Composition Function 6	COMPOSITION6	
	35	Composition Function 7	COMPOSITION7	
	36	Composition Function 8	COMPOSITION8	
Search Space: $[-100, 100]^D$, $f_{opt} = 100$				

12.3 Unimodal Functions

12.3.1 Shifted and Rotated Sphere Function

$$f_1(\mathbf{x}) = \sum_{i=1}^{D} \mathbf{z}_i^2 + f_{opt}, \tag{12.1}$$

where $\mathbf{z} = \mathbf{R}(\mathbf{x} - \mathbf{x}^{opt})$.

Properties: Unimodal; Nonseparable; Highly symmetric, in particular rotationally invariant.

Table 12.2 Speedup (Single Precision) With Different Dimensions

D	No. 3	No. 4	No. 5	No. 8	No. 9	No. 10	No. 11	No. 13	No. 14	No. 15
10	0.59	0.20	0.18	12.23	0.49	0.28	0.31	0.32	0.14	0.77
32	3.82	2.42	2.00	47.19	3.54	1.67	3.83	5.09	2.06	3.54
64	4.67	2.72	2.29	50.17	3.56	0.93	3.06	2.88	2.20	3.39
94	13.40	10.10	8.50	84.31	11.13	1.82	9.98	9.66	8.75	6.73

D	No. 16	No. 17	No. 19	No. 20	No. 21	No. 22	No. 23	No. 24	No. 25	No. 26
10	0.80	3.25	0.36	0.20	0.26	0.45	0.63	0.44	2.80	0.52
32	5.57	10.04	3.46	1.22	1.42	6.44	3.95	3.43	11.47	3.36
64	5.45	13.19	3.27	2.10	2.27	3.81	4.62	3.07	14.17	3.34
96	14.38	23.68	11.32	8.26	8.49	11.60	13.67	10.64	30.11	10.71

D	No. 27	No. 28	No. 29	No. 30	No. 31	No. 32	No. 33	No. 34	No. 35	No. 36
10	0.65	0.72	0.70	0.55	0.71	3.49	3.50	0.84	1.28	0.70
32	2.73	3.09	3.63	3.10	4.10	12.39	12.51	5.25	5.19	3.33
64	3.86	4.01	3.21	2.67	3.38	12.68	12.63	3.80	5.27	3.13
96	12.04	11.32	8.15	6.27	8.49	23.67	23.64	9.50	11.79	7.93

Table 12.3 Speedup (Double Precision) With Different Dimensions

D	No. 3	No. 4	No. 5	No. 8	No. 9	No. 10	No. 11	No. 13	No. 14	No. 15
10	0.56	0.19	0.17	9.04	0.43	0.26	0.29	0.30	0.14	0.75
32	3.78	2.43	1.80	33.37	3.09	1.59	3.52	4.81	1.97	3.53
64	4.34	2.49	1.93	30.82	3.15	0.92	2.87	2.74	2.11	3.29
96	12.27	9.24	6.95	46.01	9.72	1.78	9.62	8.74	7.87	5.92

D	No. 16	No. 17	No. 19	No. 20	No. 21	No. 22	No. 23	No. 24	No. 25	No. 26
10	0.79	2.32	0.34	0.18	0.26	0.45	0.59	0.43	1.97	0.52
32	5.10	6.79	3.28	1.13	1.29	6.10	3.63	3.14	8.15	3.23
64	4.75	8.29	3.06	1.99	2.18	3.32	4.02	2.77	9.80	2.92
96	11.91	13.81	9.75	7.37	7.78	10.24	11.55	9.57	20.81	9.40

D	No. 27	No. 28	No. 29	No. 30	No. 31	No. 32	No. 33	No. 34	No. 35	No. 36
10	0.79	2.32	0.34	0.18	0.26	0.45	0.59	0.43	1.97	0.52
32	5.10	6.79	3.28	1.13	1.29	6.10	3.63	3.14	8.15	3.23
64	4.75	8.29	3.06	1.99	2.18	3.32	4.02	2.77	9.80	2.92
96	11.91	13.81	9.75	7.37	7.78	10.24	11.55	9.57	20.81	9.40

12.3.2 Shifted and Rotated Ellipsoid Function

$$f_2(\mathbf{x}) = \sum_{i=1}^{D} i \cdot \mathbf{z}_i^2 + f_{opt}, \tag{12.2}$$

where $\mathbf{z} = \mathbf{R}(\mathbf{x} - \mathbf{x}^{opt})$.

Properties: Unimodal; Nonseparable.

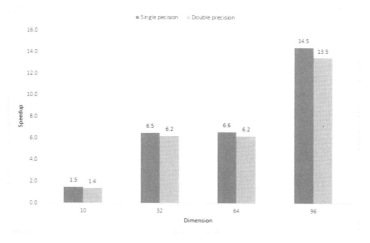

Fig. 12.1 Overall Speedup With Different Dimensions

Table 12.4 Baseline Results for Standard PSO

NO.	0	1	2	3	4	5	6	7	8	9	10	11
avg	1.00E+02	1.00E+02	7.11E+05	7.15E+02	1.87E+03	1.00E+02	1.06E+02	1.07E+02	1.31E+02	1.00E+02	2.42E+02	2.59E+02
std	3.45E−13	4.10E−13	3.71E+05	6.08E+02	2.47E+03	2.73E−05	4.36E+00	3.65E+00	4.93E+00	4.31E−03	2.94E+01	6.95E+01

12	13	14	15	16	17	18	19	20	21	22	23	24
1.12E+02	1.30E+02	1.58E+02	6.86E+03	1.20E+04	1.03E+02	3.92E+02	1.21E+02	1.00E+02	1.00E+02	1.27E+02	5.78E+05	1.65E+03
3.19E+00	1.20E+01	3.86E+01	1.10E+03	9.34E+02	3.74E−01	2.49E+01	5.87E−02	9.17E−02	3.70E−02	5.96E−01	1.42E+06	1.62E+03

25	26	27	28	29	30	31	32	33	34	35	36
1.46E+02	5.31E+03	5.13E+04	2.62E+02	3.76E+02	7.89E+02	4.05E+02	2.01E+02	5.78E+02	2.56E+03	3.04E+07	5.10E+06
1.88E+00	3.18E+03	3.67E+04	1.50E+02	6.75E+00	8.28E+01	1.73E+01	1.55E−01	1.21E+01	2.51E+02	1.72E+06	8.58E+05

12.3.3 Shifted and Rotated High-Conditioned Elliptic Function

$$f_3(\mathbf{x}) = \sum_{i=1}^{D} (10^6)^{\frac{i-1}{D-1}} z_i^2 + f_{opt}, \tag{12.3}$$

where $\mathbf{z} = \mathbf{R}(\mathbf{x} - \mathbf{x}^{opt})$.

Properties: Unimodal; Nonseparable; Quadratic ill-conditioned; Smooth local irregularities.

12.3.4 Shifted and Rotated Discus Function

$$f_4(\mathbf{x}) = 10^6 \cdot z_1^2 + \sum_{i=2}^{D} z_i^2 + f_{opt}, \tag{12.4}$$

where $\mathbf{z} = \mathbf{R}(\mathbf{x} - \mathbf{x}^{opt})$.

Properties: Unimodal; Nonseparable; Smooth local irregularities; With One sensitive direction.

12.3.5 Shifted and Rotated Bent Cigar Function

$$f_5(\mathbf{x}) = \mathbf{z}_1^2 + 10^6 \cdot \sum_{i=2}^{D} \mathbf{z}_i^2 + f_{opt}, \qquad (12.5)$$

where $\mathbf{z} = \mathbf{R}(\mathbf{x} - \mathbf{x}^{opt})$.

Properties: Unimodal; Nonseparable; Optimum located in a smooth but very narrow valley.

12.3.6 Shifted and Rotated Different Powers Function

$$f_6(\mathbf{x}) = \sqrt{\sum_{i=1}^{D} |\mathbf{z}_i|^{2+4\frac{i-1}{D-1}}} + f_{opt}, \qquad (12.6)$$

where $\mathbf{z} = \mathbf{R}(0.01(\mathbf{x} - \mathbf{x}^{opt}))$.

Properties: Unimodal; Nonseparable; Sensitivities of the $\mathbf{z}_i$ variables are different.

12.3.7 Shifted and Rotated Sharp Valley Function

$$f_7(\mathbf{x}) = \mathbf{z}_i^2 + 100 \cdot \sqrt{\sum_{i=2}^{D} \mathbf{z}_i^2} + f_{opt}, \qquad (12.7)$$

where $\mathbf{z} = \mathbf{R}(\mathbf{x} - \mathbf{x}^{opt})$.

Properties: Unimodal; Nonseparable; Global optimum located in a sharp (nondifferentiable) ridge.

12.4 Basic Multimodal Functions

12.4.1 Shifted and Rotated Step Function

$$f_8(\mathbf{x}) = \sum_{i=1}^{D} \lfloor \mathbf{z}_i + 0.5 \rfloor^2 + f_{opt}, \qquad (12.8)$$

where $\mathbf{z} = \mathbf{R}(\mathbf{x} - \mathbf{x}^{opt})$.

Properties: Many Plateaus of different sizes; Nonseparable.

12.4.2 Shifted and Rotated Weierstrass Function

$$f_9(\mathbf{x}) = \sum_{i=1}^{D} \left(\sum_{k=0}^{k_{max}} a^k \cos\left(2\pi b^k (\mathbf{z}_i + 0.5)\right) \right) - D \cdot \sum_{k=0}^{k_{max}} a^k \cos\left(2\pi b^k \cdot 0.5\right) + f_{opt},$$

(12.9)

where $a = 0.5$, $b = 3$, $k_{max} = 20$, $\mathbf{z} = \mathbf{R}(0.005 \cdot (\mathbf{x} - \mathbf{x}^{opt}))$.

Properties: Multimodal; Nonseparable; Continuous everywhere but only differentiable on a set of points.

12.4.3 Shifted and Rotated Griewank Function

$$f_{10}(\mathbf{x}) = \sum_{i=1}^{D} \frac{\mathbf{z}_i^2}{4000} - \prod_{i=1}^{D} \cos\left(\frac{\mathbf{z}_i}{\sqrt{i}}\right) + 1 + f_{opt},$$

(12.10)

where $\mathbf{z} = \mathbf{R}(6 \cdot (\mathbf{x} - \mathbf{x}^{opt}))$.

Properties: Multimodal; Nonseparable; With many regularly distributed local optima.

12.4.4 Shifted Rastrigin Function

$$f_{11}(\mathbf{x}) = \sum_{i=1}^{D} \left(\mathbf{z}_i^2 - 10\cos(2\pi \mathbf{z}_i)\right) + 10 \cdot D + f_{opt},$$

(12.11)

where $\mathbf{z} = 0.0512 \cdot (\mathbf{x} - \mathbf{x}^{opt})$.

Properties: Multimodal; Separable; With many regularly distributed local optima.

12.4.5 Shifted and Rotated Rastrigin Function

$$f_{12}(\mathbf{x}) = \sum_{i=1}^{D} \left(\mathbf{z}_i^2 - 10\cos(2\pi \mathbf{z}_i) + 10\right) + f_{opt},$$

(12.12)

where $\mathbf{z} = \mathbf{R}(0.0512 \cdot (\mathbf{x} - \mathbf{x}^{opt}))$.

Properties: Multimodal; Nonseparable; With many regularly distributed local optima.

12.4.6 Shifted Rotated Schaffer's F7 Function

$$f_{13}(\mathbf{x}) = \left(\frac{1}{D-1} \sum_{i=1}^{D-1} \left((1 + \sin^2(50 \cdot \mathbf{w}_i^{0.2})) \cdot \sqrt{\mathbf{w}_i} \right) \right)^2 + f_{opt}, \qquad (12.13)$$

where $\mathbf{w}_i = \sqrt{\mathbf{z}_i^2 + \mathbf{z}_{i+1}^2}$, $\mathbf{z} = \mathbf{R}(\mathbf{x} - \mathbf{x}^{opt})$.

Properties: Multimodal; Nonseparable.

12.4.7 Expanded Griewank Plus Rosenbrock Function

Rosenbrock Function: $g_2(x,y) = 100(x^2 - y)^2 + (x - 1)^2$
Griewank Function: $g_3(x) = x^2/4000 - \cos(x) + 1$

$$f_{14}(\mathbf{x}) = \sum_{i=1}^{D-1} g_3(g_2(\mathbf{z}_i, \mathbf{z}_{i+1})) + g_3(g_2(\mathbf{z}_D, \mathbf{z}_1)) + f_{opt}, \qquad (12.14)$$

where $\mathbf{z} = \mathbf{R}(0.05 \cdot (\mathbf{x} - \mathbf{x}^{opt})) + \mathbf{1}$.

Properties: Multimodal; Nonseparable.

12.4.8 Shifted and Rotated Rosenbrock Function

$$f_{15}(\mathbf{x}) = \sum_{i=1}^{D-1} \left(100 \cdot (\mathbf{z}_i^2 - \mathbf{z}_{i+1})^2 + (\mathbf{z}_i - 1)^2 \right) + f_{opt}, \qquad (12.15)$$

where $\mathbf{z} = \mathbf{R}(0.02048 \cdot (\mathbf{x} - \mathbf{x}^{opt})) + \mathbf{1}$.

Properties: Multimodal; Nonseparable; With a long, narrow, parabolic shaped flat valley from local optima to global optima.

12.4.9 Shifted Modified Schwefel Function

$$f_{16}(\mathbf{x}) = 418.9829 \times D - \sum_{i=1}^{D} g_1(\mathbf{w}_i), \qquad \mathbf{w}_i = \mathbf{z}_i + 420.9687462275036, \tag{12.16}$$

$$g_1(\mathbf{w}_i) = \begin{cases} \mathbf{w}_i \cdot \sin(\sqrt{|\mathbf{w}_i|}) & \text{if } |\mathbf{w}_i| \le 500 \\ (500 - \mod(\mathbf{w}_i, 500)) \cdot \sin\left(\sqrt{500 - \mod(\mathbf{w}_i, 500)} \right) - \frac{(\mathbf{w}_i - 500)^2}{10000 D} & \text{if } \mathbf{w}_i > 500 \\ (\mod(-\mathbf{w}_i, 500) - 500) \cdot \sin\left(\sqrt{500 - \mod(-\mathbf{w}_i, 500)} \right) - \frac{(\mathbf{w}_i + 500)^2}{10000 D} & \text{if } \mathbf{w}_i < -500 \end{cases},$$
$$\tag{12.17}$$

where $\mathbf{z} = 10 \cdot (\mathbf{x} - \mathbf{x}^{opt})$.

Properties: Multimodal; Separable; Having many local optima with the second better local optima far from the global optima.

12.4.10 Shifted Rotated Modified Schwefel Function

$$f_{17}(\mathbf{x}) = 418.9829 \times D - \sum_{i=1}^{D} g_1(\mathbf{w}_i), \qquad \mathbf{w}_i = \mathbf{z}_i + 420.9687462275036,$$

(12.18)

where $\mathbf{z} = \mathbf{R}(10 \cdot (\mathbf{x} - \mathbf{x}^{opt}))$ and $g_1(\cdot)$ is defined as Eq. (12.17).

Properties: Multimodal; Nonseparable; Having many local optima with the second better local optima far from the global optima.

12.4.11 Shifted Rotated Katsuura Function

$$f_{18}(\mathbf{x}) = \frac{10}{D^2} \prod_{i=1}^{D} (1 + i \sum_{j=1}^{32} \frac{|2^j \cdot \mathbf{z}_i - [2^j \cdot \mathbf{z}_i]|}{2^j})^{\frac{10}{D^{1.2}}} - \frac{10}{D^2} + f_{opt},$$

(12.19)

where $\mathbf{z} = \mathbf{R}(0.05 \cdot (\mathbf{x} - \mathbf{x}^{opt}))$.

Properties: Multimodal; Nonseparable; Continuous everywhere but differentiable nowhere.

12.4.12 Shifted and Rotated Lunacek Bi-Rastrigin Function

$$f_{19}(\mathbf{x}) = \min \left(\sum_{i=1}^{D} (\mathbf{z}_i - \mu_1)^2, dD + s \sum_{i=1}^{D} (\mathbf{z}_i - \mu_2)^2) \right)$$
$$+ 10 \cdot (D - \sum_{i=1}^{D} \cos(2\pi(\mathbf{z}_i - \mu_1))) + f_{opt},$$

(12.20)

where $\mathbf{z} = \mathbf{R}(0.1 \cdot (\mathbf{x} - \mathbf{x}^{opt}) + 2.5 * \mathbf{1})$, $\mu_1 = 2.5$, $\mu_2 = -2.5$, $d = 1$, $s = 0.9$.

Properties: Multimodal; Nonseparable; With two funnel around $\mu_1 \mathbf{1}$ and $\mu_2 \mathbf{1}$.

12.4.13 Shifted and Rotated Ackley Function

$$f_{20}(\mathbf{x}) = -20 \cdot \exp \left(-0.2 \sqrt{\frac{1}{D} \sum_{i=1}^{D} \mathbf{x}_i^2} \right) - \exp \left(\frac{1}{D} \sum_{i=1}^{D} \cos(2\pi \mathbf{x}_i) \right) + 20 + e + f_{opt},$$

(12.21)

where $\mathbf{z} = \mathbf{R}(\mathbf{x} - \mathbf{x}^{opt})$.

Properties: Multimodal; Nonseparable; Having many local optima with the global optima located in a very small basin.

12.4.14 Shifted Rotated HappyCat Function

$$f_{21}(\mathbf{x}) = |\sum_{i=1}^{D} \mathbf{z}_i^2 - D|^{0.25} + (\frac{1}{2} \sum_{j=1}^{D} \mathbf{z}_j^2 + \sum_{j=1}^{D} \mathbf{z}_j)/D + 0.5 + f_{opt}, \qquad (12.22)$$

where $\mathbf{z} = \mathbf{R}(0.05 \cdot (\mathbf{x} - \mathbf{x}^{opt})) - \mathbf{1}$.

Properties: Multimodal; Nonseparable; Global optima located in curved narrow valley.

12.4.15 Shifted Rotated HGBat Function

$$f_{22}(\mathbf{x}) = |(\sum_{i=1}^{D} \mathbf{z}_i^2)^2 - (\sum_{j=1}^{D} \mathbf{z}_j)^2|^{0.5} + (\frac{1}{2} \sum_{j=1}^{D} \mathbf{z}_j^2 + \sum_{j=1}^{D} \mathbf{z}_j)/D + 0.5 + f_{opt}, \quad (12.23)$$

where $\mathbf{z} = \mathbf{R}(0.05 \cdot (\mathbf{x} - \mathbf{x}^{opt})) - \mathbf{1}$.

Properties: Multimodal; Nonseparable; Global optima located in curved narrow valley.

12.4.16 Expanded Schaffer's F6 Function

$$\text{Schaffer's F6 Function: } g_4(x,y) = \frac{\sin^2(\sqrt{x^2 + y^2}) - 0.5}{(1 + 0.001 \cdot (x^2 + y^2))^2} + 0.5,$$

$$f_{23}(\mathbf{x}) = \sum_{i=1}^{D-1} g_4(\mathbf{z}_i, \mathbf{z}_{i+1}) + g_4(\mathbf{z}_D, \mathbf{z}_1) + f_{opt}, \qquad (12.24)$$

where $\mathbf{z} = \mathbf{R}(\mathbf{x} - \mathbf{x}^{opt})$.

Properties: Multimodal; Nonseparable.

12.5 Hybrid Functions

Hybrid functions are created according to [109]. For each hybrid function, the variables are randomly divided into subcomponents and different basic functions (unimodal and multimodal) are used for different subcomponents, as depicted in Eq. (12.25)

$$F(\mathbf{x}) = \sum_{i=1}^{N} G_i(\mathbf{R}_i \cdot \mathbf{z}^i) + f^{opt}, \tag{12.25}$$

where $F(\cdot)$ is the constructed hybrid function, $G_i(\cdot)$ is the ith basic function used, and N is the number of basic functions. $\mathbf{z}_i$ is constructed as follows:

$$\mathbf{y} = \mathbf{x} - \mathbf{x}^{opt}$$
$$\mathbf{z}^1 = [\mathbf{y}_{S_1}, \mathbf{y}_{S_2}, \ldots, \mathbf{y}_{S_{n_1}}]$$
$$\mathbf{z}^2 = [\mathbf{y}_{S_{n_1+1}}, \mathbf{y}_{S_{n_1+2}} \cdots \mathbf{y}_{S_{n_1+n_2}}]$$
$$\vdots$$
$$\mathbf{z}^N = [\mathbf{y}_{S_{(\Sigma_{i=1}^{N-1} n_i)+1}}, \mathbf{y}_{S_{(\Sigma_{i=1}^{N-1} n_i)+2}}, \ldots, \mathbf{y}_{S_{n_D}}]$$

where S is a permutation of $(1 : D)$, such that $\mathbf{z} = [\mathbf{z}^1, \mathbf{z}^2, \ldots, \mathbf{z}^N]$ forms the transformed vector and $n_i, i = 1, \ldots, N$, are the dimensions of the basic functions, which is derived as Eq. (12.26)

$$n_i = \lceil p_i D \rceil (i = 1, 2, \cdots, N-1), n_N = D - \sum_{i=1}^{N-1} n_i, \tag{12.26}$$

where p_i is used to control the percentage of each basic functions.

12.5.1 Hybrid Function 1

- $N = 3$
- $p = [0.3, 0.3, 0.4]$
- G_1: Modified Schwefel's Function
- G_2: Rastrigin Function
- G_3: High Conditioned Elliptic Function

12.5.2 Hybrid Function 2

- $N = 5$
- $p = [0.3, 0.3, 0.4]$
- G_1: Bent Cigar Function
- G_2: HGBat Function
- G_3: Rastrigin Function

12.5.3 Hybrid Function 3

- $N = 4$
- $p = [0.2, 0.2, 0.3, 0.3]$
- G_1: Griewank Function
- G_2: Weierstrass Function
- G_3: Rosenbrock Function
- G_4: Expanded Scaffer's F6 Function

12.5.4 Hybrid Function 4

- $N = 4$
- $p = [0.2, 0.2, 0.3, 0.3]$
- G_1: HGBat Function
- G_2: Discus Function
- G_3: Expanded Griewank plus Rosenbrock Function
- G_4: Rastrigin Function

12.5.5 Hybrid Function 5

- $N = 5$
- $p = [0.1, 0.2, 0.2, 0.2, 0.3]$
- G_1: Expanded Scaffer's F6 Function
- G_2: HGBat Function
- G_3: Rosenbrock Function
- G_4: Modified Schwefel's Function
- G_5: High Conditioned Elliptic Function

12.5.6 Hybrid Function 6

- $N = 5$
- $p = [0.1, 0.2, 0.2, 0.2, 0.3]$
- G_1: Katsuura Function
- G_2: HappyCat Function
- G_3: Expanded Griewank plus Rosenbrock Function
- G_4: Modified Schwefel's Function
- G_5: Ackley Function

12.6 Composition Functions

Composition functions are constructed in the same manner as in [110, 109]

$$F(\mathbf{x}) = \sum_{i=1}^{N} \left[\omega_i * (\lambda \cdot G_i(\mathbf{x}) + bias_i) \right] + f^{opt}, \tag{12.27}$$

where

- $F(\cdot)$: the constructed composition function
- $G_i(\cdot)$: ith basic function
- N: number of basic functions used
- $bias_i$: define which optimum is the global optimum
- σ_i: control $G_i(\cdot)$'s coverage range, a small σ_i gives a narrow range for $G_i(\cdot)$
- λ_i: control $G_i(\cdot)$'s height
- ω_i: weighted value for $G_i(\cdot)$, calculated as follows:

$$w_i = \frac{1}{\sqrt{\sum_{j=1}^{D}(\mathbf{x}_j - \mathbf{x}_j^{opt,i})^2}} \exp(-\frac{\sum_{j=1}^{D}(\mathbf{x}_j - \mathbf{x}_j^{opt,i})^2}{2D\sigma_i^2}) \qquad (12.28)$$

where $\mathbf{x}^{opt,i}$ represents the optimum position for $G_i(\cdot)$. Then normalize w_i to get ω_i: $\omega_i = w_i / \sum_{i=1}^{N} w_i$.

When $\mathbf{x} = \mathbf{x}^{opt,i}$, $\omega_j = \begin{cases} 1 & j = i \\ 0 & j \neq i \end{cases}$ $(j = 1, 2, \cdots, N)$, such that $F(\mathbf{x}) = bias_i + f^{opt,i}$.

The constructed functions are multimodal and nonseparable and merge the properties of the subfunctions better and maintains continuity around the global/local optima. The local optimum which has the smallest bias value is the global optimum. The optimum of the third basic function is set to the origin as a trip in order to test the algorithms' tendency to converge to the search center.

Note that the landscape not only changes along with the selection of basic function, but the optima and σ and λ can effect it greatly.

12.6.1 Composition Function 1

- $N = 5$
- $\sigma = [10, 20, 30, 40, 50]$
- $\lambda = [1e - 10, 1e - 6, 1e - 26, 1e - 6, 1e - 6]$
- $bias = [0, 100, 200, 300, 400]$
- G_1: Rotated Rosenbrock Function
- G_2: High Conditioned Elliptic Function
- G_3: Rotated Bent Cigar Function
- G_4: Rotated Discus Function
- G_5: High Conditioned Elliptic Function

12.6.2 Composition Function 2

- $N = 3$
- $\sigma = [15, 15, 15]$
- $\lambda = [1, 1, 1]$
- $bias = [0, 100, 200]$
- G_1: Expanded Schwefel Function
- G_2: Rotated Rstrigin Function
- G_3: Rotated HGBat Function

12.6.3 Composition Function 3

- $N = 3$
- $\sigma = [20, 50, 40]$
- $\lambda = [0.25, 1, 1e - 7]$
- $bias = [0, 100, 200]$
- G_1: Rotated Schwefel Function
- G_2: Rotated Rastrigin Function
- G_3: Rotated High Conditioned Elliptic Function

12.6.4 Composition Function 4

- $N = 5$
- $\sigma = [20, 15, 10, 10, 40]$
- $\lambda = [2.5e - 2, 0.1, 1e - 8, 0.25, 1]$
- $bias = [0, 100, 200, 300, 400]$
- G_1: Rotated Schwefel Function
- G_2: Rotated HappyCat Function
- G_3: Rotated High Conditioned Elliptic Function
- G_4: Rotated Weierstrass Function
- G_5: Rotated Griewank Function

12.6.5 Composition Function 5

- $N = 5$
- $\sigma = [15, 15, 15, 15, 15]$
- $\lambda = [10, 10, 2.5, 2.5, 1e - 6]$
- $bias = [0, 100, 200, 300, 400]$
- G_1: Rotated HGBat Function

- G_2: Rotated Rastrigin Function
- G_5: Rotated Schwefel Function
- G_4: Rotated Weierstrass Function
- G_3: Rotated High Conditioned Elliptic Function

12.6.6 Composition Function 6

- $N = 5$
- $\sigma = [10, 20, 30, 40, 50]$
- $\lambda = [2.5, 10, 2.5, 5e - 4, 1e - 6]$
- $bias = [0, 100, 200, 300, 400]$
- G_1: Rotated Expanded Griewank plus Rosenbrock Function
- G_2: Rotated HappyCat Function
- G_3: Rotated Schwefel Function
- G_4: Rotated Expanded Scaffer's F6 Function
- G_5: High Conditioned Elliptic Function

12.6.7 Composition Function 7

- $N = 3$
- $\sigma = [10, 30, 50]$
- $\lambda = [1, 1, 1]$
- $bias = [0, 100, 200]$
- G_1: Hybrid Function 1
- G_2: Hybrid Function 2
- G_3: Hybrid Function 3

12.6.8 Composition Function 8

- $N = 3$
- $\sigma = [10, 30, 50]$
- $\lambda = [1, 1, 1]$
- $bias = [0, 100, 200]$
- G_1: Hybrid Function 4
- G_2: Hybrid Function 5
- G_3: Hybrid Function 6

12.7 Summary

This chapter describes cuROB, a GPU-based benchmark for real parameter optimization problems. cuROB is very flexible. It supports any dimension within the limit of hardware. Powered by the highly parallelled GPU, cuROB can be very efficient which makes it a handy benchmark for testing high dimension problems.

Appendix: Figures for 2D Functions

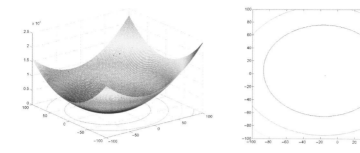

Fig. A.1 Sphere Function

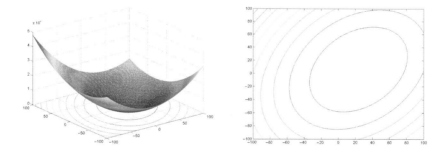

Fig. A.2 Ellipsoid Function

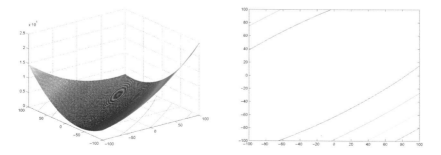

Fig. A.3 Elliptic Function

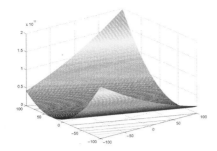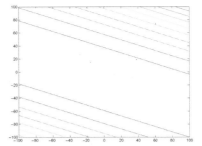

Fig. A.4 Discus Function

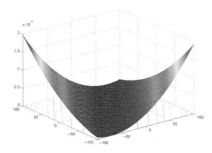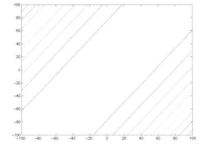

Fig. A.5 Bent Cigar Function

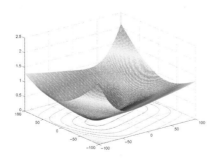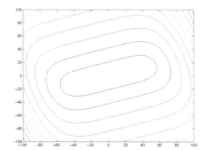

Fig. A.6 Different Powers Function

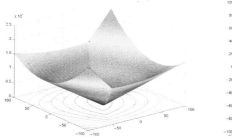 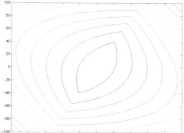

Fig. A.7 Sharp Valley Function

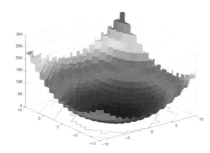 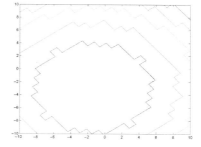

Fig. A.8 Step Function

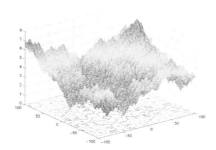 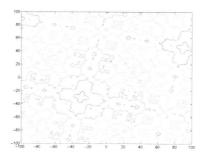

Fig. A.9 Weierstrass Function

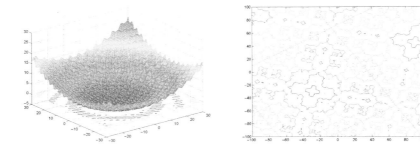

Fig. A.10 Weierstrass Function

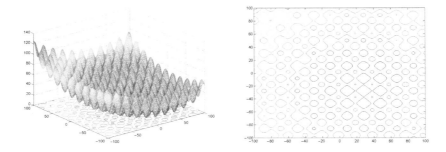

Fig. A.11 Rastrigin Function

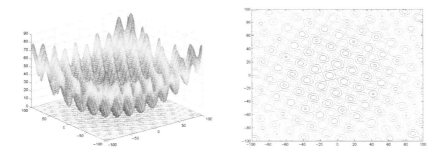

Fig. A.12 Rotated Rastrigin Function

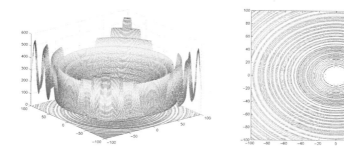

Fig. A.13 Schaffer's F7 Function

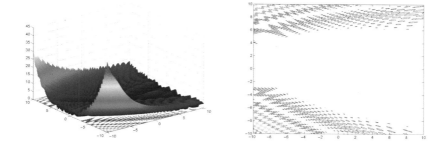

Fig. A.14 Expanded Griewank Rosenbrock Function

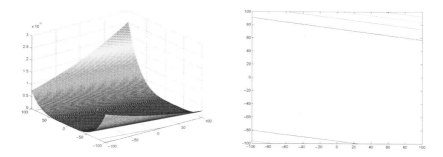

Fig. A.15 Rosenbrock Function

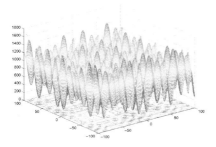 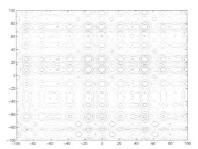

Fig. A.16 Schwefel Function

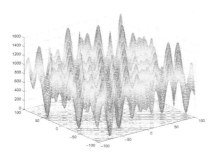 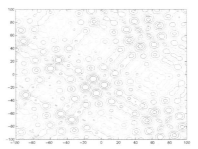

Fig. A.17 Rotated Schwefel Function

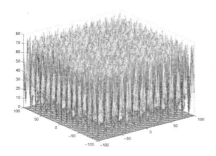 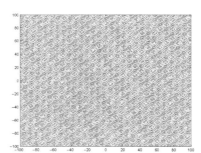

Fig. A.18 Katsuura Function

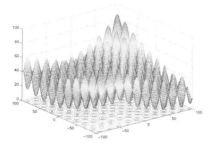 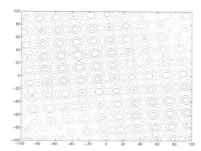

Fig. A.19 Lunacek Function

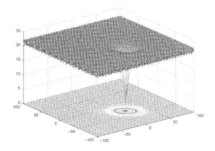 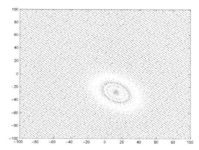

Fig. A.20 Ackley Function

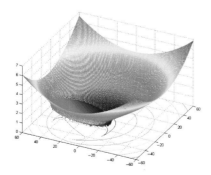 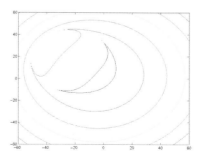

Fig. A.21 HappyCat Function

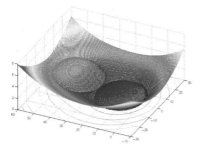 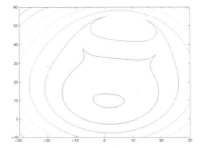

Fig. A.22 HGBat Function

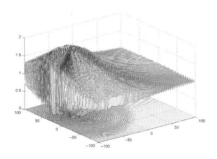 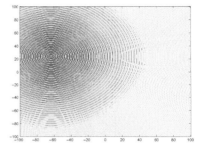

Fig. A.23 Expanded Scaffers' F6 Function

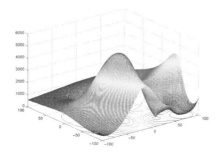 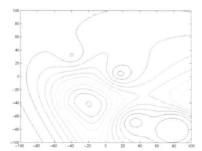

Fig. A.24 Composition Function 1

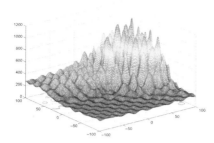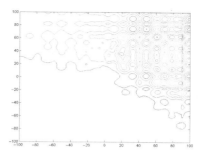

Fig. A.25 Composition Function 2

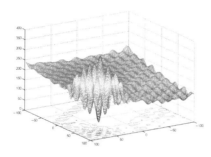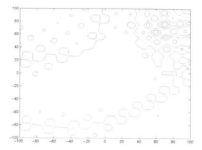

Fig. A.26 Composition Function 3

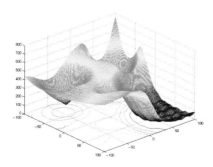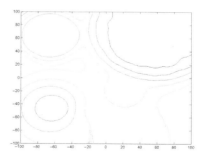

Fig. A.27 Composition Function 4

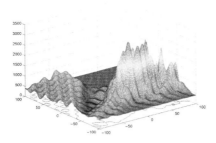 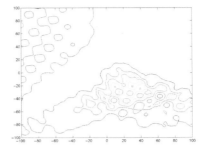

Fig. A.28 Composition Function 5

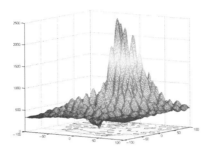 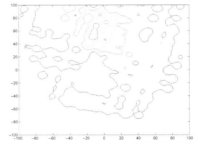

Fig. A.29 Composition Function 6

Appendix A
Figures and Tables

List of Figures

List of Tables

Appendix B
Resources

B.1 Internet Resources

1. Fireworks Algorithm Research Forum : http://www.cil.pku.edu.cn/research/fwa/index.html
2. Source Codes of Fireworks Algorithm and its Variants: http://www.cil.pku.edu.cn/research/fwa/resources/index.html
3. 2014 International Conference on Swarm Intelligence Competition on Single Objective Optimization (ICSI-2014-BS): http://www.ic-si.org/competition/
4. IEEE CEC 2014 Competition Benchmark Functions: http://www.ntu.edu.sg/home/EPNSugan/index_files/CEC2013/CEC2013.htm
5. IEEE CEC 2013 Competition Benchmark Functions: http://www.ntu.edu.sg/home/EPNSugan/index_files/CEC2014/CEC2014.htm
6. A CUDA-Based Real Parameter Optimization Benchmark: https://github.com/DingKe/cuROB

B.2 Organizations

1. Computational Intelligence Laboratory of Peking University: http://www.cil.pku.edu.cn
2. IEEE Computational Intelligence Society: http://cis.ieee.org/
3. ACM SIGEVO: sigevo-members@ACM.ORG
4. World Federation on Soft Computing: http://www.softcomputing.org/
5. IEEE Systems, Man, and Cybernetics Society: http://www.ieeesmc.org/

B.3 Journals

1. International Journal of Swarm Intelligence Research
2. International Journal of Artificial Intelligence
3. International Journal of Swarm Intelligence
4. IEEE Transactions on Evolutionary Computation
5. IEEE Transactions on Cyberlnetics
6. Softcomputing
7. Applied Softcomputing

8. International Journal of Computational Intelligence and Pattern Recognition
9. CAAI Transactions on Intelligent Systems

B.4 Conferences

1. International Conference on Swarm Intelligence (ICSI): http://www.ic-si.org
2. IEEE Symposium on Swarm Intelligence
3. IEEE Congress on Evolutionary Computation (CEC)
4. IEEE International Conference on System, Man and Cybernetics (IEEE SMC)
5. IEEE-INNS, International Joint Conference on Neural Networks (IJCNN)
6. IEEE World Congress on Computational Intelligence
7. ACM The Genetic and Evolutionary Computation Conference (GECCO)

Appendix C
Table of Symbols

Table C.1: **Table of Symbols**

Symbols	Meanings
$f()$	optimization function f
D	dimension
x_i	variable
x_{ij}	the jth dimension value of variable x_i
x_{UB}	the upper bound of variable x
x_{LB}	the lower bound of variable x
$x_{UB,k}$	the kth dimension upper bound value of variable x
$x_{LB,k}$	the kth dimension lower bound value of variable x
$evals_{max}$	the maximum evaluation times
$maxIter$	the maximum iteration number
N	fireworks number
m	explosion sparks number
$\hat{m}$	Gaussian mutation sparks number
X_i	the location of the ith firework in the fireworks swarm
X_{ik}	the kth dimension value of firework X_i
$f(X_i)$	the function fitness of firework X_i
A_i	the explosion amplitude of the ith firework
$\hat{A}$	coefficient in the calculation of explosion amplitudes
S_i	the explosion sparks number of the ith firework
$U(a,b)$	a random value generated between (a,b) with uniform distribution
$\mathcal{N}(\mu,\sigma)$	a random value generated with Gaussian distribution with mean μ and variance σ
g	$\mathcal{N}(1,1)$
e	$\mathcal{N}(0,1)$
K	candidates set, in general, it contains fireworks, explosion sparks and Gaussian mutation sparks.
$d(.,.)$	distance measure
ε	machine smallest value
x_j	the position of jth individual in candidates set
$x_{j,k}$	the kth dimension value of x_j
$R(x_i)$	the sum distances between individual x_i and the rest individuals in candidates K
$p(x_i)$	the probability that individual x_i is selected as firework

Continued

Table C.1 Table of Symbols

Symbols	Meanings
s^*	the best spark generated by firework X
X_B	the best firework
X_{elite}	the generated elite solution
$\hat{x}_b$	the explosion sparks with minimal fitness among all the explosion sparks
CF	the firework with best function fitness
$nonCF$	the fireworks except for CF
X_{CF}	the location of CF
$X_{CF,k}$	the kth dimension value of X_{CF}
A_{CF}	the explosion amplitude of CF
C_a	amplification factor for explosion amplitude of CF
C_r	reduction factor for explosion amplitude of CF
A_{init}	the initial explosion amplitude
A_{final}	the final explosion amplitude
$\|\cdot\|_F$	F norm
$\|\cdot\|_\infty$	infinite norm
SI	shift index
SV	shift value
round(.)	round operation
E_t	the current evaluation times
$o(.)$	low order
$\%$	modular arithmetic operation
C'	coverage measure
A	objective matrix
W	reduced rank nonnegative factors matrix
H	reduced rank nonnegative factors matrix
D	distance matrix
w_i^r	the ith row of W
h_j^c	the jth column of H
a_i^r	the ith row of A
a_j^c	the ith column of A
L	the length of the root
p_a	the probability that a solution is accepted
θ	parameter which controls the p_a
Ω_S	the super volume of region S
F_{Max}	maximum fitness
r_t	radius of the target
R_i	the ith robot
$P_i(t)$	robot i's position
$V_i(t)$	robot i's velocity
$G_i(t)$	grouping component
$H_i(t)$	history component

References

1. The boost random number library. URL http://www.boost.org/doc/libs/1_55_0/doc/html/boost_random.html
2. Open accelerators. URL http://www.openacc.org
3. In: Handbook of Computational Statistics, Springer Handbooks of Computational Statistics (2012)
4. Alba, E., Luque, G., Nesmachnow, S.: Parallel metaheuristics: recent advances and new trends. International Transactions in Operational Research **20**(1), 1–48 (2013). DOI 10.1111/j.1475-3995.2012.00862.x
5. AMD Inc.: Application showcase. URL http://developer.amd.com/community/application-showcase/
6. AMD Inc.: Core Math Library (ACML). URL http://developer.amd.com/tools-and-sdks/cpu-development/amd-core-math-library-acml/
7. Amdahl, G.M.: Validity of the single processor approach to achieving large scale computing capabilities. In: Proceedings of the April 18-20, 1967, Spring Joint Computer Conference, AFIPS '67 (Spring), pp. 483–485. ACM, New York, NY, USA (1967). DOI 10.1145/1465482.1465560
8. Arun, J., Mishra, M., Subramaniam, S.: Parallel implementation of mopso on gpu using opencl and cuda. In: High Performance Computing (HiPC), 2011 18th International Conference on, pp. 1–10 (2011). DOI 10.1109/HiPC.2011.6152719
9. Bai, H., Ouyang, D., Li, X., He, L., Yu, H.: Max-min ant system on gpu with cuda. In: Innovative Computing, Information and Control (ICICIC), 2009 Fourth International Conference on, pp. 801–804 (2009)
10. Ballou, K., Mohammad Mousa, N.: Opencuda+mpi. Tech. Rep. Paper 14, Student Research Initiative (2013)
11. Bastos-Filho, C., Junior, M.O., Nascimento, D.: Running particle swarm optimization on graphic processing units. Search Algorithms and Applications (2011)
12. Bastos-Filho, C.J.A., Andrade, J., Pita, M., Ramos, A.: Impact of the quality of random numbers generators on the performance of particle swarm optimization. In: Systems, Man and Cybernetics, 2009. SMC 2009. IEEE International Conference on, pp. 4988–4993 (2009). DOI 10.1109/ICSMC.2009.5346366
13. Bastos-Filho, C.J.A., Oliveira, M., Nascimento, D.N.O., Ramos, A.D.: Impact of the random number generator quality on particle swarm optimization algorithm running on graphic processor units. In: Hybrid Intelligent Systems (HIS), 2010 10th International Conference on, pp. 85–90 (2010). DOI 10.1109/HIS.2010.5601073
14. Batcher, K.E.: Sorting networks and their applications. In: Proceedings of the April 30–May 2, 1968, Spring Joint Computer Conference, AFIPS '68 (Spring), pp. 307–314. ACM, New York, NY, USA (1968). DOI 10.1145/1468075.1468121
15. Bell, N., Garland, M.: Efficient sparse matrix-vector multiplication on cuda. Tech. rep., NVIDIA Technical Report NVR-2008-004, NVIDIA Corporation (2008)
16. Blecic, I., Cecchini, A., Trunfio, G.A.: Fast and accurate optimization of a gpu-accelerated ca urban model through cooperative coevolutionary particle swarms. Procedia Computer Science **29**(0), 1631–1643 (2014). DOI http://dx.doi.org/10.1016/j.procs.2014.05.148. 2014 International Conference on Computational Science
17. Blelloch, G.E.: Prefix sums and their applications. Tech. Rep. CMU-CS-90-190, School of Computer Science, Carnegie Mellon University (1990)
18. Box, G.E.P., Muller, M.E.: A note on the generation of random normal deviates. Ann. Math. Statist. **29**(2), 610–611 (1958)
19. Bratton, D., Kennedy, J.: Defining a standard for particle swarm optimization. In: Swarm Intelligence Symposium, 2007. SIS 2007. IEEE, pp. 120–127 (2007). DOI 10.1109/SIS.2007.368035
20. Brown, L.G.: A survey of image registration techniques. ACM Comput. Surv. **24**(4), 325–376 (1992)

21. Buck, I., Foley, T., Horn, D., Sugerman, J., Fatahalian, K., Houston, M., Hanrahan, P.: Brook for gpus: stream computing on graphics hardware. ACM Trans. Graph. **23**(3), 777–786 (2004). DOI 10.1145/1015706.1015800

22. Bura, W., Boryczka, M.: The parallel ant vehicle navigation system with cuda technology. In: Computational Collective Intelligence. Technologies and Applications, *Lecture Notes in Computer Science*, vol. 6923, pp. 505–514. Springer Berlin Heidelberg (2011)

23. Bureerat, S.: Hybrid population-based incremental learning using real codes. In: Learning and Intelligent Optimization, *Lecture Notes in Computer Science*, vol. 6683, pp. 379–391. Springer Berlin Heidelberg (2011)

24. Cagnoni, S., Bacchini, A., Mussi, L.: Opencl implementation of particle swarm optimization: A comparison between multi-core cpu and gpu performances. In: Applications of Evolutionary Computation, *Lecture Notes in Computer Science*, vol. 7248, pp. 406–415. Springer Berlin Heidelberg (2012). DOI 10.1007/978-3-642-29178-4_41

25. Calazan, R., Nedjah, N., Macedo Mourelle, L.: Swarm grid: A proposal for high performance of parallel particle swarm optimization using gpgpu. In: Computational Science and Its Applications C ICCSA 2012, *Lecture Notes in Computer Science*, vol. 7333, pp. 148–160. Springer Berlin Heidelberg (2012). DOI 10.1007/978-3-642-31125-3_12

26. Calazan, R., Nedjah, N., Macedo Mourelle, L.: Three alternatives for parallel gpu-based implementations of high performance particle swarm optimization. In: Advances in Computational Intelligence, *Lecture Notes in Computer Science*, vol. 7902, pp. 241–252. Springer Berlin Heidelberg (2013). DOI 10.1007/978-3-642-38679-4_23

27. Canalys: Tablets to make up 50% of pc market in 2014. http://www.canalys.com (2013)

28. Cano, A., Olmo, J.L., Ventura, S.: Parallel multi-objective ant programming for classification using gpus. Journal of Parallel and Distributed Computing **73**(6), 713–728 (2013)

29. Cano, E.G., Rodríguez, K.: A parallel pso algorithm for a watermarking application on a gpu. Computación y Sistemas **17**, 381–390 (2013)

30. Cárdenas-Montes, M., Vega-Rodríguez, M.A., Rodríguez-Vázquez, J.J., Gómez-Iglesias, A.: Accelerating particle swarm algorithm with gpgpu. In: Parallel, Distributed and Network-Based Processing (PDP), 2011 19th Euromicro International Conference on, pp. 560–564 (2011). DOI 10.1109/PDP.2011.33

31. Catala, A., Jaen, J., Mocholi, J.: Strategies for accelerating ant colony optimization algorithms on graphical processing units. In: Evolutionary Computation, 2007. CEC 2007. IEEE Congress on, pp. 492–500 (2007)

32. Cecilia, J.M., Garcła, J.M., Nisbet, A., Amos, M., Ujaldón, M.: Enhancing data parallelism for ant colony optimization on gpus. Journal of Parallel and Distributed Computing **73**(1), 42–51 (2013)

33. Cecilia, J.M., Garcła, J.M., Ujaldón, M., Nisbet, A., Amos: Parallelization strategies for ant colony optimisation on gpus. In: Parallel and Distributed Processing Workshops and Phd Forum (IPDPSW), 2011 IEEE International Symposium on, pp. 339–346 (2011)

34. Cecilia, J.M., Nisbet, A., Amos, M., García, J.M., Ujaldón, M.: Enhancing gpu parallelism in nature-inspired algorithms. The Journal of Supercomputing **63**(3), 773–789 (2013)

35. Chandrakasan, A.P., Potkonjak, M., Mehra, R., Rabaey, J., Brodersen, R.W.: Optimizing power using transformations. Computer-Aided Design of Integrated Circuits and Systems, IEEE Transactions on **14**(1), 12–31 (1995)

36. Chen, R.B., Hsieh, D.N., Hung, Y., Wang, W.: Optimizing latin hypercube designs by particle swarm. Statistics and Computing **23**(5), 663–676 (2013). DOI 10.1007/s11222-012-9363-3

37. Clerc, M.: List-based optimisers: Experiments and open questions. International Journal of Swarm Intelligence Research (IJSIR) **4**(4), 23–38 (2013)

38. Coates, A., Huval, B., Wang, T., Wu, D., Catanzaro, B., Andrew, N.: Deep learning with cots hpc systems. In: S. Dasgupta, D. McAllester (eds.) Proceedings of the 30th International Conference on Machine Learning (ICML-13), vol. 28, pp. 1337–1345. JMLR Workshop and Conference Proceedings (2013)

39. Das, S., Suganthan, P.N.: Differential evolution: a survey of the state-of-the-art. Evolutionary Computation, IEEE Transactions on **15**(1), 4–31 (2011)

40. Datta, D., Mehta, S., Shalivahan, Srivastava, R.: Cuda based particle swarm optimization for geophysical inversion. In: Recent Advances in Information Technology (RAIT), 2012 1st International Conference on, pp. 416–420 (2012). DOI 10.1109/RAIT.2012.6194456

41. Dawson, L., Stewart, I.A.: Improving ant colony optimization performance on the gpu using cuda. In: Evolutionary Computation (CEC), 2013 IEEE Congress on, pp. 1901–1908 (2013). DOI 10.1109/CEC.2013.6557791

42. Dawson, L., Stewart, I.A.: Accelerating ant colony optimization-based edge detection on the gpu using cuda. In: Evolutionary Computation (CEC), 2014 IEEE Congress on, pp. 1901–1908 (2014)

43. Dean, J., Ghemawat, S.: MapReduce: simplified data processing on large clusters. Communications of the ACM **51**(1), 107–113 (2008)

44. Deb, K., Thiele, L., Laumanns, M., Zitzler, E.: Scalable test problems for evolutionary multiobjective optimization. In: A. Abraham, L. Jain, R. Goldberg (eds.) Evolutionary Multiobjective Optimization, Advanced Information and Knowledge Processing, pp. 105–145. Springer London (2005). DOI 10.1007/1-84628-137-7_6

45. Delisle, P.: Parallel ant colony optimization: Algorithmic models and hardware implementations. In: Ant Colony Optimization - Techniques and Applications. InTech (2013)

46. Demirovic, D., Serifovic-Trbalic, A., Cattin, P.C.: Evaluation of opencl native math functions for image processing algorithms. In: Information, Communication and Automation Technologies (ICAT), 2013 XXIV International Symposium on, pp. 1–5 (2013). DOI 10.1109/ICAT.2013.6684093

47. Ding, K., Tan, Y.: Comparison of random number generators in particle swarm optimization algorithm. In: the Proceeding of 2014 IEEE Congress on Evolutionary Computation, (IEEE CEC 2014), pp. 2664–2671 (2014)

48. Ding, K., Tan, Y.: cuROB: A GPU-based test suit for real-parameter optimization. In: Advances in Swarm Intelligence, Lecture Notes in Computer Science, pp. 66–78. Springer Berlin Heidelberg (2014)

49. Ding, K., Zheng, S., Tan, Y.: A GPU-based parallel fireworks algorithm for optimization. In: Proceeding of the fifteenth annual conference on Genetic and evolutionary computation conference, GECCO '13, pp. 9–16. ACM, New York, NY, USA (2013). DOI 10.1145/2463372.2463377

50. Dorigo, M., Birattari, M.: Ant colony optimization. In: Encyclopedia of Machine Learning, pp. 36–39. Springer (2010)

51. Dorigo, M., Blum, C.: Ant colony optimization theory: A survey. Theoretical Computer Science **344**(2C3), 243–278 (2005)

52. Dorigo, M., Gambardella, L.: Ant colony system: a cooperative learning approach to the traveling salesman problem. Evolutionary Computation, IEEE Transactions on **1**(1), 53–66 (1997)

53. Du, P., Weber, R., Luszczek, P., Tomov, S., Peterson, G., Dongarra, J.: From cuda to opencl: Towards a performance-portable solution for multi-platform gpu programming. Parallel Computing **38**(8), 391–407 (2012)

54. Eberhart, R.C., Shi, Y., Kennedy, J.: Swarm Intelligence. Morgan Kaufmann (2001)

55. Engelbrecht, A.P.: Fundamentals of Computational Swarm Intelligence. John Wiley & Sons, Ltd (2005)

56. Eshelman, L.J., Caruana, R., Schaffer, J.D.: Biases in the crossover landscape. In: Proceedings of the 3rd International Conference on Genetic Algorithms, George Mason University, Fairfax, Virginia, USA, June 1989, pp. 10–19 (1989)

57. Filho, C.J.A.B., de Lima Neto, F.B., Lins, A.J.C.C., Nascimento, A.I.S., Lima, M.P.: A novel search algorithm based on fish school behavior. In: Systems, Man and Cybernetics, 2008. SMC 2008. IEEE International Conference on, pp. 2646–2651 (2008). DOI 10.1109/ICSMC.2008.4811695

58. Finck, S., Hansen, N., Ros, R., Auger, A.: Real-parameter black-box optimization benchmarking 2010: Noiseless functions definitions. Tech. Rep. 2009/20, Research Center PPE (2010)

59. Franz, W., Thulasiraman, P., Thulasiram, R.: Memory efficient multi-swarm pso algorithm in opencl on an apu. In: Algorithms and Architectures for Parallel Processing, *Lecture Notes in Computer Science*, vol. 8285, pp. 236–246. Springer International Publishing (2013). DOI 10.1007/978-3-319-03859-9_20

60. Franz, W., Thulasiraman, P., Thulasiram, R.: Optimization of an opencl-based multi-swarm pso algorithm on an apu. In: Parallel Processing and Applied Mathematics, Lecture Notes in Computer Science, pp. 140–150. Springer Berlin Heidelberg (2014). DOI 10.1007/978-3-642-55195-6_13

61. Fu, J., Lei, L., Zhou, G.: A parallel ant colony optimization algorithm with gpu-acceleration based on all-in-roulette selection. In: Advanced Computational Intelligence (IWACI), 2010 Third International Workshop on, pp. 260–264 (2010)

62. Gao, H., Diao, M.: Cultural firework algorithm and its application for digital filters design. International Journal of Modelling, Identification and Control **14**(4), 324–331 (2011)

63. Gaster, B., Howes, L., Kaeli, D.R., Mistry, P., Schaa, D.: Heterogeneous Computing with OpenCL. Morgan Kaufamnn (2011)

64. Gieseke, F., Heinermann, J., Oancea, C., Igel, C.: Buffer kd trees: processing massive nearest neighbor queries on gpus. In: Proceedings of The 31st International Conference on Machine Learning, pp. 172–180 (2014)

65. Goldberg, D.: What every computer scientist should know about floating-point arithmetic. ACM Computing Surveys **23**(1), 5–48 (1991)

66. Gupta, K., Stuart, J., Owens, J.: A study of persistent threads style gpu programming for gpgpu workloads. In: Innovative Parallel Computing (InPar), 2012, pp. 1–14 (2012). DOI 10.1109/InPar.2012.6339596

67. Hallmans, D., Sandstrom, K., Lindgren, M., Nolte, T.: Gpgpu for industrial control systems. In: Emerging Technologies Factory Automation (ETFA), 2013 IEEE 18th Conference on, pp. 1–4 (2013). DOI 10.1109/ETFA.2013.6648166

68. Harris, M., Sengupta, S., Owens, J.D.: GPU Gems, vol. 3, chap. Parallel prefix sum (scan) with CUDA, pp. 851–876. Addison-Wesley Professional (2007)

69. He, B., Govindaraju, N.K., Luo, Q., Smith, B.: Efficient gather and scatter operations on graphics processors. In: Proceedings of the 2007 ACM/IEEE Conference on Supercomputing, SC '07, pp. 46:1–46:12, ACM, New York, NY (2007). DOI 10.1145/1362622.1362684

70. He, W., Mi, G., Tan, Y.: Parameter optimization of local-concentration model for spam detection by using fireworks algorithm. In: Advances in Swarm Intelligence, *Lecture Notes in Computer Science*, vol. 7928, pp. 439–450. Springer Berlin Heidelberg (2013). DOI 10.1007/978-3-642-38703-6_52

71. Holland, J.H.: Adaptation in Natural and Artificial Systems: An Introductory Analysis with Ppplications to Biology, Control, and Artificial Intelligence. Univ. Michigan Press, Oxford, England (1975)

72. Horn, D.R., Sugerman, J., Houston, M., Hanrahan, P.: Interactive k-d tree gpu raytracing. In: Proceedings of the 2007 symposium on Interactive 3D graphics and games, I3D '07, pp. 167–174. ACM, New York, NY, USA (2007). DOI 10.1145/1230100.1230129

73. Howes, L., Thomas, D.:

74. Hsieh, H.T., Chu, C.H.: Particle swarm optimisation (pso)-based tool path planning for 5-axis flank milling accelerated by graphics processing unit (gpu). International Journal of Computer Integrated Manufacturing **24**(7), 676–687 (2011). DOI 10.1080/0951192X.2011.570792

75. Husselmann, A.V., Hawick, K.A.: Parallel parametric optimisation with firefly algorithms on graphical processing units. In: Proc. Int. Conf. on Genetic and Evolutionary Methods (GEM12), CSTN-141, pp. 77–83. CSREA, Las Vegas, USA (2012)

76. Intel Corp.: The Math Kernel Library: Reference Manual (2007). URL http://software.intel.com/en-us/intel-mkl

77. Janecek, A., Tan, Y.: Using population based algorithms for initializing nonnegative matrix factorization. In: Advances in Swarm Intelligence, *Lecture Notes in Computer Science*, vol. 6729, pp. 307–316. Springer Berlin Heidelberg (2011)

78. Jaqueline S. Angelo, D.A.A., Barbosa, H.J.C.: Pstrategies for parallel ant colony optimization on graphics processing units. In: Ant Colony Optimization - Techniques and Applications. InTech (2013)
79. Jaros, J., Pospichal, P.: A fair comparison of modern cpus and gpus running the genetic algorithm under the knapsack benchmark. In: Applications of Evolutionary Computation, *Lecture Notes in Computer Science*, vol. 7248, pp. 426–435. Springer Berlin Heidelberg (2012). DOI 10.1007/978-3-642-29178-4_43
80. Jeong, H., Lee, W., Pak, J., jong Choi, K., Park, S.H., sik Yoo, J., Kim, J.H., Lee, J., Lee, Y.W.: Performance of kepler gtx titan gpus and xeon phi system. In: Proceedings of 31st International Symposium on Lattice Field Theory. Mainz, Germany (2013)
81. Jia, Y., Shelhamer, E., Donahue, J., Karayev, S., Long, J., Girshick, R., Guadarrama, S., Darrell, T.: Caffe: Convolutional architecture for fast feature embedding. In: Proceedings of the ACM International Conference on Multimedia, MM '14, pp. 675–678. ACM, New York, NY, USA (2014). DOI 10.1145/2647868.2654889
82. Jin, Y., Olhofer, M., Sendhoff, B.: Dynamic weighted aggregation for evolutionary multi-objective optimization: Why does it work and how? (2011)
83. Jovanovic, R., Tuba, M.: Parallelization of the cuckoo search using cuda architecture. In: 7th International Conference on Applied Mathematics, Simulation, Modelling (ASM 13). Cambridge, USA (2013)
84. Kalivarapu, V., Winer, E.: Implementation of digital pheromones in pso accelerated by commodity graphics hardware. In: 12th AIAA/ISSMO Multidisciplinary Analysis and Optimization Conference. the American Institute of Aeronautics and Astronautics, Inc., Victoria, British Columbia Canada (2008)
85. Kalivarapu, V., Winer, E.: Digital pheromone implementation of pso with velocity vector accelerated by commodity graphics hardware. In: 5th AIAA/AS ME/ASCE/AHS/ASC Structures, Structural Dynamics, and Materials Conference. the American Institute of Aeronautics and Astronautics, Inc., Palm Springs, California, USA (2009)
86. Kapasi, U.J., Rixner, S., Ahn, W.J.D.B.K.J.H., Mattson, P., Owens, J.D.: Programmable stream processors. Computer **36**(8), 54–62 (2003)
87. Kennedy, J., Eberhart, R.: Particle swarm optimization. In: Neural Networks, 1995. Proceedings., IEEE International Conference on, vol. 4, pp. 1942–1948 vol.4 (1995). DOI 10.1109/ICNN.1995.488968
88. Khronos OpenCL Working Group: The OpenCL 1.2 Specification (2011). URL http://www.khronos.org/registry/cl/specs/opencl-1.2.pdf
89. Kilic, O., El-Araby, E., Nguyen, Q., Dang, V.: Bio-inspired optimization for electromagnetic structure design using full-wave techniques on gpus. International Journal of Numerical Modelling: Electronic Networks, Devices and Fields **26**(6), 649–669 (2013). DOI 10.1002/jnm.1878
90. Kirk, D.B., mei W. Hwu, W.: Programming Massively Parallel Processors: A Hands-on Approach. Tsinghua University Press, Beijing, China (2010)
91. Kirkpatrick, S., Stoll, E.P.: A very fast shift-register sequence random number generator. Journal of Computational Physics **40**(2), 517–526 (1981)
92. Knuth, D.E.: The Art of Computer Programming, volume 3: Sorting and Searching, 2nd edn. Addison-Wesley Professional (1996)
93. Knuth, D.E.: The Art of Computer Programming, volume 2: Seminumerical Algorithms, 3rd edn. Addison-Wesley Professional (1997)
94. Kristiadi, A., Pranowo, P., Mudjihartono, P.: Parallel particle swarm optimization for image segmentation. In: The Second International Conference on Digital Enterprise and Information Systems (DEIS2013), pp. 129–135. Kuala Lumpur, Malaysia (2013)
95. Krömer, P., Platoš, J., Snášel, V.: A brief survey of advances in particle swarm optimization on graphic processing units. In: Nature and Biologically Inspired Computing (NaBIC), 2013 World Congress on, pp. 182–188 (2013). DOI 10.1109/NaBIC.2013.6617859
96. Krömer, P., Platoš, J., Snášel, V.: Nature-inspired meta-heuristics on modern gpus: State of the art and brief survey of selected algorithms. International Journal of Parallel Programming pp. 1–29 (2013). DOI 10.1007/s10766-013-0292-3

97. Krömer, P., Snåšel, V., Platoš, J., Abraham, A.: Many-threaded implementation of differential evolution for the cuda platform. In: Proceedings of the 13th annual conference on Genetic and evolutionary computation, GECCO '11, pp. 1595–1602. ACM, New York, NY, USA (2011). DOI 10.1145/2001576.2001791

98. Laguna-Sánchez, G.A., Olguín-Carbajal, M., Cruz-Cortés, N., Barrón-Fernández, R., Álvarez Cedillo, J.A.: Comparative study of parallel variants for a particle swarm optimization. Journal of Applied Research and Technology 7(3), 292–309 (2009)

99. Langdon, W.B.: A fast high quality pseudo random number generator for nvidia cuda. In: Proceedings of the 11th Annual Conference Companion on Genetic and Evolutionary Computation Conference: Late Breaking Papers, GECCO '09, pp. 2511–2514. ACM, New York, NY, USA (2009). DOI 10.1145/1570256.1570353

100. L'Ecuyer, P.:

101. L'Ecuyer, P.: Good parameters and implementations for combined multiple recursive random number generators. Operations Research 47(1), 159–164 (1999)

102. L'Ecuyer, P.: Tables of linear congruential generators of different sizes and good lattice structure. Math. Comput. 68(225), 249–260 (1999). DOI 10.1090/S0025-5718-99-00996-5

103. L'Ecuyer, P., Simard, R.: Testu01: A c library for empirical testing of random number generators. ACM Trans. Math. Softw. 33(4) (2007). DOI 10.1145/1268776.1268777

104. Lee, V.W., Kim, C., Chhugani, J., Deisher, M., Kim, D., Nguyen, A.D., Satish, N., Smelyanskiy, M., Chennupaty, S., Hammarlund, P., Singhal, R., Dubey, P.: Debunking the 100x gpu vs. cpu myth: an evaluation of throughput computing on cpu and gpu. ACM SIGARCH Computer Architecture News 38(3), 451–460 (2010)

105. Lewis, T.G., Payne, W.H.: Generalized feedback shift register pseudorandom number algorithm. Journal of the ACM 20(3), 456–468 (1973). DOI 10.1145/321765.321777

106. Li, J., Wan, D., Chi, Z., Hu, X.: A parallel particle swarm intelligence algorithm based on fine-grained model with gpu-accelerating. Journal of Harbin Institute of Technology 38(12), 2162–2166 (2006)

107. Li, J., Wan, D., Chi, Z., Hu, X.: An efficient fine-grained parallel particle swarm optimization method based on gpu-acceleration. International Journal of Innovative Computing, Information and Control 3(6(B)), 1707–1714 (2007)

108. Li, J., Zheng, S., Tan, Y.: Adaptive fireworks algorithm. In: Evolutionary Computation (CEC), 2014 IEEE Congress on, pp. 3214–3221 (2014). DOI 10.1109/CEC.2014.6900418

109. Liang, J.J., Qu, B.Y., Suganthan, P.N.: Problem definitions and evaluation criteria for the cec 2014 special session and competition on single objective real-parameter numerical optimization. Tech. Rep. 201311, Computational Intelligence Laboratory, Zhengzhou University and Nanyang Technological University, Singapore (2013)

110. Liang, J.J., Qu, B.Y., Suganthan, P.N., Hernández-Díaz, A.G.: Problem definitions and evaluation criteria for the cec 2013 special session and competition on real-parameter optimization. Tech. Rep. 201212, Computational Intelligence Laboratory, Zhengzhou University and Nanyang Technological University, Singapore (2013)

111. Lins, A.J.C.C., Bastos-Filho, C.J.A., Nascimento, D.N.O., Junior, M.A.C.O., de Lima-Neto, F.B.: Analysis of the performance of the fish school search algorithm running in graphic processing units. In: Theory and New Applications of Swarm Intelligence, pp. 17–32. InTech, Shanghai, China (2012)

112. Lu, G., jian Tan, D., ming Zhao, H.: Improvement on regulating definition of antibody density of immune algorithm. In: Neural Information Processing, 2002. ICONIP '02. Proceedings of the 9th International Conference on, vol. 5, pp. 2669–2672 vol.5 (2002). DOI 10.1109/ICONIP.2002.1201980

113. Luo, G.H., Huang, S.K., Chang, Y.S., Yuan, S.M.: A parallel bees algorithm implementation on gpu. Journal of Systems Architecture 60(3), 271–279 (2014)

114. Maghazeh, A., Bordoloi, U.D., Eles, P., Peng, Z.: General purpose computing on low-power embedded gpus : Has it come of age? Tech. rep., Linköping University, The Institute of Technology (2013)

115. Majd, A., Sahebi, G.: A survey on parallel evolutionary computing and introduce four general frameworks to parallelize all ec algorithms and create new operation for migration. Journal of Information and Computing Science **9**(2), 97–105 (2014)
116. Marsaglia, G.: Xorshift rngs. Journal of Statistical Software **8**(14), 1–6 (2003)
117. Matsumoto, M., Nishimura, T.: Mersenne twister: a 623-dimensionally equidistributed uniform pseudo-random number generator. ACM Transactions on Modeling and Computer Simulation (TOMACS) **8**(1), 3–30 (1998)
118. Matsumoto, M., Nishimura, T.: Dynamic creation of pseudorandom number generators. In: Monte Carlo and Quasi-Monte Carlo Methods 1998, pp. 56–69. Springer Berlin Heidelberg (2000)
119. Mitchell, T.: Machine Learning, 1st edn. McGraw Hill, New York, USA (1997)
120. Monniaux, D.: The pitfalls of verifying floating-point computations. ACM Transactions on Programming Languages and Systems **30**(3), 12:1–12:41 (2008)
121. Muñoz, D., Llanos, C., Coelho, L., Ayala-Rincon, M.: Comparison between two fpga implementations of the particle swarm optimization algorithm for high-performance embedded applications. In: Bio-Inspired Computing: Theories and Applications (BIC-TA), 2010 IEEE Fifth International Conference on, pp. 1637–1645 (2010). DOI 10.1109/BICTA.2010. 5645256
122. Muñoz, D., Llanos, C., dos S Coelho, L., Ayala-Rincon, M.: Hardware particle swarm optimization based on the attractive-repulsive scheme for embedded applications. In: Reconfigurable Computing and FPGAs (ReConFig), 2010 International Conference on, pp. 55–60 (2010). DOI 10.1109/ReConFig.2010.73
123. Munshi, A., Gaster, B., Mattson, T.G., Fung, J., Ginsburg, D.: OpenCL Programming Guide. Addison-Wesley Professional (2011)
124. Mussi, L., Cagnoni, S., Cardarelli, E., Daolio, F., Medici, P., Porta, P.: Gpu implementation of a road sign detector based on particle swarm optimization. Evolutionary Intelligence **3**(3-4), 155–169 (2010). DOI 10.1007/s12065-010-0043-y
125. Mussi, L., Cagnoni, S., Daolio, F.: Gpu-based road sign detection using particle swarm optimization. In: Intelligent Systems Design and Applications, 2009. ISDA '09. Ninth International Conference on, pp. 152–157 (2009). DOI 10.1109/ISDA.2009.88
126. Mussi, L., Daolio, F., Cagnoni, S.: Evaluation of parallel particle swarm optimization algorithms within the cuda^{TM} architecture. Information Sciences **181**(20), 4642–4657 (2011). DOI http://dx.doi.org/10.1016/j.ins.2010.08.045
127. Mussi, L., Ivekovic, S., Cagnoni, S.: Markerless articulated human body tracking from multiview video with gpu-pso. In: Evolvable Systems: From Biology to Hardware, *Lecture Notes in Computer Science*, vol. 6274, pp. 97–108. Springer Berlin Heidelberg (2010). DOI 10. 1007/978-3-642-15323-5_9
128. Mussi, L., Nashed, Y.S., Cagnoni, S.: Gpu-based asynchronous particle swarm optimization. In: Proceedings of the 13th annual conference on Genetic and evolutionary computation, GECCO '11, pp. 1555–1562. ACM, New York, NY, USA (2011). DOI 10.1145/2001576. 2001786
129. Narasimhan, H.: Parallel artificial bee colony (pabc) algorithm. In: Nature Biologically Inspired Computing, 2009. NaBIC 2009. World Congress on, pp. 306–311 (2009). DOI 10.1109/NABIC.2009.5393726
130. Nashed, Y.S., Ugolotti, R., Mesejo, P., Cagnoni, S.: libcudaoptimize: An open source library of gpu-based metaheuristics. In: Proceedings of the Fourteenth International Conference on Genetic and Evolutionary Computation Conference Companion, GECCO Companion '12, pp. 117–124. ACM, New York, NY, USA (2012). DOI 10.1145/2330784.2330803
131. Nobile, M., Besozzi, D., Cazzaniga, P., Mauri, G., Pescini, D.: A gpu-based multi-swarm pso method for parameter estimation in stochastic biological systems exploiting discrete-time target series. In: Evolutionary Computation, Machine Learning and Data Mining in Bioinformatics, *Lecture Notes in Computer Science*, vol. 7246, pp. 74–85. Springer Berlin Heidelberg (2012). DOI 10.1007/978-3-642-29066-4_7
132. Nobile, M.S., Besozzi, D., Cazzaniga, P., Mauri, G., Pescini, D.: Estimating reaction constants in stochastic biological systems with a multi-swarm pso running on gpus. In:

Proceedings of the fourteenth international conference on Genetic and evolutionary computation conference companion, GECCO Companion '12, pp. 1421–1422. ACM, New York, NY, USA (2012). DOI 10.1145/2330784.2330964

133. NVIDIA Corp.: Nvidia geforce 8800 gpu architecture overview. Tech. rep. (2006)
134. NVIDIA Corp.: Nvidia's next generattion cuda^{TM} compute architecture: Fermi^{TM} (2009)
135. NVIDIA Corp.: CUDA C Best Practices Guide v7.0 (2015). URL http://docs.nvidia.com/cuda/cuda-c-best-practices-guide/
136. NVIDIA Corp.: CUDA C Programming Guide v7.0 (2015). URL http://docs.nvidia.com/cuda/cuda-c-programming-guide/
137. NVIDIA Corp.: CURAND Library Programming Guide v7.0 (2015). URL http://docs.nvidia.com/cuda/curand/
138. NVIDIDA Corp.: Cuda in action - research & apps. URL https://developer.nvidia.com/cuda-action-research-apps
139. OpenACC Standards Group: The OpenACC® Application Programming Interface (version 2.0) (2013). URL http://www.openacc.org
140. Owens, J., Houston, M., Luebke, D., Green, S., Stone, J., Phillips, J.: Gpu computing. Proceedings of the IEEE **96**(5), 879–899 (2008). DOI 10.1109/JPROC.2008.917757
141. Owens, J.D., Luebke, D., Govindaraju, N., Harris, M., Krger, J., Lefohn, A.E., Purcell, T.J.: A survey of general-purpose computation on graphics hardware. Computer Graphics Forum **26**(1), 80–113 (2007). DOI 10.1111/j.1467-8659.2007.01012.x
142. de P. Veronese, L., Krohling, R.A.: Swarm's flight: Accelerating the particles using c-cuda. In: Evolutionary Computation, 2009. CEC '09. IEEE Congress on, pp. 3264–3270 (2009). DOI 10.1109/CEC.2009.4983358
143. Parsopoulos, K.E., Tasoulis, D.K., Vrahatis, M.N., Words, K.: Multiobjective optimization using parallel vector evaluated particle swarm optimization. In: In Proceedings of the IASTED International Conference on Artificial Intelligence and Applications (AIA 2004, pp. 823–828. ACTA Press (2004)
144. Parsopoulos, K.E., Vrahatis, M.N.: Particle swarm optimization method in multiobjective problems. In: Proceedings of the 2002 ACM Symposium on Applied Computing, SAC '02, pp. 603–607. ACM, New York, NY, USA (2002)
145. Passino, K.: Biomimicry of bacterial foraging for distributed optimization and control. Control Systems, IEEE **22**(3), 52–67 (2002). DOI 10.1109/MCS.2002.1004010
146. Pedemonte, M., Nesmachnow, S., Cancela, H.: A survey on parallel ant colony optimization. Applied Soft Computing **11**(8), 5181–5197 (2011)
147. Pei, Y., Zheng, S., Tan, Y., Takagi, H.: An empirical study on influence of approximation approaches on enhancing fireworks algorithm. In: Systems, Man, and Cybernetics (SMC), 2012 IEEE International Conference on, pp. 1322–1327 (2012). DOI 10.1109/ICSMC.2012.6377916
148. Pham, D., Ghanbarzadeh, A., Koc, E., Otri, S., Rahim, S., Zaidi, M.: The bees algorithm–a novel tool for complex optimisation problems. In: Proceedings of the 2nd Virtual International Conference on Intelligent Production Machines and Systems (IPROMS 2006), pp. 454–459 (2006)
149. Platos, J., Snasel, V., Jezowicz, T., Kromer, P., Abraham, A.: A pso-based document classification algorithm accelerated by the cuda platform. In: Systems, Man, and Cybernetics (SMC), 2012 IEEE International Conference on, pp. 1936–1941 (2012). DOI 10.1109/ICSMC.2012.6378021
150. Pospichal, P., Jaros, J., Schwarz, J.: Parallel genetic algorithm on the cuda architecture. In: Proceedings of the 2010 International Conference on Applications of Evolutionary Computation - Volume Part I, EvoApplicatons'10, pp. 442–451. Springer-Verlag, Berlin, Heidelberg (2010)
151. Price, K., Storn, R.M., Lampinen, J.A.: Differential evolution: a practical approach to global optimization. Springer Science & Business Media (2006)
152. Rabinovich, M., Kainga, P., Johnson, D., Shafer, B., Lee, J., Eberhart, R.: Particle swarm optimization on a gpu. In: Electro/Info- rmation Technology (EIT), 2012 IEEE International Conference on, pp. 1–6 (2012). DOI 10.1109/EIT.2012.6220761

153. Reguera-Salgado, J., Martin-Herrero, J.: High performance gcp-based particle swarm optimization of orthorectification of airborne pushbroom imagery. In: Geoscience and Remote Sensing Symposium (IGARSS), 2012 IEEE International, pp. 4086–4089 (2012). DOI 10.1109/IGARSS.2012.6350729

154. Reyes, R., de Sande, F., López, I.: Frangollo: A run-time library for openacc support. Tech. Rep. 04/2013, Universidad de La Laguna (2013)

155. Reyes-Sierra, M., Coello, C.C.: Multi-objective particle swarm optimizers: A survey of the state-of-the-art. International journal of computational intelligence research **2**(3), 287–308 (2006)

156. Rice, J.A.: Mathematical Statistics and Data Analysis. Thomson Higher Education, Belmont, CA USA (2007)

157. Roberge, V., Tarbouchi, M.: Efficient parallel particle swarm optimizers on gpu for real-time harmonic minimization in multilevel inverters. In: IECON 2012 - 38th Annual Conference on IEEE Industrial Electronics Society, pp. 2275–2282. Montreal, QC (2012)

158. Roberge, V., Tarbouchi, M.: Parallel particle swarm optimization on graphical processing unit for pose estimation. WSEAS TRANSACTIONS on COMPUTERS **11**(6), 170–179 (2012)

159. Roberge, V., Tarbouchi, M.: Comparison of particle swarm optimization for graphical processing units and multicore processors. International Journal of Computational Intelligence and Applications **12**(1), 1–20 (2013). DOI 10.1142/S1469026813500065

160. Ross, P.: Why cpu frequency stalled. Spectrum, IEEE **45**(4), 72 (2008). DOI 10.1109/MSPEC.2008.4476447

161. Rymut, B., Kwolek, B.: Gpu-supported object tracking using adaptive appearance models and particle swarm optimization. In: Computer Vision and Graphics, *Lecture Notes in Computer Science*, vol. 6375 (2010)

162. Rymut, B., Kwolek, B.: Real-time multiview human body tracking using gpu-accelerated pso. In: Parallel Processing and Applied Mathematics, Lecture Notes in Computer Science, pp. 458–468. Springer Berlin Heidelberg (2014). DOI 10.1007/978-3-642-55224-3_43

163. Rymut, B., Kwolek, B., Krzeszowski, T.: Gpu-accelerated human motion tracking using particle filter combined with pso. In: Advanced Concepts for Intelligent Vision Systems, *Lecture Notes in Computer Science*, vol. 8192, pp. 426–437. Springer International Publishing (2013). DOI 10.1007/978-3-319-02895-8_38

164. Saito, M., Matsumoto, M.: Simd-oriented fast mersenne twister: a 128-bit pseudorandom number generator. In: Monte Carlo and Quasi-Monte Carlo Methods 2006, pp. 607–622. Springer Berlin Heidelberg (2008). DOI 10.1007/978-3-540-74496-2_36

165. Saito, M., Matsumoto, M.: Variants of mersenne twister suitable for graphic processors. ACM Trans. Math. Softw. **39**(2), 12:1–12:20 (2013). DOI 10.1145/2427023.2427029

166. Schaffer, J.D.: Multiple objective optimization with vector evaluated genetic algorithms. In: Proceedings of the 1st International Conference on Genetic Algorithms, pp. 93–100. L. Erlbaum Associates Inc., Hillsdale, NJ, USA (1985)

167. Segal, M., Akeley, K.: The OpenGL® Graphics System: A Specification (Version 4.4). The Khronos Group Inc. (2013)

168. Shainer, G., Ayoub, A., Lui, P., Liu, T., Kagan, M., Trott, C., Scantlen, G., Crozier, P.: The development of mellanox/nvidia gpudirect over infinibandła new model for gpu to gpu communications. Computer Science - Research and Development **26**(3-4), 267–273 (2011). DOI 10.1007/s00450-011-0157-1

169. Sharma, B., Thulasiram, R., Thulasiraman, P.: Portfolio management using particle swarm optimization on gpu. In: Parallel and Distributed Processing with Applications (ISPA), 2012 IEEE 10th International Symposium on, pp. 103–110 (2012). DOI 10.1109/ISPA.2012.22

170. Sharma, B., Thulasiram, R., Thulasiraman, P.: Normalized particle swarm optimization for complex chooser option pricing on graphics processing unit. The Journal of Supercomputing **66**(1), 170–192 (2013). DOI 10.1007/s11227-013-0893-z

171. Shen, Z., Wang, K., Wang, F.Y., Chen, C.L.P.: Gpu based genetic algorithms for the dynamic sub-area division problem of the transportation system. In: The International Federation of Automatic Control. Cape Town, South Africa (2014)

172. Sheng, W., Szymanski, P., Leupers, R., Ascheid, G.: Software migration for parallel execution on a multicore tablet: A case study. In: Embedded Multicore Socs (MCSoC), 2013 IEEE 7th International Symposium on, pp. 1–6 (2013). DOI 10.1109/MCSoC.2013.17

173. Shi, Y.: Reevaluating amdahl's law and gustafson's law. Tech. rep., Computer Sciences Department, Temple University (MS: 38-24) (1996)

174. Shi, Y.: Brain storm optimization algorithm. In: Advances in Swarm Intelligence, *Lecture Notes in Computer Science*, vol. 6728, pp. 303–309. Springer Berlin Heidelberg (2011). DOI 10.1007/978-3-642-21515-5_36

175. Solomon, S., Thulasiraman, P., Thulasiram, R.: Collaborative multi-swarm pso for task matching using graphics processing units. In: Proceedings of the 13th annual conference on Genetic and evolutionary computation, GECCO '11, pp. 1563–1570. ACM, New York, NY, USA (2011). DOI 10.1145/2001576.2001787

176. Solomon, S., Thulasiraman, P., Thulasiram, R.: Scheduling using multiple swarm particle optimization with memetic features on graphics processing units. In: Massively Parallel Evolutionary Computation on GPGPUs, Natural Computing Series, pp. 149–178. Springer Berlin Heidelberg (2013). DOI 10.1007/978-3-642-37959-8_8

177. Souza, D.L., Teixeira, O., Monteiro, D.C., Oliveira, R.C.L.: A new cooperative evolutionary multi-swarm optimizer algorithm based on cuda architecture applied to engineering optimization. In: Combinations of Intelligent Methods and Applications, *Smart Innovation, Systems and Technologies*, vol. 23, pp. 95–115. Springer Berlin Heidelberg (2013). DOI 10.1007/978-3-642-36651-2_6

178. Stanković, S., Astola, J.: GPU Computing with Applications in Digital Logic, chap. An Overview of Miscellaneous Applications of GPU Computing, pp. 191–215. Tampere International Center for Signal Processing (2012)

179. Tan, Y.: Particle swarm optimizer algorithms inspired by immunity-clonal mechanism and their application to spam detection. International Journal of Swarm Intelligence Research **1**(1), 64–86 (2010)

180. Tan, Y.: Fireworks Algorithm. Springer, New York (2015)

181. Tan, Y.: An Introduction to Fireworks Algorithm. Science Press, Beijing, China (2015)

182. Tan, Y., Ding, K.: Survey of GPU-based implementation of swarm intelligence algorithms. Cybernetics, IEEE Trans. on **6**(5), 1–14 (2016). DOI 10.1109/TCYB.2015.2460261

183. Tan, Y., Xiao, Z.: Clonal particle swarm optimization and its applications. In: Evolutionary Computation, 2007. CEC 2007. IEEE Congress on, pp. 2303–2309 (2007)

184. Tan, Y., Yu, C., Zheng, S., Ding, K.: Introduction to fireworks algorithm. International Journal of Swarm Intelligence Research **4**(4), 39–70 (2013). DOI 10.4018/ijsir.2013100103

185. Tan, Y., Zhu, Y.: Fireworks algorithm for optimization. In: Advances in Swarm Intelligence, *Lecture Notes in Computer Science*, vol. 6145, pp. 355–364. Springer Berlin Heidelberg (2010). DOI 10.1007/978-3-642-13495-1_44

186. The Numerical Algorithms Group Ltd: Nag library manual, mark 23 (2011). URL http://www.nag.co.uk/numeric/fl/nagdoc_fl23/xhtml/FRONTMATTER/manconts.xml

187. Tsutsui, S.: Aco on multiple gpus with cuda for faster solution of qaps. In: C. Coello, V. Cutello, K. Deb, S. Forrest, G. Nicosia, M. Pavone (eds.) Parallel Problem Solving from Nature - PPSN XII, *Lecture Notes in Computer Science*, vol. 7492, pp. 174–184. Springer Berlin Heidelberg (2012)

188. Tsutsui, S., Fujimoto, N.: Aco with tabu search on a gpu for solving qaps using move-cost adjusted thread assignment. In: Proceedings of the 13th Annual Conference on Genetic and Evolutionary Computation, GECCO '11, pp. 1547–1554. ACM, New York, NY, USA (2011)

189. Tsutsui, S., Fujimoto, N.: Fast qap solving by aco with 2-opt local search on a gpu. In: Evolutionary Computation (CEC), 2011 IEEE Congress on, pp. 812–819 (2011)

190. Tsutsui, S., Fujimoto, N.: Aco with tabu search on gpus for fast solution of the qap. In: S. Tsutsui, P. Collet (eds.) Massively Parallel Evolutionary Computation on GPGPUs, Natural Computing Series, pp. 179–202. Springer Berlin Heidelberg (2013). DOI 10.1007/978-3-642-37959-8_9

191. Uchida, A., Ito, Y., Nakano, K.: An efficient gpu implementation of ant colony optimization for the traveling salesman problem. In: Networking and Computing (ICNC), 2012 Third International Conference on, pp. 94–102 (2012)

192. Ugolotti, R., Nashed, Y., Cagnoni, S.: Real-time gpu based road sign detection and classification. In: Parallel Problem Solving from Nature - PPSN XII, *Lecture Notes in Computer Science*, vol. 7491, pp. 153–162. Springer Berlin Heidelberg (2012). DOI 10.1007/ 978-3-642-32937-1_16

193. Ugolotti, R., Nashed, Y.S., Mesejo, P., Špela Ivekovič, Mussi, L., Cagnoni, S.: Particle swarm optimization and differential evolution for model-based object detection. Applied Soft Computing **13**(6), 3092–3105 (2013). DOI http://dx.doi.org/10.1016/j.asoc.2012.11.027

194. Valdez, F., Melin, P., Castillo, O.: Bio-inspired optimization methods on graphic processing unit for minimization of complex mathematical functions. In: O. Castillo, P. Melin, J. Kacprzyk (eds.) Recent Advances on Hybrid Intelligent Systems, *Studies in Computational Intelligence*, vol. 451, pp. 313–322. Springer Berlin Heidelberg (2013). DOI 10.1007/978-3-642-33021-6_25

195. de Veronese, L., Krohling, R.: Differential evolution algorithm on the gpu with c-cuda. In: Evolutionary Computation (CEC), 2010 IEEE Congress on, pp. 1–7 (2010). DOI 10.1109/ CEC.2010.5586219

196. Wachowiak, M.P., Foster, A.E.L.: Gpu-based asynchronous global optimization with particle swarm. Journal of Physics: Conference Series **385**(1), 012,012 (2012)

197. Wang, H., Potluri, S., Luo, M., Singh, A., Sur, S., Panda, D.: Mvapich2-gpu: optimized gpu to gpu communication for infiniband clusters. Computer Science - Research and Development **26**(3-4), 257–266 (2011). DOI 10.1007/s00450-011-0171-3

198. Wang, J., Dong, J., Zhang, C.: Implementation of ant colony algorithm based on gpu. In: Computer Graphics, Imaging and Visualization, 2009 Sixth International Conference on, pp. 50–53 (2009)

199. Weber, R., Gothandaraman, A., Hinde, R., Peterson, G.: Comparing hardware accelerators in scientific applications: A case study. Parallel and Distributed Systems, IEEE Transactions on **22**(1), 58–68 (2011). DOI 10.1109/TPDS.2010.125

200. Weiss, R.M.: GPU Computing Gems, chap. GPU-Accelerated Ant Colony Optimization, pp. 325–340. Morgan Kaufamnn (2011)

201. Weiss, R.M.: Accelerating swarm intelligence algorithms with gpu-computing. In: GPU Solutions to Multi-scale Problems in Science and Engineering, Lecture Notes in Earth System Sciences, pp. 503–515. Springer Berlin Heidelberg (2013). DOI 10.1007/ 978-3-642-16405-7_31

202. Yang, X., Tan, Y.: Sample index based encoding for clustering using evolutionary computation. In: Advances in Swarm Intelligence, *Lecture Notes in Computer Science*, vol. 8794, pp. 489–498. Springer International Publishing (2014). DOI 10.1007/ 978-3-319-11857-4_55

203. Yang, X.S.: Swarm intelligence based algorithms: a critical analysis. Evolutionary Intelligence **7**(1), 17–28 (2014). DOI 10.1007/s12065-013-0102-2

204. Yang, X.S., Deb, S.: Cuckoo search via lévy flights. In: Nature Biologically Inspired Computing, 2009. NaBIC 2009. World Congress on, pp. 210–214 (2009). DOI 10.1109/NABIC. 2009.5393690

205. Zhang, C., Mei, H.C., Yang, H.: A parallel way to select the parameters of svm based on the ant optimization algorithm. arXiv (2014). URL http://arxiv.org/abs/1405.4589

206. Zhang, J., Tan, Y., Ni, L., Xie, C., Tang, Z.: Hybrid uniform distribution of particle swarm optimizer. IEICE Transactions on Fundamentals of Electronics, Communications and Computer Sciences **E93-A**(10), 1782–1791 (2010)

207. Zhang, J., Tan, Y., Ni, L., Xie, C., Tang, Z.: AMT-PSO: An adaptive magnification transformation based particle swarm optimizer. IEICE Transactions on Fundamentals of Electronics, Communications and Computer Sciences **E94-D**(4), 786–797 (2011)

208. Zhang, Z., Seah, H.S.: Cuda acceleration of 3d dynamic scene reconstruction and 3d motion estimation for motion capture. In: Parallel and Distributed Systems (ICPADS), 2012 IEEE 18th International Conference on, pp. 284–291 (2012). DOI 10.1109/ICPADS.2012.47

209. Zhao, J., Wang, W., Pedrycz, W., Tian, X.: Online parameter optimization-based prediction for converter gas system by parallel strategies. Control Systems Technology, IEEE Transactions on **20**(3), 835–845 (2012). DOI 10.1109/TCST.2011.2134098

210. Zheng, S., Janecek, A., Tan, Y.: Enhanced fireworks algorithm. In: Evolutionary Computation (CEC), 2013 IEEE Congress on, pp. 2069–2077 (2013). DOI 10.1109/CEC.2013.6557813

211. Zheng, S., Janecek, A., Tan, Y.: Dynamic search in fireworks algorithm. In: Evolutionary Computation (CEC), 2014 IEEE Congress on, pp. 3222–3229 (2014)

212. Zheng, S., Li, J., Janecek, A., Tan, Y.: A cooperative framework for fireworks algorithm. IEEE/ACM Transactions on Computational Biology and Bioinformatics (TCBB), (2016). DOI 10.1109/TCBB.2015.2497227

213. Zhou, Y., Tan, Y.: GPU-based parallel particle swarm optimization. In: Evolutionary Computation, 2009. CEC '09. IEEE Congress on, pp. 1493–1500 (2009). DOI 10.1109/CEC.2009.4983119

214. Zhou, Y., Tan, Y.: Particle swarm optimization with triggered mutation and its implementation based on gpu. In: Proceedings of the 12th annual conference on Genetic and evolutionary computation, GECCO '10, pp. 1–8. ACM, New York, NY, USA (2010). DOI 10.1145/1830483.1830485

215. Zhou, Y., Tan, Y.: GPU-based parallel multi-objective particle swarm optimization. International Journal of Artificial Intelligence **7**(A11), 125–141 (2011)

216. Zhu, W., Curry, J.: Parallel ant colony for nonlinear function optimization with graphics hardware acceleration. In: Systems, Man and Cybernetics, 2009. SMC 2009. IEEE International Conference on, pp. 1803–1808 (2009)

217. Zhu, W., Curry, J.: Particle swarm with graphics hardware acceleration and local pattern search on bound constrained problems. In: Swarm Intelligence Symposium, 2009. SIS '09. IEEE, pp. 1–8 (2009). DOI 10.1109/SIS.2009.4937837

218. Zitzler, E., Deb, K., Thiele, L.: Comparison of multiobjective evolutionary algorithms: Empirical results. Evol. Comput. **8**(2), 173–195 (2000)

Index